BEGINNER GUITAR: NO WIMPS!

a Metal Guitar Academy MGA Publication

Brett Miller

Copyright © 2018, 2021

All rights reserved. No part of this publication may be reproduced, stored in a retrieval system, or transmitted, in any form or by any means, electronic, mechanical, photocopying, recording, or otherwise, without the prior written permission of the publisher.

SESSION 01 – HOLDING THE GUITAR, LEFT HAND, RIGHT HAND, STRING NAMES, TABLATURE	01
SESSION 02 – PLAYING NOTES, FRET MARKERS, METRONOME	08
SESSION 03 – CHORDS, POWER CHORDS, HAMMER-ONS, CHORD BOXES, INTERVALS	12
SESSION 04 – OPEN CHORDS, PULL-OFFS, FINDING NOTES, MEASURES	19
SESSION 05 – CHORD CHANGES, LEGATO, SCALE DIAGRAMS	27
SESSION 06 – STRUMMING, ALTERNATE PICKING, SCALES, MINOR PENTATONIC SCALE	33
SESSION 07 – CHORD CHANGES, MINOR PENTATONIC SCALE	38
SESSION 08 – POWER CHORDS, SLIDES, PALM MUTING, NOTE VALUES	42
SESSION 09 – RHYTHMIC STRUMS, MINOR PENTATONIC (FORM #2), STRING BENDING, RESTS, TIES	49
SESSION 10 – MINOR PENTATONIC (FORM #3), RYTHMIC STRUMS, TIME SIGNATURES, LICKS & RIFFS	56
SESSION 11 – BARRE CHORDS (3-STRING), MINOR PENTATONIC (FORMS #4, #5), BUILDING CHORDS	63
SESSION 12 – TRIADS (SET 1), TREMOLO PICKING, UNISON BENDS, SCALE THEORY	69
SESSION 13 – BARRE CHORDS (4-STRING), MAJOR SCALE, DOTTED RHYTHMS	76
SESSION 14 – GUITAR SOLO, LEGATO EXERCISES, CHORDS & SCALES	80
SESSION 15 – DIATONIC TRIADS, MAJOR SCALE, KEYS	84
SESSION 16 – MAJOR SCALE, BARRE CHORDS (6-STRING MAJOR), MINOR SCALE	89
SESSION 17 – MAJOR SCALE, BARRE CHORDS (5 AND 6-STRING), MINOR KEYS	94
SESSION 18 – 3 AND 4-NOTE SEQUENCES, TRIADS (SET 2), RELATIVE MINOR	100
SESSION 19 – MINOR PENTATONIC SEQUENCES, TRIADS (SET 3), ROOT NOTE LOCATIONS	107
SESSION 20 – NAVIGATING THE NECK (MINOR PENTATONIC), TRIADS (SET 4), RIFF CONSTRUCTION	113
SESSION 21 – NAVIGATING THE NECK (MAJOR SCALE)	118
APPENDIX A – TUNING THE GUITAR	A
APPENDIX B – AWESOME GUITAR PLAYERS TO CHECK OUT	B

Introduction

There's a lot of beginning guitar books out there - you've probably noticed this, and maybe even had a difficult time picking out this one over the others. You also may have noticed how many of these beginning tomes call themselves a "method" book. Now, what could that mean - "method"?

Well, to most of us, "method" would imply a certain way of doing things - a choice between many options. Martial arts is a good example; while most of the time we think of the different types (like Kung Fu, Aikido, Judo, etc.) as "styles", they are really methods: different techniques for accomplishing the same goal of self defense. And they certainly seem pretty different from one another when you see skilled practitioners using them.

But, at the level of beginner, are these martial arts methods so different? While I'm no fighting expert, I would argue that they're not. Master instructors of any of these disciplines understand that there is a *basic set of skills*, both physical and mental, that a brand new student needs to master, *must* master. Punches, kicks, stamina and conditioning exercises - these foundations tend to look the same, regardless of style or method. These guys know their stuff, and they know that what their beginning students need to learn are the *foundations*.

Most beginning *guitar* method books, however, seem *not* to have come to the same conclusion. Have I seen every single one out there? Of course not. But in my close to 20 years of private instruction experience, have I seen *way* more than most people ever will? Absolutely.

With guitar, just like in martial arts, there is no "style" at the beginning level, no choice about what *should* and *shouldn't* be learned. There are basic skills, both physical and mental, that need to be imparted by the teacher, and mastered by the student. Unfortunately, *every* beginning guitar book that I've seen fails miserably at both tasks. The one you now hold in your hands is different, and aims to fix this widespread and systemic failure within the guitar instructional community. You've chosen wisely.

How the Book is Organized

As its title implies, this book is written for the intensity-ready, complete beginner. There is a lesson for each Session, a total of twenty one. Each of these lessons consists of two distinct parts:

1. Physical

This aspect of each lesson is all about increasing your strength, stamina, and technical ability. These exercises and techniques will prepare you for the *real* arena of playing guitar - for playing the songs you'll actually want to play (not "Polly Wolly Doodle" or "Mary Had a Little Lamb"). Playing the guitar is a physical skill, and like any other skill, repetition is the key. Some of the exercises and techniques will be harder for you to master than others, so take as many days as you need before moving on to the next Session. Always remember that your focus should be on *results*, not a timetable.

2. Mental

This portion of each lesson is of extreme importance, because it provides a *context* for what you're playing. Far too many times, a student misses the big picture - learns techniques and specific chords, scales, etc., and then has no idea *how* to use them, or *why* they work with other things. You'll be presented with a bird's-eye view of music and the guitar right from the beginning, setting you up for the later successes that, unfortunately, elude many players forever.

Attitude

One more thing: as soon as you pick up that guitar and play that first note, you're officially a guitarist; so it's important to start thinking of yourself as one! Take it from me (a pro player who's been playing for 30 years) - there's going to be ups and downs. There will be plateaus, where you'll feel like it's taking forever to make progress. This is *normal* - so, as corny as it sounds, you've got to *enjoy the journey*, and not get too hung up about the destination. Your destination always changes depending upon your skill level, but the journey is constant and never-ending....and with the right mindset, it can be one of the most exciting and rewarding journeys of your life. It certainly is for me!

Now enough talk - time to get to work and have some fun!

Brett Miller
Metal Guitar Academy MGA

P.S. - Visit **MetalGuitarAcademy.com** and sign up for the FREE **90-Minute Beginner Bootcamp** video! It's a great companion piece to this book, where you'll see me demonstrating many of the important technique concepts in detail. Don't miss out on this extremely useful Bonus Content - go get it right away!

SESSION 01

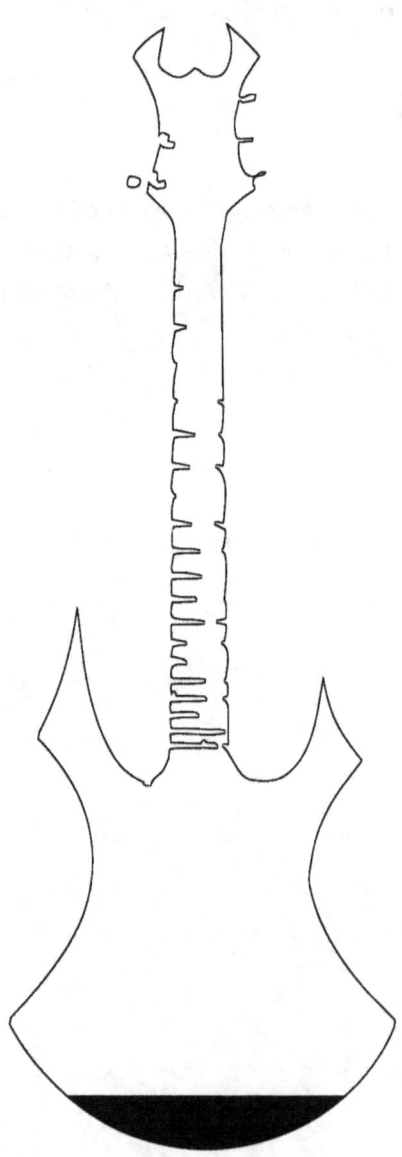

PHYSICAL

As a guitarist, it's important to get used to playing both **sitting down**, and **standing up**. You'll find yourself in situations where one (or maybe even both) are called for. When sitting with the guitar, keep your back fairly straight, but not rigidly so (don't slouch!) Set the curved part of the guitar onto your right leg, and let the neck of the guitar stick out at about a **45 degree angle** - no need to get out the protractor, just eyeball it! The body of the guitar should be pressed comfortably and lightly against your torso. *Resist the urge to crane your neck* to try and see the strings on the guitar; it's natural to just see the strings as a "blur" when you look down, and in fact this will be an advantage - with time, you'll know which strings you're on **just by the feel of your hands and fingers**.

Sitting

Neck Placement

When standing, adjust the strap length so that the guitar is at a height **close to where it would be if you were sitting comfortably**. "Low slung" guitars look cool, but they're hard to play!

Standing

You should consider purchasing some **strap locks**. These are replacements for the strap buttons that came with your guitar, and are an inexpensive way to protect your instrument. With normal strap buttons, it's possible for the strap to become twisted without you noticing it, and to fall right off the button - with the result of your guitar crashing to the floor. Strap locks are designed to attach to any guitar strap, and to lock in place. Unless your strap itself breaks (unlikely), or the screws themselves fall out of your guitar (again, unlikely) that strap is going to stay attached to your guitar, preventing what could be a nasty fall.

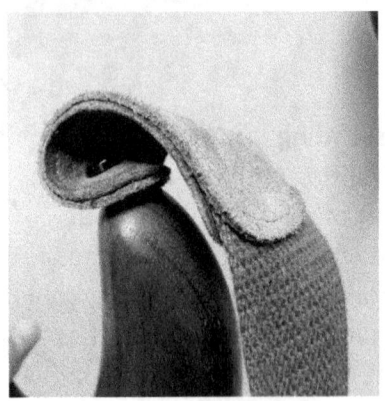 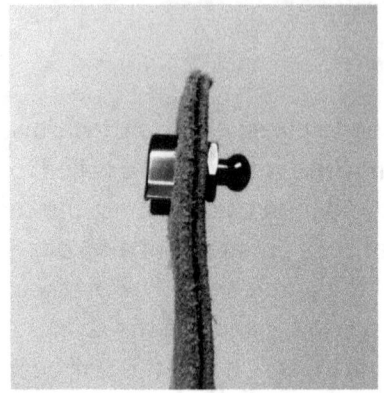 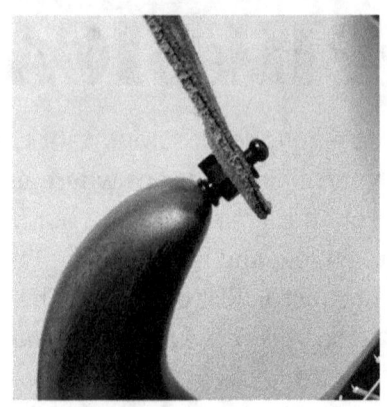

There are some **variations** on the way to sit with the guitar, which you're encouraged to experiment with. For example, you may find that the guitar is too low. If your left wrist or forearm is **resting on your leg** (a no-no that will *restrict movement*), then this may be the case. To bring the guitar up a bit higher, you can either **cross your right leg** over your left, or else use a small **footstool** underneath your right foot:

Another way that you'll see some guitarists sit, will be to place the guitar on the **left leg**, with a footstool underneath the **left foot**. Why this variation? The guitar will be in a position *more closely resembling its position when standing*. If you're wearing a strap, try sitting in this position and then standing up - you'll see what I mean. This way of sitting is also preferred by most **classical guitar players**.

So, which way should *you* sit? Start with the "standard" way on the previous page - because as the old axiom says, *"If it ain't broke, don't fix it!"* This is a great way to learn, and is the most common way to sit.

Once you've got the basics down though, I encourage you to try **playing while standing up** once in a while. If you ever play on stage, chances are you'll be standing - and playing this way *does* feel a little different from sitting. When you've gotten used to standing up, *then* try the method of **sitting with the guitar on the left leg**. You'll have enough experience to decide which sitting position is the most comfortable for you!

Most beginning guitar players look at the speed and pyrotechnics of a seasoned player's *left* hand, and leap to the conclusion that this hand is going to be the hardest to master. In fact, for beginners, it's most often the *right* hand (picking hand) that presents the biggest challenge - so here's how to set yourself up for success:

First, make sure to grip the pick between the side of your index finger, and your thumb. Make a relaxed "thumbs up" sign with your right hand, and notice the crease created by your joint nearest your finger tip. Place the pick, with the tip pointing straight out, directly over that crease in your finger. Then, lay your thumb flat over the pick. Don't bend your thumb joint, keep it relaxed:

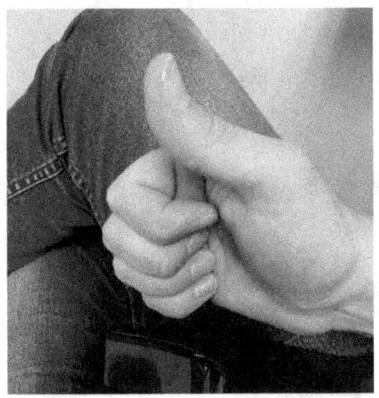 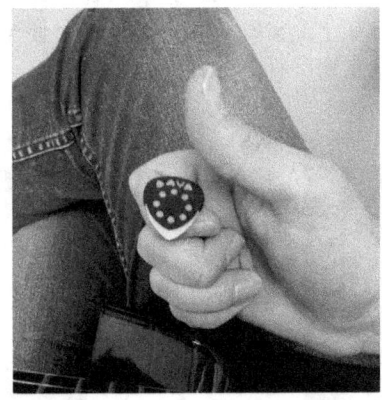 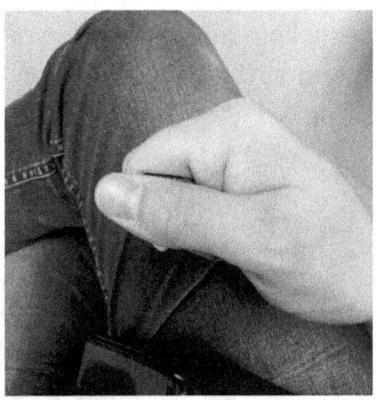

Notice the small amount of pick sticking out; it's important to "choke up" on the pick like this. Too much sticking out makes it difficult to cross the strings efficiently. Next, place your right hand onto the guitar. Rest your hand lightly behind the strings at the bridge, where your wrist meets the bottom portion of your hand. Let the joints by the tips of your ring and pinky fingers touch the higher strings. You'll feel them touch the strings as you play, and that's okay:

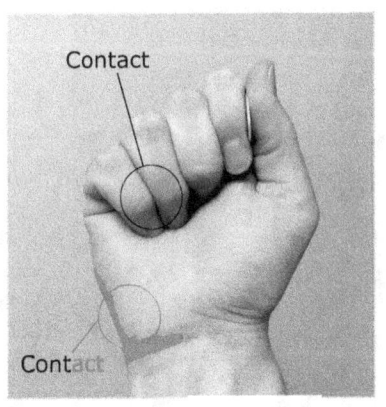 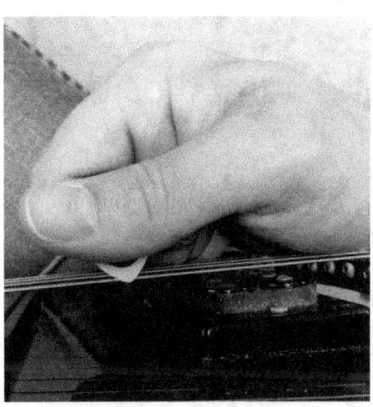

This is your correct right hand position! Why is it important to do this? Well, if you were to just grab the pick between the *tips* of your index finger and thumb (most people's first instinct), since your finger joint itself can move up and down, no matter how hard you grip the pick, it will wobble when picking fast or aggressively. Your finger joint can't move sideways though, so by placing the pick on the side of the finger, you'll have much more control over the pick.

[Keep in mind that some players' positioning will vary slightly. Some will fan out their middle, ring, and pinky fingers a bit, some will rest their pinky underneath the thinnest string, etc. The above principles will set you up for success now, and you can always experiment with variations along the way. Visit *MetalGuitarAcademy.com* for some even more detailed video explanation of right hand positioning.]

Also, if you just *floated* the hand over the strings (didn't rest it on the bridge like you should), you'd find that **there's no way of knowing which string your pick is about to hit** - unless you stare at your right hand, which is a no-no! By resting the hand on the bridge and strings, with some practice you begin to actually *feel* the distances involved when picking - therefore, *you gain control without having to stare at your pick*. The other reason for resting the hand is that it creates a *fulcrum point* of sorts - you'll have more economy of motion when you begin picking fast. If you were floating your hand *above* the bridge, you'd be dragging your entire forearm around - very cumbersome!

Now that you've got your right hand in the correct position, try picking each string one at a time. Let your hand move *with the pick*; don't curve your wrist to get the pick to that thinnest string! Check this by making sure that your pick is pretty *flat* against each string, not angled. After you pick a string, make sure that the pick is *hovering in between* the two strings - you don't want the pick to fall onto the next string:

Excellent job! Next, let's get your *left* hand off to a good start. First, place your thumb on the back of the neck, pointing straight up (think "thumbs up" sign). The pad of your thumb should be pressing against the neck, behind your index and middle fingers - **don't** bend your thumb at the joint, **don't** hook your thumb over the neck, and **don't** point your thumb down the neck.

Correct Thumb Position

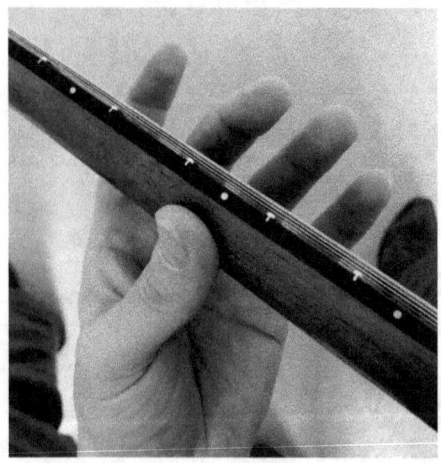
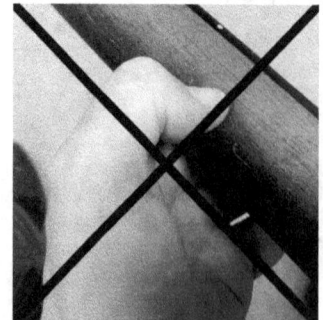
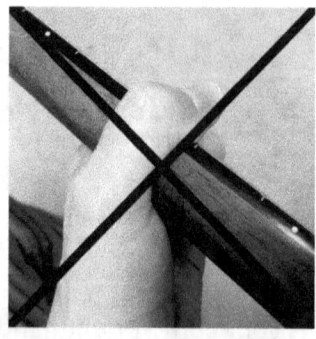
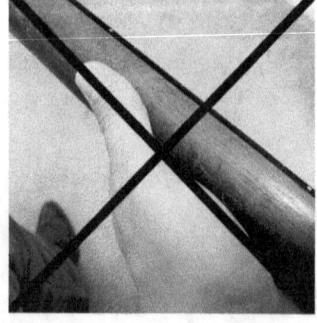

Try to **relax** while practicing your thumb placement. Everyone's hands are shaped and sized a bit differently, so use these photos and descriptions as a guide - there's no need to get out the protractor and start measuring precise angles! Stay comfortable, take your time, and **keep your arm and shoulder relaxed**. You'll get it!

Next, find your **5th fret** and press the thickest string *straight down with the tip* of your middle finger. Make your hand very "claw-like" - your fingers should be arched so that just the tip of the finger makes contact with the string. Press down in the *center* of the fret; don't get too close to the metal fret wire. Press firmly, but without your hand feeling stiff or "locked up". It should feel like you're **pinching the guitar neck** between your thumb and middle finger.

Finger Position

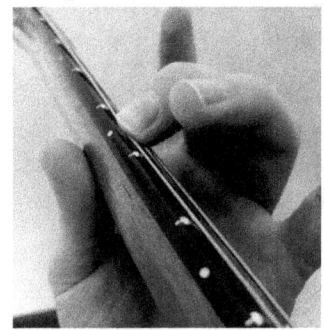

Great! Now, keep pressing that string down against the wood. Put your right hand in its proper position, and **pick that string**. Hold it down until the sound stops ringing out.

Congratulations! You just played your first official note as a guitarist! Try pressing the same note down with **each of your other fingers**, one at a time, to really get used to how this feels. Use more strength than you think you need to at first. This way, you'll get a clear sound, with no string "buzz".

MENTAL

Any music you've ever heard is made up of **pitches** - high or low frequencies that our brains interpret as musical tones. There are 12 specific pitches that we use to make music, and we use 7 letters of the alphabet to identify them. You're probably thinking "Why not 12 letters?" Good question! We'll answer it soon enough. For now though, just remember that the letters **A B C D E F and G** represent certain musical tones. Your guitar strings are **tuned** so that when vibrating, they produce some of these notes. In fact, each string is named after the note that it makes when played **open** - that is, without being pressed down anywhere. It's very important to memorize the string names, so here they are:

Low (thick) ——— E   A   D   G   B   E ——— High (thin)

Notice that there are two E strings on the guitar: the low and high. When you hear "directional" terms like this (high, low, up, down) remember that it's usually referring to the pitch - not physical direction! The low E string is physically higher, but has a lower pitch - hence it's name. Here's a good way to remember the names: **E**d **A**te **D**ynamite, **G**ood **B**ye **E**d!

Now in order to practice, you'll need a way to know what strings to pick, and where to press down. Luckily, we've got that covered! There's a system for this called **tablature**, and it's a fantastic way to write down music and exercises. **[Note: beware of any "guitar teacher" that speaks negatively about tablature - these hacks will try to tell you that it's not "as good" as standard music notation. That's totally wrong, and this belief is generally the mark of a "jack of all trades" music instructor - a little trumpet, a little piano, a little guitar, etc. Avoid these people like the plague. They will steer you in the wrong direction.]**

Okay, now that's out of the way - so let's explain how tablature (or TABs) work! Here's some blank TAB:

There are 6 lines, each of which represents one of your **guitar strings**. The one on the bottom is the low E string (the thick one). While this might seem backwards at first, think of it this way: the low E string has a lower sound, so it's weighted and pulled downwards. Remember, things like "up and down" on guitar have to do with sound, not physical direction. Here's the same TAB, this time labeled with the strings:

Knowing which string to play is only half of the equation though. You'll also need to know which **fret** to press the string down onto. Luckily, there's an easy way to notate this - we simply use **numbers.** Each fret gets it's own number, from 1 (the biggest fret, by the tuning pegs) to 21, 22, or 24 (depending on the type of guitar you have). We just plop the numbers right on the lines, depending upon which string we want to play. Here's an example of some TAB with six notes indicated:

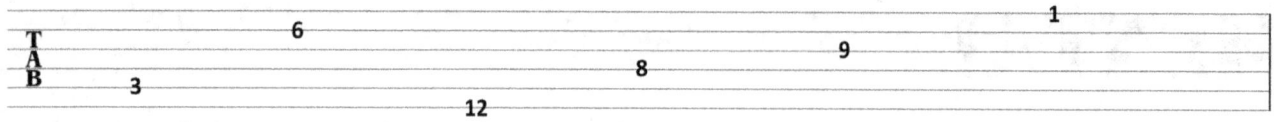

With tablature, we read the notes from left to right, like if you were reading a book; it doesn't matter which notes are physically higher or lower. So in this case, 3rd fret A string is the first note, 6th fret B string is the second note, and so on. Try finding and playing each of the above notes - use any left hand finger you want for now, but make sure you're using the correct left and right hand positions!

Here are a few more TAB examples for you to practice finding and playing. Use this opportunity to start strengthening all of your fingers - use a good combination of index, middle, ring, and pinky when holding these notes down.

1.

2.

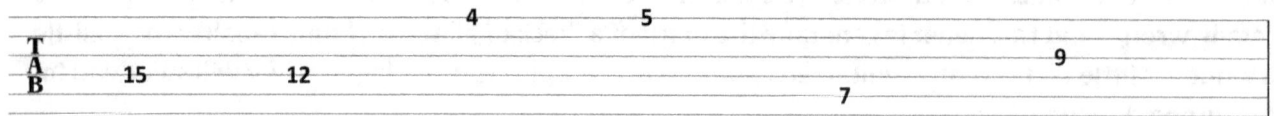

3.

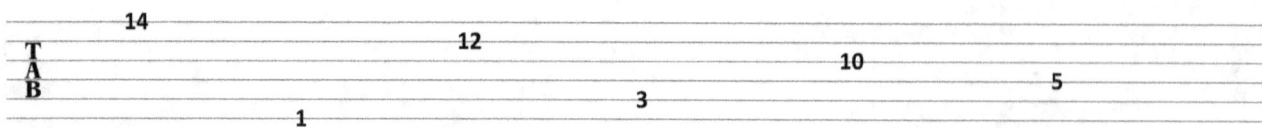

SESSION 02

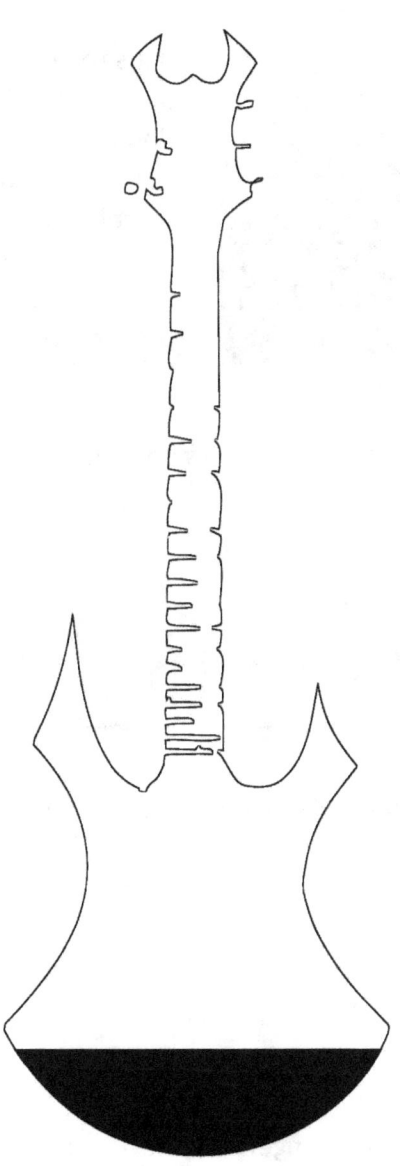

PHYSICAL

Hand coordination is the name of the game today. In order to play accurately and cleanly, your two hands have to work together seamlessly. The exercises below will target this, and will also get your left hand fingers working independently from one another.

In the first example, you'll play four notes per string. Notice the letters above the TAB notes; these stand for your left hand fingers: **i**ndex, **m**iddle, **r**ing, and **p**inky. Since you'll be using one finger per fret, and the frets are all right next to each other, you'll be playing **in position** - stretching neither forwards nor backwards with your fingers.

You'll only have one finger pressing down at a time when playing these exercises. As soon as you press down a note, **stop holding the previous one**. Also, before you play the first note, set yourself up for success by *hovering* your other three fingers above their "assigned" frets. Remember to keep your thumb in the correct position (on the back of the neck), in order to make this easier:

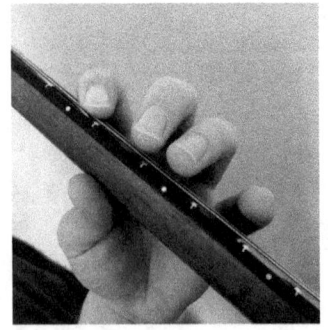 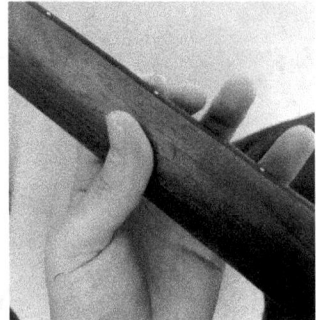

If it's too much of a stretch right now for your pinky or ring fingers to hover over their frets, don't worry! Before using them to press down at the 7th and 8th frets, **you can move your thumb closer to your pinky**. The thumb is not set in stone - it can move around a bit to help support your ring and pinky fingers as they press down.

Let's give this exercise a shot! Take your time, and press down firmly enough to get a clear, ringing sound (no buzz)!

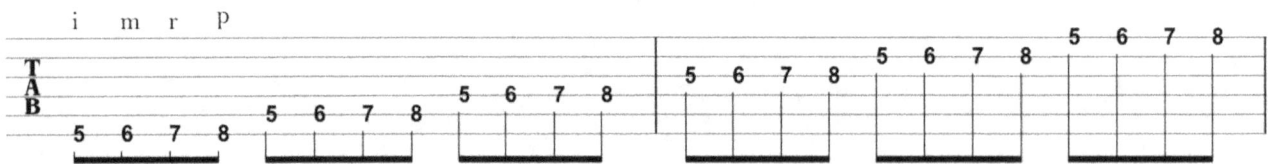

Now, try going backwards - or **descending**. Lead with your pinky finger on each string.

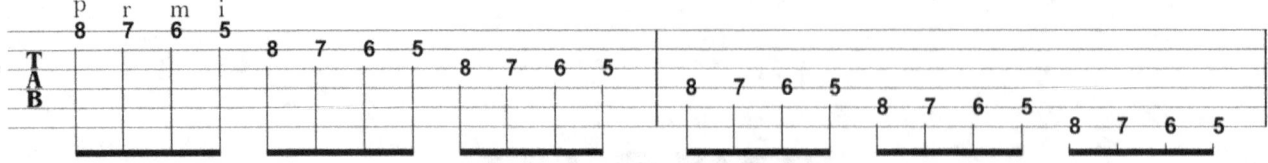

Make sure that your **pick** and your **left hand fingers** are moving *at exactly the same time!* Your finger should **touch and press** the string at the *exact same moment* that your pick connects with the string - not before, and not after. A great way to practice this is to *count to four* as you play. Every time that you say "one", move both your pick and your finger. Let the note ring as you say "two, three, four", then **pick and press** again on "one". Go as slowly as you need to - precision and accuracy are what you're going for here, not speed! Try these similar exercises, and remember that *repetition is the mother of skill*. Beginners often don't realize just how much repetition is involved in learning to play well. With guitar, you'll quickly realize how much truth there is in the statement *"you get out what you put in"*!

This exercise has you playing up at the **high frets.** The distances between the frets shrink, so keep those fingers closer together. Also, most people tend to freak out a bit when first attempting to play high up on the neck. Don't contort your body, overbend your wrist, or take your thumb off of the neck (sounds funny now, but wait until you find yourself doing it)! Just stay relaxed - **your thumb and hand positions are no different in this area of the neck than anywhere else**.

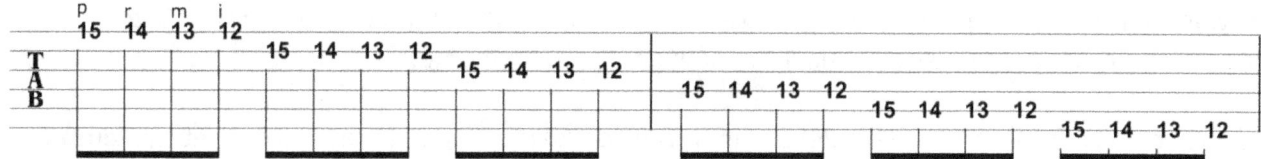

These next two exercises are more confusing for the fingers - and that means you'll get even more out of them! Take your time, and remember to focus on **even rhythm** (each note lasts exactly the same amount of time) and **good tone** (no string buzz, even volume):

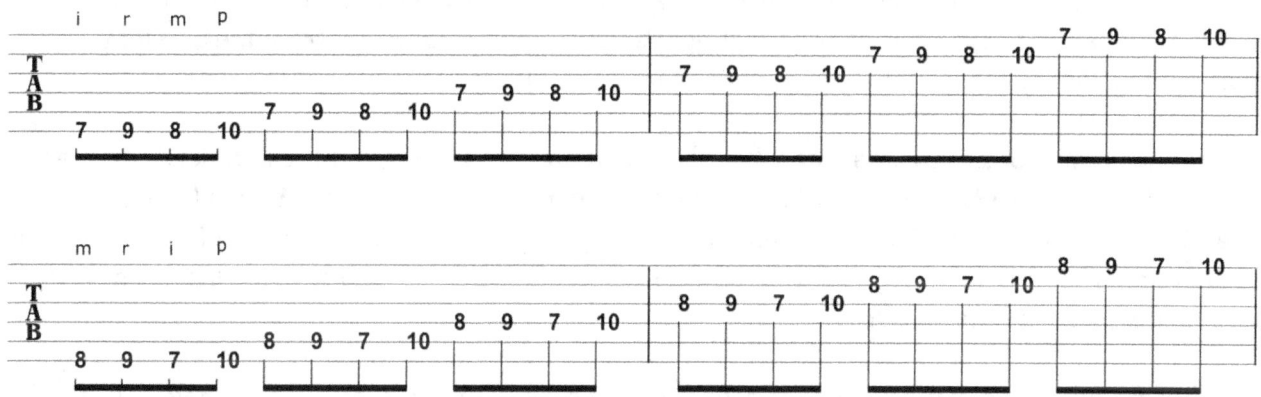

MENTAL

Now that you're rockin' the frets all over the place, it's time to start finding your way around the neck! You've probably noticed by now the dots on your guitar neck - on the side, and also (usually, but not always) on the frets themselves *[Note: I'll refer to these fret markers as "dots" because that's the most common design - but you could have trapezoids, fins, skulls, etc. on your guitar, depending on the make and model. Don't worry; they all serve the same purpose!]*

So, what are these for? They're simply there to serve as a **visual cue**; to let you know *what fret you're on*. They're not like "training wheels" either - you'll use 'em forever. If you're playing down by the 3rd fret, and all of a sudden you've got to jump quickly to the 15th fret, those dots will save the day. It's very difficult to navigate around without them - for beginners and pros alike!

You'll need to *memorize* where the dots are (what number frets they're on). There are a few reasons for this, but the pressing one is that you're reading TAB now...and TAB is about fret numbers! The faster you can find those frets, the better. So here's where those dots are:

3, 5, 7, 9 / 12, 15, 17, 19 / 21, 24

To be honest, there's no magical way to memorize this - they aren't laid out like a phone number or anything like that, and they're not even symmetrical all the time (sometimes one fret in between, sometimes two). So do the best you can! Like so many other things with guitar, repetition is the key.

Speaking of numbers, it's time to get really, really, good at **counting**. You've been counting to four in order to be accurate with your hand coordination exercises, and that's great. But what happens when you want to go a bit faster - and you don't want to keep saying the numbers that quickly? Enter a gadget that will be absolutely essential from now on: the **metronome**.

A metronome is simply a little device that clicks. The cool part though, is that you can set the **tempo**, or speed of the clicks, and they will be evenly and precisely spaced apart. Think of it like a ticking clock that can click as fast or slow as you want! The goal is to let the metronome do the counting for you, so that your brain becomes synced up with it - it sets your "internal clock" so to speak. Like the Force, you and the metronome will become One!

There are many kinds of metronomes (mechanical, quartz, digital) and you should definitely pick one up. But an easy way to start getting used to it right away is to download a **metronome app** for your smart phone. There's plenty out there, so find one with good reviews.

Every metronome works the same way - you dial in a number, and the higher the number, the faster the click. If you dial in 88, then it will click **88 times in one minute**. We call that **88 bpm** (beats per minute). If you look at guitar TABs in a magazine, in books, or online, in the beginning of the song you'll see a number like this. It's telling you what to dial in on your metronome, so that you'll know how fast the song is supposed to be played...

But we're getting ahead of ourselves. For right now, you'll be using the metronome to help **keep track of your speed**, and to **play evenly** when practicing the upcoming exercises throughout this book. If you're a guitar player who's *serious* about making progress, the metronome will quickly become your best friend!

Here's a couple of examples of what a metronome looks like - you may also see a type that looks like a pendulum swinging back and forth; while these are cool and retro, it's best to avoid them - the click can get out of whack over time, due to the device's mechanical nature.

SESSION 03

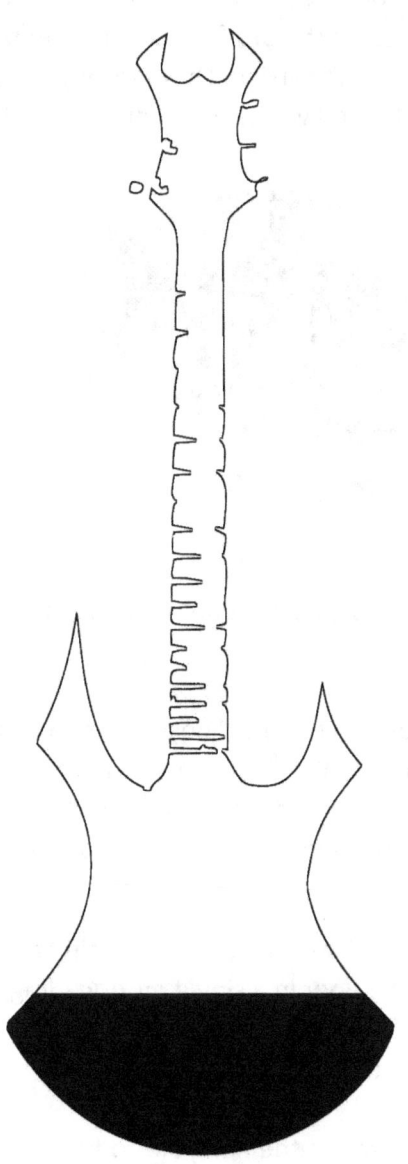

PHYSICAL

Ever see a guitar player put their fingers into a weird shape and start strumming? Sure you have - in fact, that's usually what most people imagine when they think "guitar player". So what are they doing? They're playing a **chord**, that's what! Chords are simply *three or more notes*, hit at exactly the same time - and you're about to play 'em.

When written in TAB, the notes in a chord are stacked up on top of each other - like this:

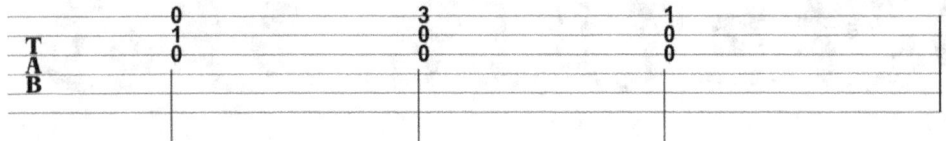

The *zero* in TAB means to play the string **open** - not pressed down anywhere. Try playing these three chords, and keep these tips in mind as you do so: First, use your **index finger** to play notes on the 1st fret, and your **ring finger** to play the note on the 3rd fret. Second, keep those fingers straight up and down, so that just the *tip* is pressing down the string. Otherwise, your finger may hit the open string, muting it. If this happens, it can't vibrate, and you won't hear the note! Keep those fingers like a claw.

  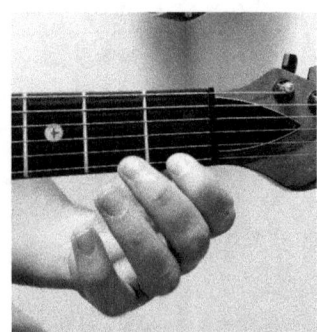

Lastly, since these are chords, the three notes are meant to sound *at the same time*. This means you are going to **strum** them.

When strumming, the right hand will be in a different position than usual: it will **float above** the bridge. While floating above the bridge is normally a no-no, when strumming, it's the proper way to do it. This allows you to move your wrist and forearm more freely; playing chords requires less right hand precision than playing single notes, so this is okay. Here's how your hand should look as you prepare to strum:

For the actual strum, you're just going to move your wrist and forearm towards the floor in a single motion, dragging the pick across all three strings. Use enough force to get one single sound, but not so much that the pick gets caught on any of the strings. Try it!

When you've got the hang of producing one continuous sound, try playing all three chords in a row. Set your metronome to a slow tempo (like **60 bpm**) and try to play a different chord every two or three beats.

If you find that you're having trouble hearing all three strings (and if you need to straighten out your fingers, so that you're not muting any open strings), keep this in mind: **Don't over-bend your wrist!** Over-bending your wrist *will* straighten out your fingers, but it's uncomfortable, bad form, and bad for your wrist. Instead, *make your fingers do the work* - use your **finger muscles** to get your fingers straighter up and down. *Don't* do it by pushing out your wrist!

Now it's time to learn one of the most useful and fun types of chords - the **power chord**. "Power chord" is really kind of a slang term, because we're only dealing with two notes; we know that a true chord has to have **at least three notes**. But who cares? That's what it's called, and if it ain't broke, don't fix it, right?

Power chords are what a lot of famous, cool **riffs** are made of, so let's jump right in and get you playing. You're going to use two fingers to play these shapes - the **index** and **ring**. Just like any chord written in TAB, the notes of a power chord will be stacked up. Here are four for you to try:

Use your index finger to play the *lower* of the two notes, and your ring finger to play the *higher*. Keep your thumb on the back of the neck, pretty much behind your middle finger:

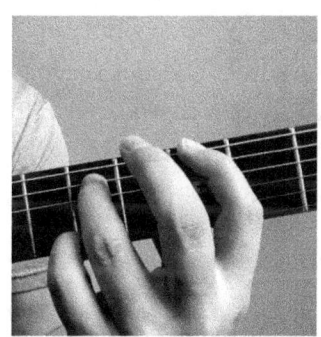
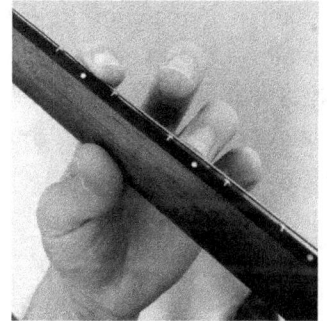

Here's an important detail to consider, regarding the position of your **index finger**. Notice in the photos that the index finger *is not* as straight up-and-down as the ring finger. In other words, **it's a bit flatter** - almost **rolled out to the side a little**. This is because *we actually want the index finger to lightly touch the next few strings.*

Why is this? Isn't muting the other strings a no-no? Well, not when you play power chords! Having your index finger lightly touching the next few strings will help to **mute** any *unwanted string noise*. As you get better at playing power chords, you'll often hit them pretty aggressively with the right hand - they're a staple of rock and Metal. Without the index finger muting some of the unplayed strings, those open strings can actually start to **vibrate sympathetically**, causing excess noise. Laying that index finger down a bit will prevent this!

One more detail regarding the index finger: when playing the power chords on the A and D strings, use the *very tip* of your index finger to **touch the low E string**. You *don't* want to *press down* the low E string - just touch it lightly.

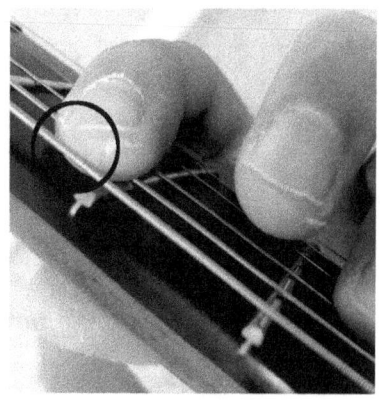

Once again, the point of this is to **mute any unwanted noise from that string**. It may seem like a small detail now, but practicing doing this right in the beginning will help make this technique second nature for you when playing power chords. So, don't neglect it!

If your fingers are having trouble reaching both notes at the same time, try these two things:

1. Lower your thumb; slide it a bit more toward the ground. This will help to increase your stretch.
2. Start by pressing your *ring finger* down first, then *reach back* with your index. You'll have more control over your index finger at first than you will your ring finger.

The great thing about power chords is that they're **movable**. This means, you can make one shape with your fingers, and just *move that same shape around the neck*. Try doing this with the first two power chords from the above example. Play the first one, then just **relax your fingers**. *Don't* take them off the strings, but don't press down either. Then, slide your fingers over the strings like you're ice skating, two frets higher to the next power chord. Try to keep your fingers spread apart as you move - you'll find that they'll want to squeeze together at first. When you get to the next power chord on the 5th fret, just press down the strings again and play it. (If you hear some *squeeky* string noise as your fingers slide, don't worry about it. This is a natural part of the sound of the guitar!)

When playing power chords, your right hand should be **resting on the bridge, just like when you play single notes**. Don't float, like you did when strumming. Power chords should be played with a quick, powerful flick of the wrist, so that your pick crosses both strings at the same time, and you hear **both notes as one sound**.

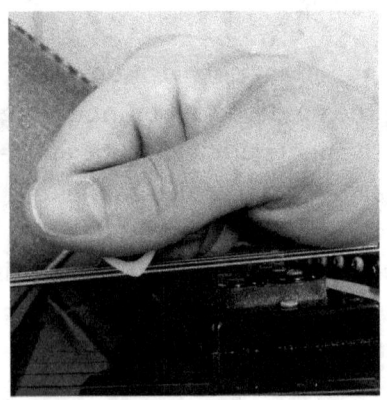

Try this exercise, designed to get you used to moving power chords all around the neck. Every other power chord is played at the **first fret**, and you'll be moving *one extra fret* each time. Play very slowly at first, but as soon as you feel like you've got the hang of it...get out that **metronome** and practice this exercise to a click!

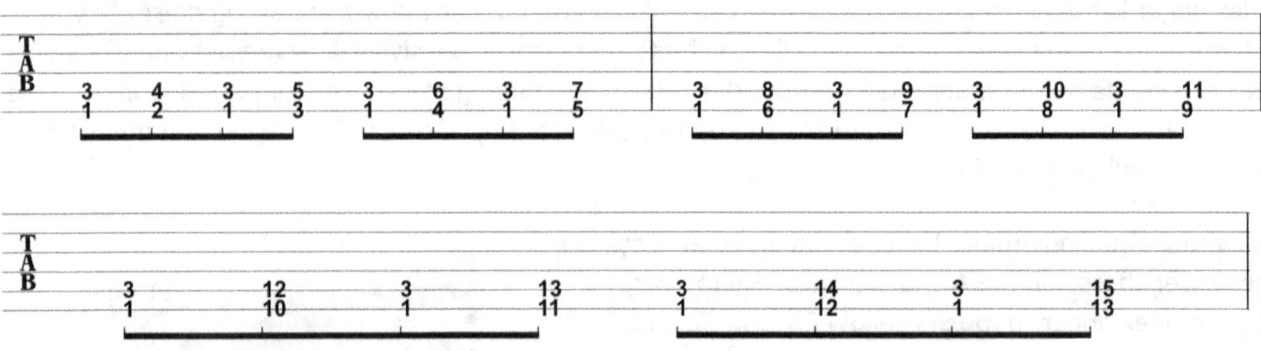

Now that you're building the skills to play some monster riffs, it's time to focus on some **lead playing**, or **soloing** skills.

This next technique is called the **hammer-on**, and practicing it will help you gain left hand strength and control.

15

The idea behind hammering (another name for the technique) is to pick one note, but then to **slap your finger tip down** onto the string for the next note - in other words to *not* pick it. This might seem strange to think about, but when you try it, you'll find that the force of your finger hammering down will actually cause the note to sound. Here's how the hammer-on technique is written in TAB; there are two hammers here, one on the **A string**, and one on the **B string**:

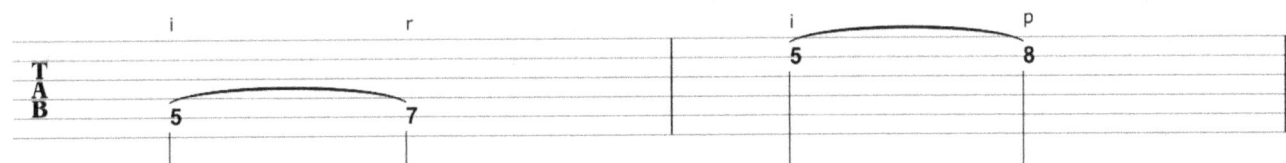

Give it a shot! Pick only the first note in each example, then hammer your finger down onto the next note, without picking it. When performing these two hammer-ons, *don't* just place your finger down onto the next note - **use some force!** Think of it like an old pirate-style flintlock pistol - your finger is like the hammer coming down, when the trigger is pulled!

The curved line connecting both notes is called a **slur**. *Whenever the hammer-on technique is called for, you will see this line connecting the notes.*

Here's something very important to keep in mind when beginning to practice the hammer-on: **don't** lift up your index finger when your other finger hammers; *you should end up with both fingers pressing down*. Here are two photos illustrating how your hand should look, first at the **beginning** of the movement, and then **at the end** (after your pinky has performed the hammer, at the 8th fret).

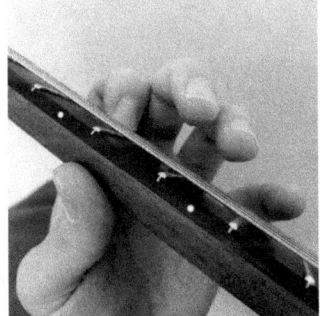
Before Hammer-On

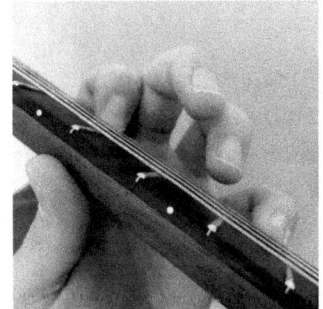
After Hammer-On

Here are a few more examples of hammer-ons to practice, using different finger combinations. Use your **metronome** with these, so that you perform them with *even rhythm* - very important!

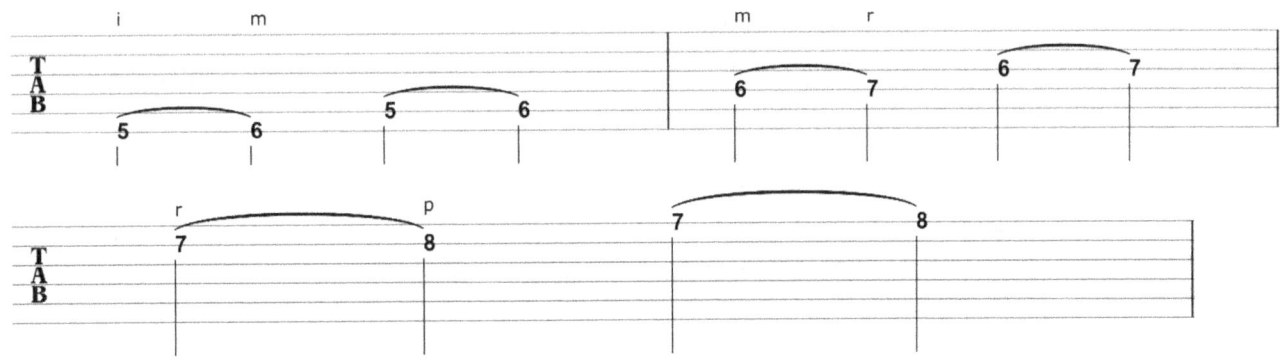

MENTAL

We've got you reading tablature pretty well now, for both single notes and chords. There's another way, though, that guitarists can read and write chords. These are called **chord diagrams** or **chord boxes**. They're pretty cool, because they're like a visual representation of how a chord looks. Lets check out a blank one:

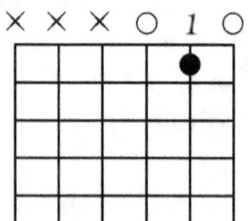

Chord diagrams are similar to TAB; the lines represent the strings. The difference, though, is that the strings are now **vertical**. The leftmost line is the **low E**, and the line on the right is the **high E**. Imagine a guitar hanging up on the wall, like in a music store, and you'll get the idea.

This of course means that the boxes represent your **frets** - there are five in this chord diagram. We use **dots** to tell you on which string and fret to place your fingers, and an **empty circle** above the string if it's to be played **open**. An **X** will float above the string if you're *not* supposed to play it:

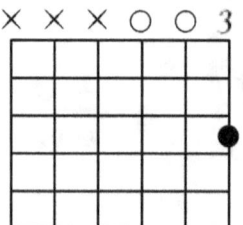

So, in this chord, the low E, A, and D strings are *not* played. The G and high E strings are played open, and the B string is pressed down at the 1st fret. You use the index finger to play it (that's what the "1" means - 1st finger).

Does this chord seem familiar? It should...it's one of the three that you played before! Both the chord diagrams and TAB can be used to write chords, and you'll often see both being used. Here's how the other two chords would look when written this way:

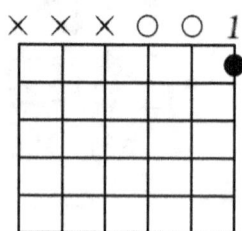

Got it? Coming up, you'll be playing bigger chords, using more fingers. Using the chord diagrams will make it easier for you to see where, and with what finger, to play the notes.

Now that you're able to figure out *where* to play notes, wouldn't it be great to also know *what* they're called? **Knowing the names of the notes** on the guitar neck is absolutely essential, but unfortunately, many players never bother to learn them. This lack of note knowledge is one of the biggest barriers to improvement, and holds back an alarming number of guitarists from achieving what they're capable of on the instrument. But not you - you're going to tackle it right away!

Remember that the name of a string simply stands for the **pitch** or **note** that it makes when played **open**. There are seven letters in music that we use to identify notes: A B C D E F G. Those notes can be found all over the neck, and there's an easy way to do it - all you need to do is learn about things called **intervals**.

In everyday language, an interval usually refers to an interval of time - like a minute, an hour, etc. In music though, it has an entirely different meaning: an interval is the **distance in pitch** between any two notes. So if one note is pretty low in pitch, and another is pretty high in pitch, those notes would be separated by a wide, or large interval. If two notes are pretty close in pitch, then they're separated by a much closer, or smaller interval.

Now, there are many types of intervals, and each interval has it's own unique sound that can be memorized. To help us find notes on the guitar though, we're only going to bother with the two smallest intervals: the **half step** and **whole step**. The half step is the smallest distance between two notes. Move by only **one fret**, and you're playing a half step. Here's a few examples:

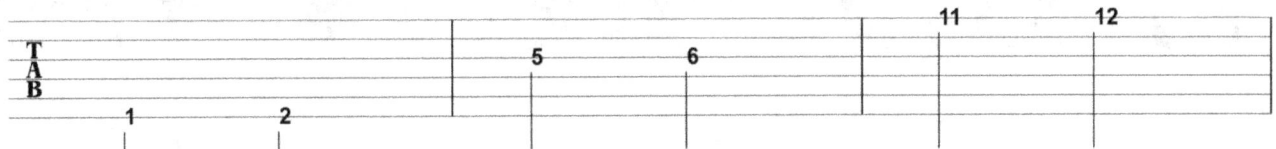

Think about the the theme from the movie *Jaws*: dahhh-dum...dahhh-dum... What you played above sounds like that, because in the movie theme, a cello plays half steps too!

A whole step is simply movement by **two frets**. Here are a few examples:

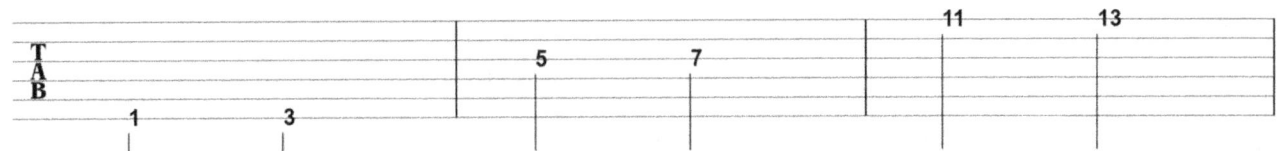

In the musical alphabet (those seven letters), sometimes moving from one letter to the next (like A to B) is a whole step, and sometimes moving from one letter to the next is a half step. If nobody tells you which is which, you wouldn't know - because they all look like they'd be the same. Here's a chart that tells you which is which - WS is "whole step", HS is "half step":

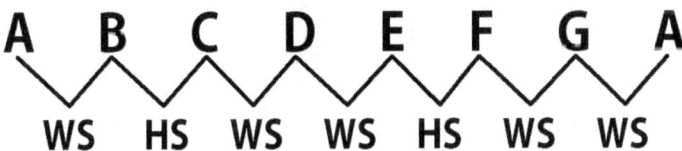

As you can see, most of the time we've got whole steps. But **B to C** and **E to F** are automatically *half steps* in music.

If you took a trumpet, or a violin, or a piano, and played B to C back and forth, it would sound like *Jaws*. Same with E to F. This is universal stuff! Memorize this - we'll be using this info to **find all the notes on the guitar...**

SESSION 04

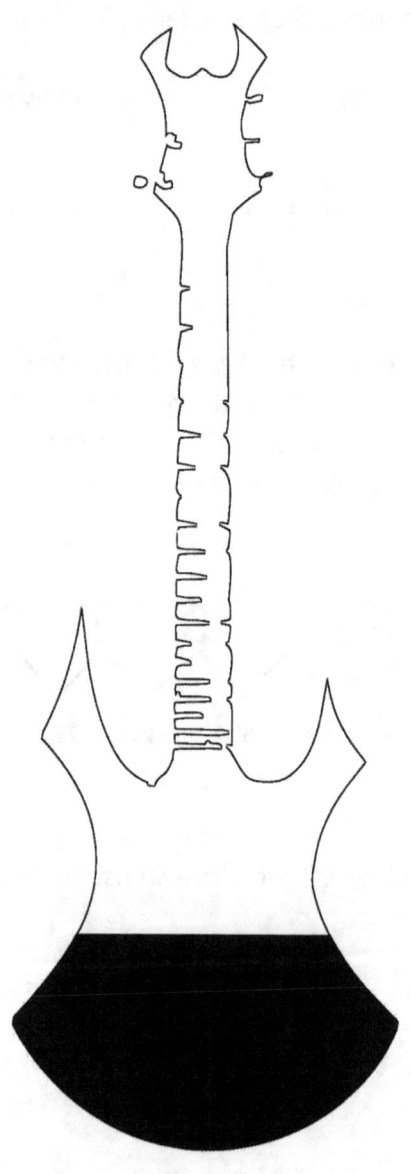

PHYSICAL

Playing chords is one of the most exciting and rewarding parts about learning guitar (especially for beginners). You'll start to feel like you're really playing some music! In fact, it's almost *guaranteed* that many of your favorite songs will use some of the chords you're about to learn. We're learning these chords first, because you'll get so much use out of them right away.

While rewarding, learning these upcoming **open chords** (so-called because they'll have open strings in them) can also be very challenging. Be patient as you practice these! Everyone has difficulty with these bigger chords at first - and you'll be no different. Practicing these chords will also help you roughen up those fingertips and get some **callouses**. Yes, your fingertips will be sore for a little while, but it goes away quickly if you just keep at it - and tough it out everyday. Here's the very first chord we're going to play - **E minor**:

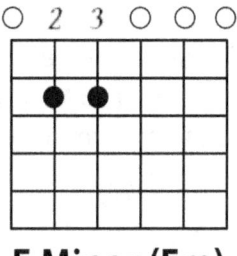

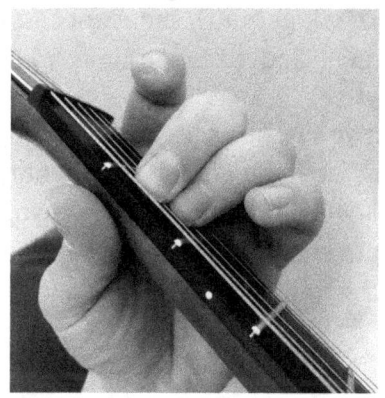

As you try this chord, keep these tips in mind: *1.* Pick all the strings *one at a time* at first, as you hold down the chord shape. This is better than just strumming it right away, because you'll hear if there are any strings that you're accidentally **muting**. *2.* Muted strings are a result of either not pressing down hard enough, pressing down too close to the metal fret wire, **touching a string with another finger, or touching a string with the inside of your hand**.

Here are two pics; the first one shows the *ring finger* touching the *G string* (which you wouldn't want to do, because it would mute it!) Notice that the ring finger is not straight enough - that's why it's hitting the string:

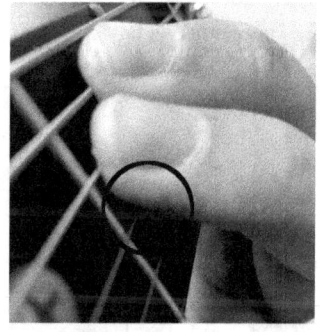

Straighten it out, to correct the problem:

Now, here are a couple of pics spotlighting another common issue: *the inside of the hand* is inadvertantly muting the *high E string*. Fix it by **opening up some space** between the hand and the guitar:

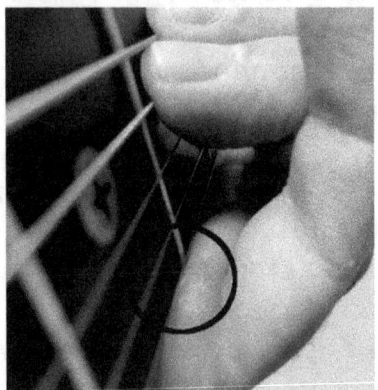 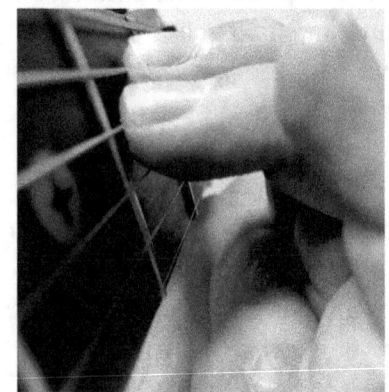

The finger movements necessary to fix these muting issues can usually be measured in **millimeters** - so relax, and take your time. You don't need to overdo the movements!

If you're having trouble hearing a certain string when playing the following chords, look carefully at what you're doing, and identify one of the aforementioned four problems. Remember to keep your fingers **straight up-and-down**, and use only the *tips* to press down. If you need to straighten your fingers, **let your fingers do the work!** Don't try to fix the problem by over-bending your wrist; it's not the right way to do it. Okay...time to play some chords!

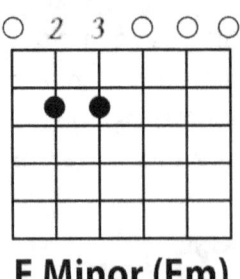

E Minor (Em)

 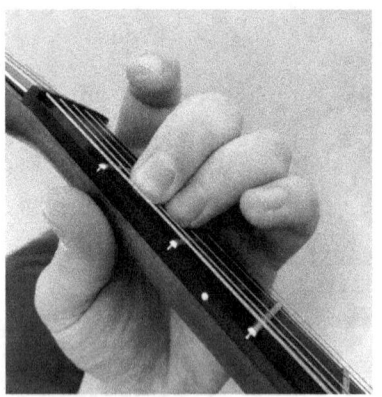

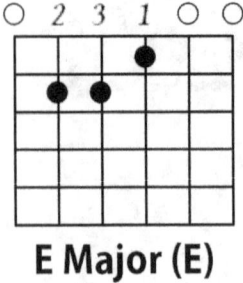

E Major (E)

 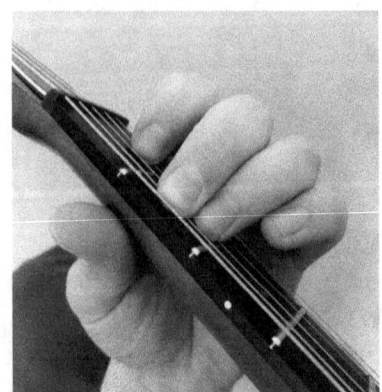

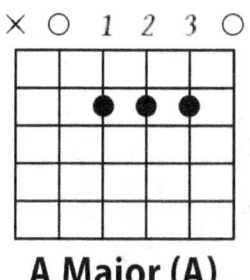
A Major (A)

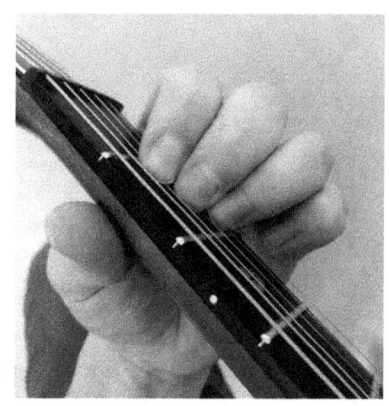

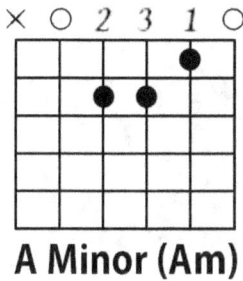
A Minor (Am)

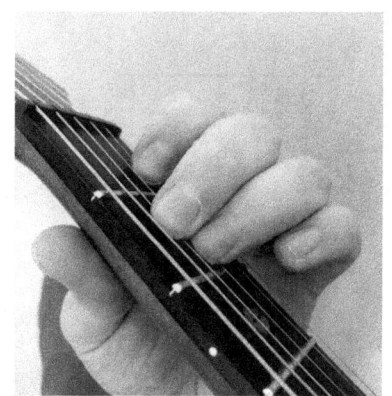

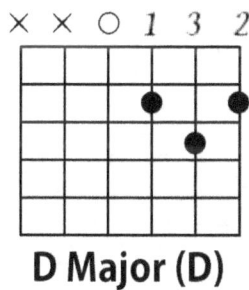
D Major (D)

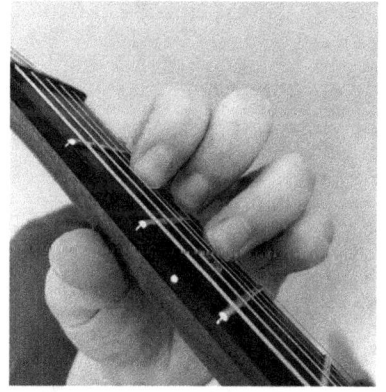

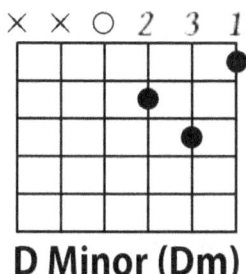
D Minor (Dm)

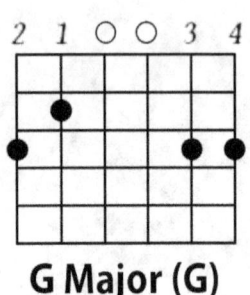
G Major (G)

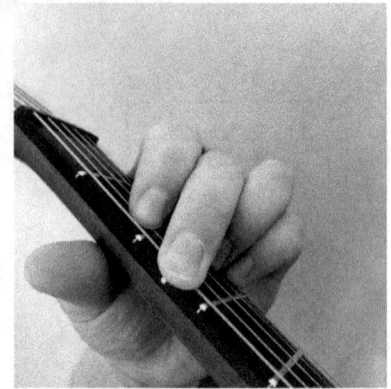

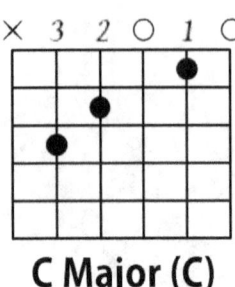
C Major (C)

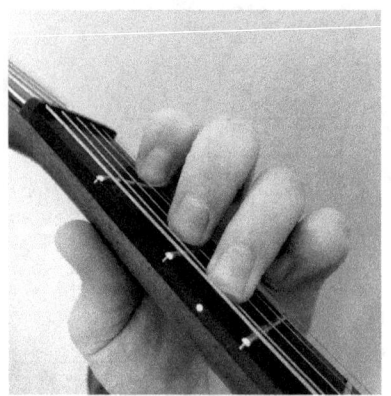

Are you chord-ed out? Let's take a break from the chords, and get back to some lead playing. What you learned about **legato** (which is the fancy, "official music" term for the hammer-on technique!) is only half of the equation. There's another aspect to *legato*; the missing 50%, commonly called **pull-offs**.

Hammer-ons are always *ascending*, but pull-offs are performed when *descending* - going from a higher to a lower note. Here are two examples, written in TAB:

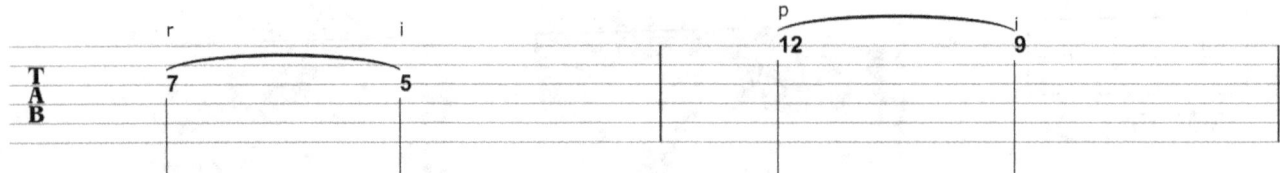

To perform a pull-off, you need to pick the higher note, and then **pluck towards the floor** with whichever finger is playing it. Don't just lift the finger; it won't be loud enough. Really pull that string! This is what will set it vibrating. **Keep the lower note clamped down the entire time** as you pluck the higher note.

Notice that the same symbol - the **slur** - is used for pull-offs as well as hammer-ons. Remember, it's the *direction* that you're going that will tell you whether to use a hammer-on or a pull-off when you see a slur.

When performing a **hammer**, you need to *end up* with both fingers pressing down, right? Well, with **pulls** you'll need to *start* with both fingers down. If you don't, there won't be a note to pull-off to!

Here are two photos showing the finger positions before and after a pull-off:

Before   After

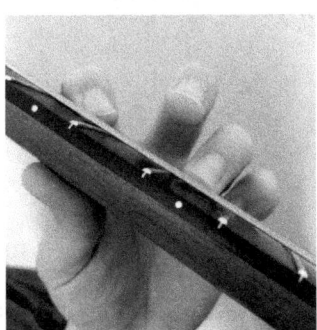 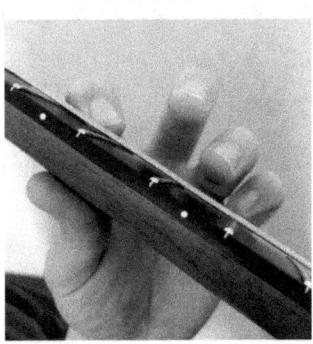

When crossing strings, the finger that's **plucking** will move to the next string *slightly before* the other finger. If they moved simultaneously, the note you pulled to would get **cut off prematurely**. Remember though, you *do* want both fingers down and ready to go *before* performing the next pull-off...so take your time and go slowly at first, to get the timing and movement right!

Here are a few more examples of pull-offs to practice, using different combinations to work those fingers. Always remember how important it is to practice with *even rhythm* - use that metronome!

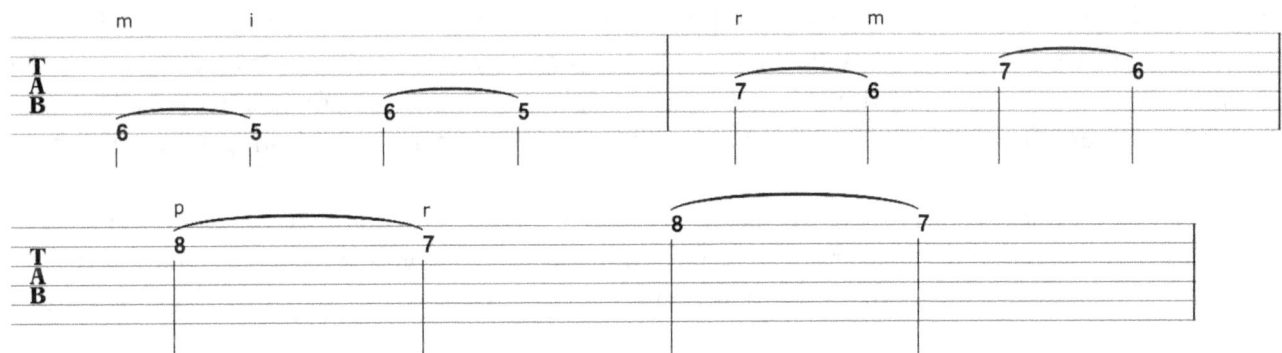

MENTAL

You know all about **half steps** and **whole steps** - the two smallest intervals in music. You've also learned that the notes B to C, and E to F, are *automatically* half steps (not just for guitar, but for every instrument). Now, let's put that knowledge to some good, practical use...it's time to find some notes on the neck!

Here's that musical alphabet again:

You're going to find all of these notes on the **A string**, moving up the neck, while *saying all of the notes as you go*. To start, we're going to pretend that there's a fret **behind** your 1st fret. Put your finger on the A string, by the tuning pegs - this will be your starting note, "A" (since it's the A string, played open):

Play the open A string, and say "A". Now, if we want to play the next note, B, move your finger to the 2nd fret. Why the 2nd? Because, *since A to B is a whole step, you'll need to move two frets.*

Now, from the 2nd fret, where do we go to play the C? Since B to C is always a half step, you simply move to the 3rd fret - one fret away. Starting to get the hang of it?

Continue on this way, saying all the notes as you go. If you do this correctly, here's what you should get:

```
    A     B     C     D     E     F     G     A
T
A   0     2     3     5     7     8     10    12
B
```

How'd you do? If you ended up at the 12th fret, and knew that it was A, then great job! The 12th fret is important on the guitar - notice that it's the **same note name as your open string**. In music, we call this an **octave**. An octave is a special interval; you can think of it as "same note name, higher pitch level". The 12th fret is usually marked with two dots, to identify it as one octave away from your open strings.

Let's do the same thing with the **G string**, for some practice. Again, put your finger on the G string, by the tuning pegs, and pretend that it's a fret. Now, play it and say "G". Work your way up the string, saying the notes as you go. Remember to think about your half steps and whole steps! Let's see how you did:

```
    G     A     B     C     D     E     F     G
T
A   0     2     4     5     7     9     10    12
B
```

Excellent! Now just one more thing, and you'll have the ability (with practice of course!) to find *any note at all* on the guitar. That one more thing is **accidentals** - more commonly called **sharps** and **flats**. Here's what the symbols for "sharp" and "flat" look like:

$$\sharp = \text{Sharp} \qquad \flat = \text{Flat}$$

Did you notice that when you were finding those notes, there were frets that you skipped over? We need to account for those frets, and that's what accidentals do. When a note is sharped (like for example, "G sharp"), its pitch gets **raised by one half step**. On the guitar, this means to play **one fret higher**. When a note is flatted (like "G flat"), its pitch gets **lowered by one half step**. This means to play **one fret lower**.

Check out these examples of **natural** (not sharped or flatted) notes, paired with their sharped and flatted versions:

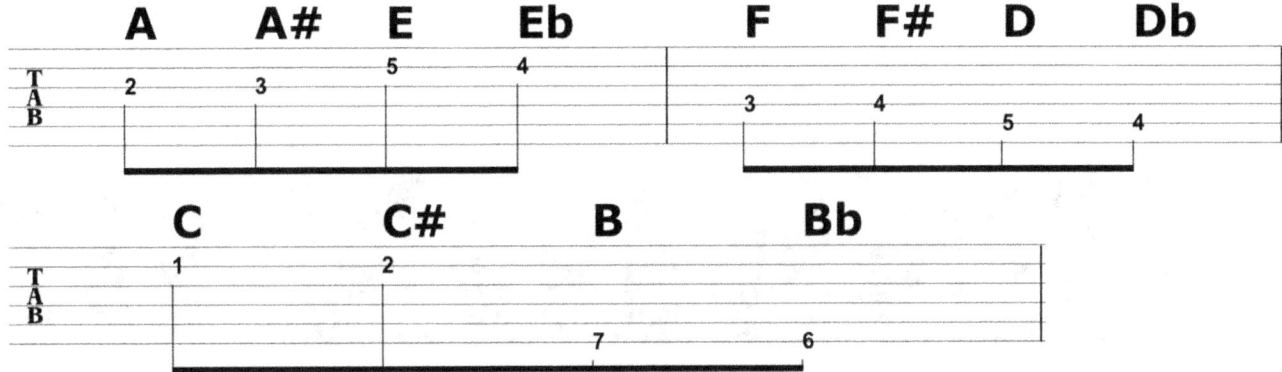

Practice finding notes for a few minutes every day. Choose a note (i.e. "C#") and find it on *every string*. Keep in mind that every sharped note can *also* be a flatted note: C# is the same pitch as Db, A# is the same as Bb, etc. The pitch is **exactly the same**, but you can call it either way - it usually depends which direction you're moving. Moving down, you'd call the note flat; moving up, you'd call it sharp.

It might not seem like a big deal now, but knowing the notes on the guitar is one of *the most important skills you'll need to have* (if you want to become really good, that is!)

Speaking of skills you'll need to have...how about being able to **play in time**, and have good **rhythm**? How important do you think *that* might be? (Hint: incredibly important!) With that in mind, let's tackle two basic concepts: **measures** and **rhythm slashes**. Understanding how these work is the first step in knowing how to **read rhythm** - another *absolutely essential* skill.

When TAB is divided into boxes, we call them **measures**. These boxes can hold a certain amount of counts or **beats**. Measures are connected one right after the other, and as you can imagine, most songs contain lots of measures. Actually, you've already seen measures being used in some of the examples so far - they help to organize the notes visually, so that everything doesn't run into everything else. Here's an example of four empty measures:

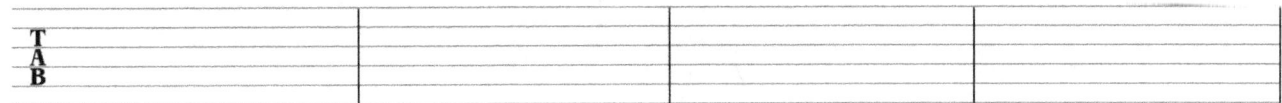

A basic (yet effective) way to use the measures is to fill them with **rhythm slashes**. These slashes will tell you how many beats to count during one measure - 2 slashes for two beats, 3 slashes for three beats, 4 for four beats, etc. Check out this example of the same four measures, this time with rhythm slashes; there are four beats in every measure:

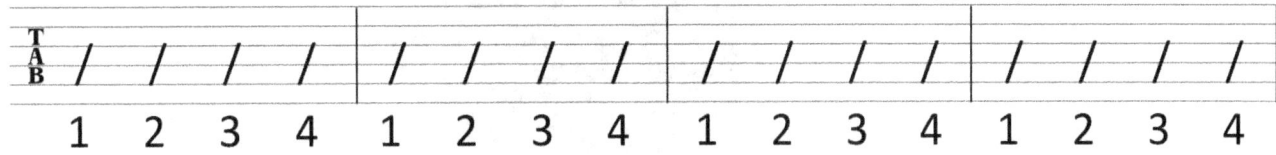

Notice that for each new measure, you start with "one" again. Each measure contains exactly four beats - no more, no less.

SESSION 05

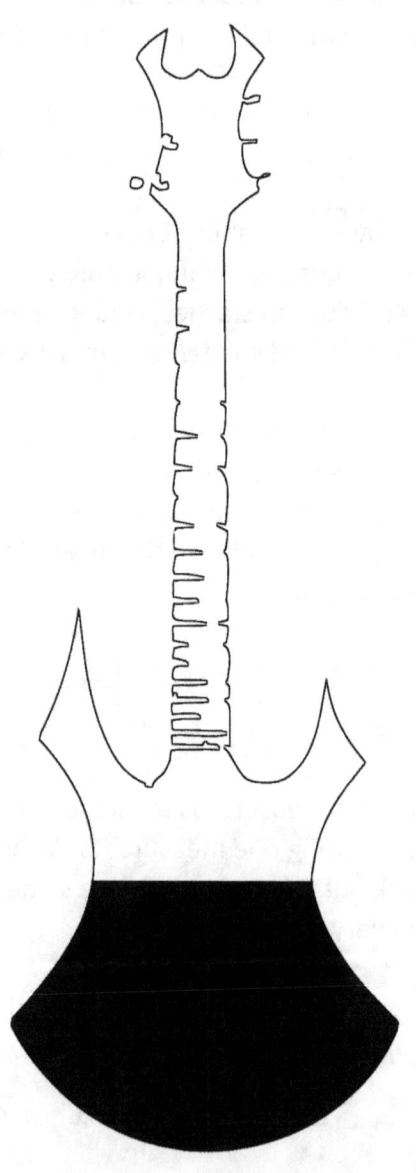

PHYSICAL

If you wrote a song that was just one chord, held it for the whole thing and strummed it over and over again, it'd be pretty awful, wouldn't it? One of the things that makes a song really cool sounding is the **chord progression** - the way one chord moves into another, and then another. Today, you'll be practicing **chord changes**, moving from one chord to the next. Get good at this, and you'll be able to play so many chord progressions and songs, it'll make your head spin!

To start, we're going to pick two chords from the eight open chords that you know. How about... **Em** and **D**? Good, glad you approve! But first, there's a couple more items to cover about playing chords. Item one? An important *exception* to the rule about **thumb position**.

Some of the chords you've learned (**A, Am, D, Dm, C**) *don't* include the low E string. When strumming these chords fast and aggressively though, it's virtually impossible to *not* hit that string with the pick. Therefore, **it becomes extremely important to mute the low E string**, so that we don't hear it ringing out when we don't want to. To accomplish this, you'll need to break one of our "rules of thumb", and **hook your thumb over the neck**. Your thumb will then be able to *lightly touch* the low E string, and stop it from vibrating! Here's what your thumb will look like when playing the **D major** chord:

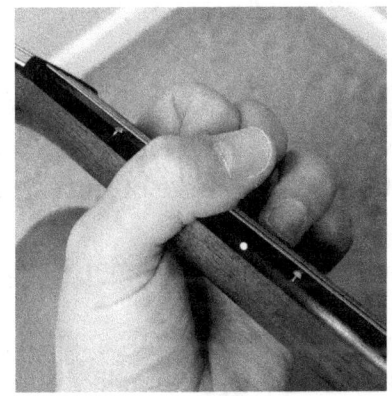

Make sure that you're **not pressing down** with your thumb - that will cause an extra note to sound! Just touch the E string lightly. Your fingers should still stay **straight up-and-down**, no different than you've been practicing.

Try this with the other chords as well - it's the way to go when strumming!

Item number two involves the **hand mechanics** of moving from chord to chord. Ideally, **all of the fingers should land on their assigned strings at the exact same time**. At first though, this is easier said than done! While it's not the end of the world to start with the ol' "one finger at a time" chord change, you can train yourself right away to get all those fingers dropping down at once by practicing the following exercise. Make the **Em chord** with your left hand, but *don't strum it*. Then lift both fingers at once, *keeping them lightly squeezed together* (so that they touch, and don't separate). Next, drop them both back down, so that **both fingers hit the strings at exactly the same time**:

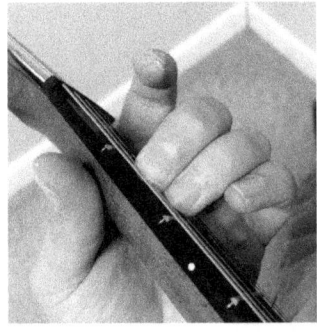
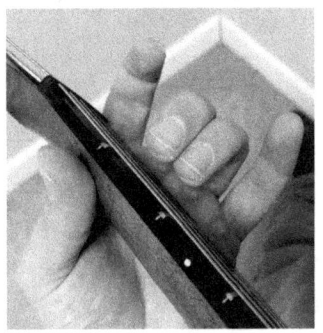
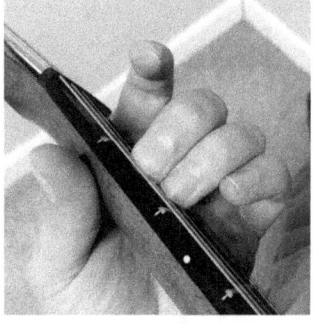

Now, try the same thing with the **D major chord**. *Make sure that your thumb is still "hooking" over the neck while your fingers are in the air* - if not, your fingers won't maintain the shape of the chord!

  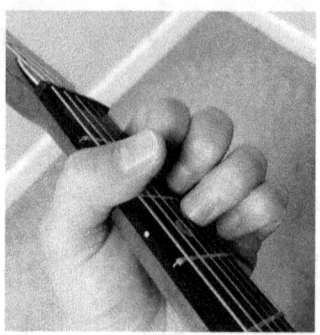

Having that thumb support is *essential* for keeping your fingers from **flying apart from each other** when in the air. Now - back to our **Em** to **D** chord change.

You're going to **count to four** (while using your metronome, of course!) Every time you say "*1*", you'll **strum one of the chords**. Here's how it looks using **rhythm slashes**:

```
   Em              D              Em              D
T |/  /  /  /  |  /  /  /  /  |  /  /  /  /  |  /  /  /  /  |
A
B
```

Don't strum on any beat except for "1" in each measure. You'll use the other three beats to *move your hand into the next chord shape*, as quickly as you can! Remember - ideally, you want to drop your fingers onto the strings **all at the same time**, like you were practicing in the previous exercises.

Don't flip out though if you can only do the "one-finger-at-a-time" chord change at first. It's normal!

Repeat these four measures over and over again. It doesn't matter (for now) if the chord rings out for all four beats or not - you can cut off the sound as you scramble to move your fingers into the next chord shape. What does matter is your **rhythmic accuracy** - make sure that you strum *exactly* on beat one, even if you think you've messed up the left hand shape. It's a lot easier to fix up your chord shape than it is to break the habit of **sloppy rhythm**, so make sure that you don't even give yourself the chance to form that habit. As you move back and forth, the chord shapes will clean themselves up (*if you concentrate!*)

When you're pretty comfortable changing chords smoothly, *don't* just crank up the metronome and try it faster - do this first:

```
   Em    D       Em    D       Em    D       Em    D
T |/  /  /  /  | /  /  /  /  | /  /  /  /  | /  /  /  /  |
A
B
```

Now you're strumming **twice** per measure, on beats *one* and *three*. This will make you move faster, that's for sure - but also, try to *hold down each chord just a little longer than you're comfortable with*. Doing this will help you begin to eliminate any pauses in the sound when changing chords. The goal is to have virtually seamless sound, from one chord to the next. Now, here's step three, strumming on beats *one* and *four*:

Em	D	Em	D	Em	D	Em	D
/ / / /	/ / / /	/ / / /	/ / / /	/ / / /	/ / / /	/ / / /	/ / / /

Make sure that you use **many different combinations** of two chords for these exercises. That's the point here - to become more comfortable changing between *all* of the chords that you've learned so far.

Switching gears from chords back into soloing, it's time to go **legato** again - and this time, you'll be combining both hammer-ons *and* pull-offs!

We're also going to up the ante by using **three fingers** for these legato exercises. This means you'll be performing *double* hammer-ons and *double* pull-offs. Because of this, it's extremely important to remember these two "golden rules" of legato: *1. When hammering, all the fingers you're using should* **end up** *pressing down | 2. When pulling,* **start** *with pressing down all the fingers you're using.*

For example, in the following exercise, this is what your fingers should look like *after* the two hammer-ons are complete:

Keep your fingers **just like this** when *beginning* the two pull-offs; that way, the two notes you'll be pulling to will **already be pressed down**. If they weren't, you'd have nothing to pull to! Your pull-off would sound sloppy, and you might even hear an **open string** by mistake.

Here's the ascending and descending example, using your index, middle, and ring fingers:

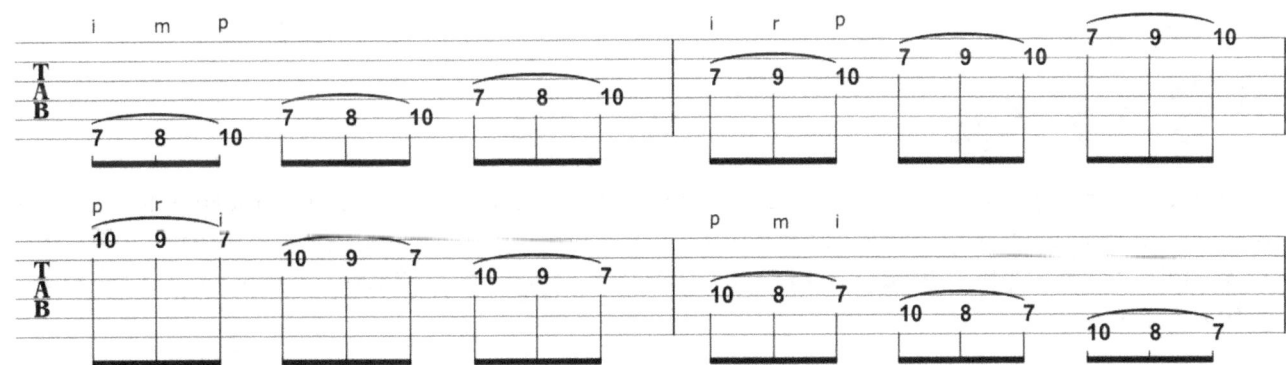

Whenever the slur is broken, *you must pick again*. In the above example, this means that you're picking **the first of every three notes**. After pulling both notes on one string, make sure that your pinky and ring (or pinky and middle) land on the next string *simultaneously*. Your index should follow them immediately, leaving you with **all three fingers down** before you pull again:

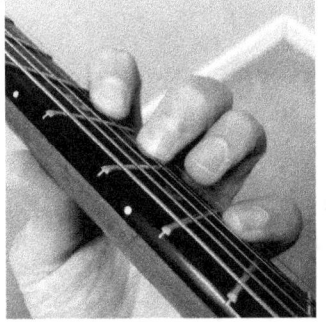

Take your time with all of this, and **play these exercises slowly**. Yes, there is a lot of detail here; that's a good thing. However, if you try to play too quickly at first, you'll skip right over these details - and then wonder why it doesn't sound good! When working on the physical movements, *don't* worry about **even rhythm** - only use the metronome when you're ready!

Now, you'll get to play some hammer-ons *followed immediately* by pull-offs. Having all three fingers down after the hammers will **set you up** for the pull-offs:

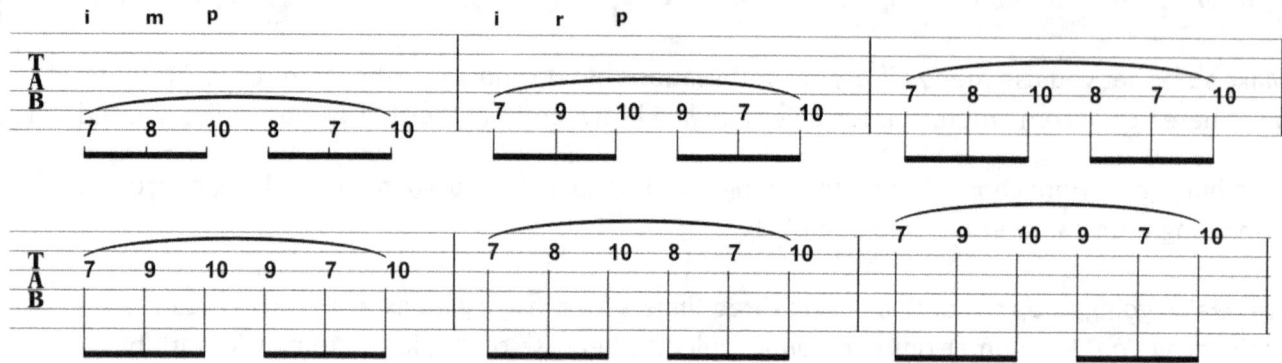

This exercise combines all four fingers, as well as **two-per-string** and **three-per-string** hammers and pulls:

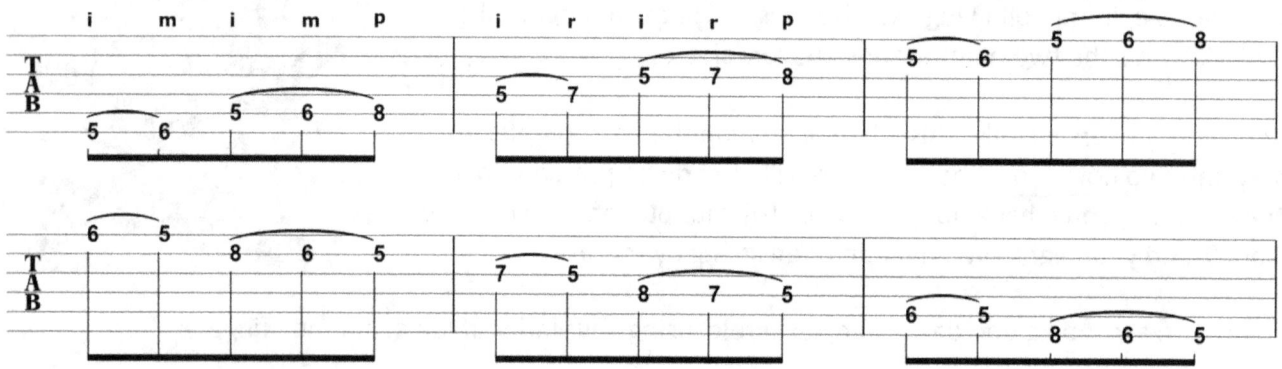

MENTAL

With the chord boxes, we have a cool visual way to see the shapes our hands must make when learning a new chord. Did you know that we can use these same boxes to learn **single note patterns**? Well, now you do! Take, for example, this pattern of notes - similar to what your left hand was playing in the legato exercises:

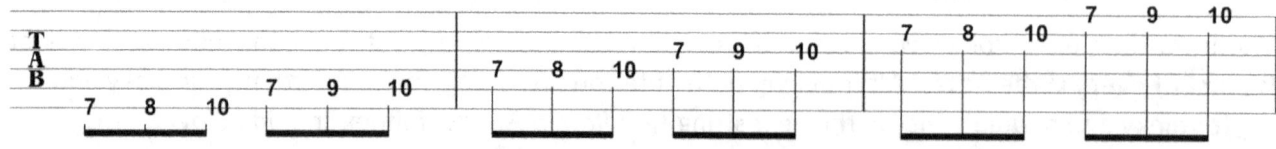

Three notes per string, covering four frets. Index, middle, pinky, then index, ring, pinky, etc. Is there a way to map out this info onto the chord box? Let's find out:

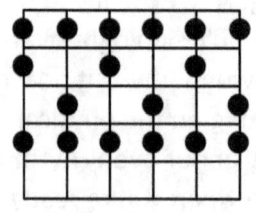

Can you see the pattern? If the top fret is your 7th fret, this means that the notes cover the 7th, 8th, 9th, and 10th frets - **three notes per string**. Because of the placement of the dots, we can also see that the notes on the low E string would be played with the index, middle, and pinky fingers. On the A string you'd use the ring finger instead, since the second dot is **shifted one fret down** (to the 9th fret).

If you can see how this works - great! If you're having a little trouble visualizing it, then try one more. Here's another diagram, followed by the same thing in TAB:

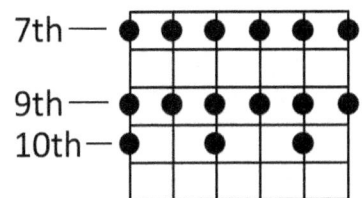

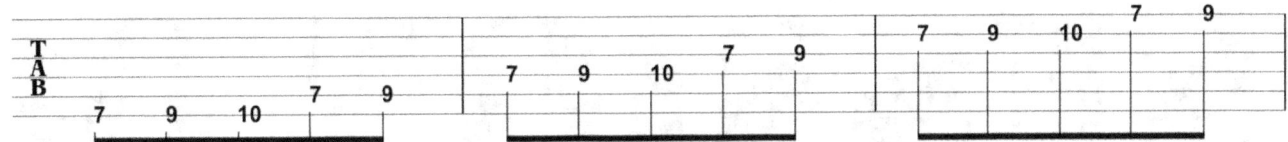

Got it now? These are like *roadmaps*; just follow each string, moving one fret at a time. The previous example has three notes on the E string, then two on the A string, etc.

So what's the advantage of writing things out this way? There are two big ones: *1.* Many finger patterns that you'll be learning on the guitar are **movable**, which means that you can play them anywhere on the neck. Using diagrams like the above can be a faster way to learn these patterns, instead of always notating specific frets using TAB. *2.* These are a more **visual** way to absorb a finger pattern; you can get a sense of the whole pattern at a glance.

You might be asking yourself, "How come the first fret in the diagram is the 7th fret?" There's actually no reason it has to be. Remember, these finger patterns are movable - **which means that you could play this pattern starting on any fret**. The 7th fret was just chosen for the heck of it! Try playing these patterns starting different places on the neck, and you'll see how it works.

As we learn more specific note patterns, it becomes even more important to know the names of all the notes you're playing. Here's a fun way to keep practicing your note finding abilities, and to get in some more chord practice at the same time!

Believe it or not, all of those big major and minor chords that you're learning are only made up of **three notes each**. The three notes in each chord are **doubled** (played in two different places), or sometimes even **tripled** - which means that one note might show up *more than once* in the chord. For example, that big **G major** chord actually has *three G notes* in it - a low, medium, and high pitched G:

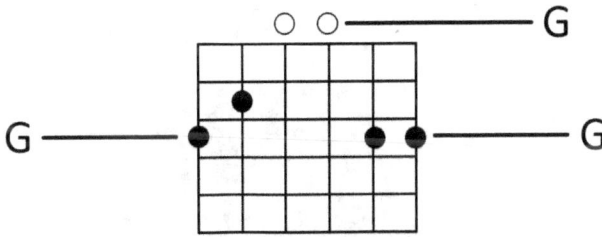

So, fully *half* of that chord shape (3 strings) is only one note! (There's another **doubled** note in the chord shape as well...can you find it?)

In a similar fashion, for all of your other major and minor chords, at least two of the strings will be making the same note...and it's your job to find them. Play each of the 8 open chords that you've learned, and *find the names of all the notes in them*. See which of the notes out of the three are **doubled** (or tripled!) Got it? Go for it!

SESSION 06

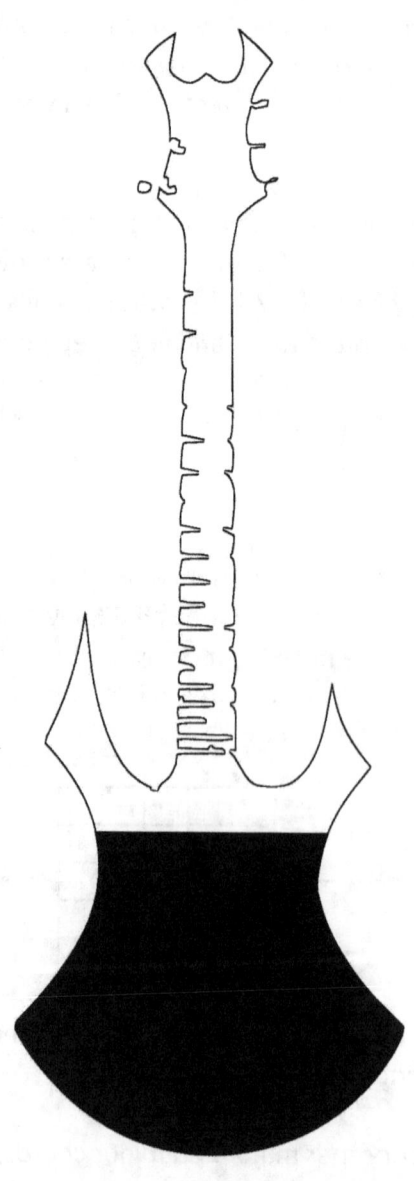

PHYSICAL

Your confidence in your chord playing ability is rising (if you've been practicing a lot, that is!) Most of that practice has been with the left hand; getting your fingers into those shapes and playing chord changes is challenging. Today's lesson, however, will get you focusing more on the *right* hand. Because with chords, it's not just about the shape...it's also about the strum.

Strums come in two types: **down** and **up**. A down strum is what you've been doing so far; moving your hand and pick towards the floor. After completing a downwards strum, you have to bring your hand **all the way back up** in order to strum downwards again. At a slow tempo, this is no big deal. But, at faster tempos, this just won't work, so...enter the *upwards* strum! Bringing your hand and pick **back up** across the strings, starting from the high E string, allows you to have a seamless *down/up* motion when strumming. This is the preferred method for playing faster.

Down strums and up strums have their own symbols, so that you'll know which to use. Here they are:

⊓ = Down   ∨ = Up

Strumming *up* can be trickier at first, because you're fighting against gravity. Keep your wrist fairly relaxed; if you're too tense, the pick can get caught on the strings, destroying the smoothness of your up strum. Let's give it a shot, with the left hand holding an **Em** chord - you'll be strumming on every beat, alternating between down and up strums:

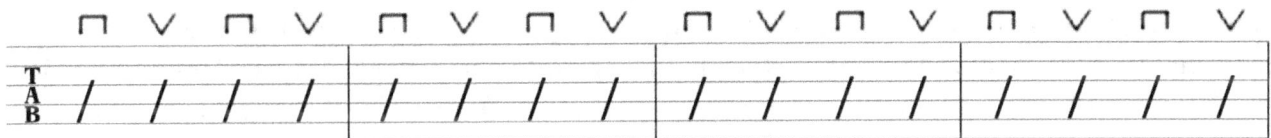

Now, try to continue this down/up strum pattern while changing chords - **Em** to **G**. The chord symbol will be written where the first rhythm slash goes. *Practice this with other combos of two chords as well!*

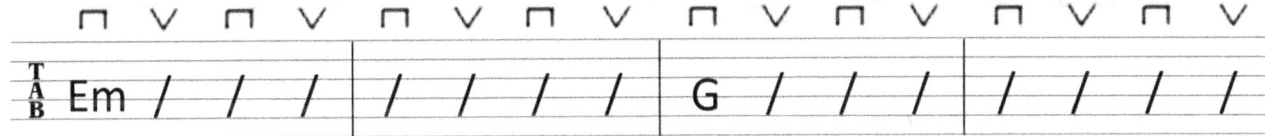

Hey, now might be a good time to ask you something - this whole "chord change" thing is hard, isn't it? It totally is (for everybody) at first. *So don't get discouraged!* Just because the material is presented in one Session, it doesn't mean that you're expected to master it in one day - or even in one week, for that matter. So there's your reality check - **don't put that kind of pressure on yourself!** Only move on to the next Session when you're ready. That advice goes for *every* Session in this book, by the way!

As a reminder, make sure you're practicing the chord changes **slowly and evenly**, using your metronome to keep your rhythm solid. *Speed is not a factor yet* - you should be concerned solely with sound, cleanliness, and rhythm. Take care of these, and your speed at changing chords is guaranteed to increase within a reasonable amount of time!

There's another use for those down/up symbols, and it has to do with **lead playing**. When playing single notes so far, you've been picking downwards, towards the floor. The name for that is a *downstroke*. **Alternate picking** is a technique where we use *upstrokes* as well - picking *up from underneath the string*. As you can tell from the name, alternate picking means that we alternate between downstrokes and upstrokes.

Why would we want to do this? Simple: speed and efficiency. As you start to increase your picking speed, you'll find that you hit a wall pretty quickly if you're only using downstrokes. *Alternating between down and upstrokes means that you've doubled your efficiency of motion*, and your picking speed can increase exponentially as a result.

The same symbols that you've used for strumming up and down are also used to indicate upstrokes and downstrokes when picking single notes. Here's a familiar exercise, but this time with the symbols thrown in:

Play through the above exercise several times, making sure that your pick *doesn't fall onto the next string* - it should hover **in between the strings** right after contact. Also, make sure that you continue to **rest your hand on the bridge**, making light contact and moving your hand and wrist with the pick as you play from thickest to thinnest strings. *Don't curve the wrist to get to the higher strings!*

Here's a simple but extremely effective exercise to get you moving with alternate picking. You'll be performing multiple pick strokes on each string, holding only *one* note at a time with the left hand - so that you can focus your full attention on your alternate picking. This technique is called **tremolo picking**, and this exercise, plus the previous one, make excellent warmups for your practice sessions.

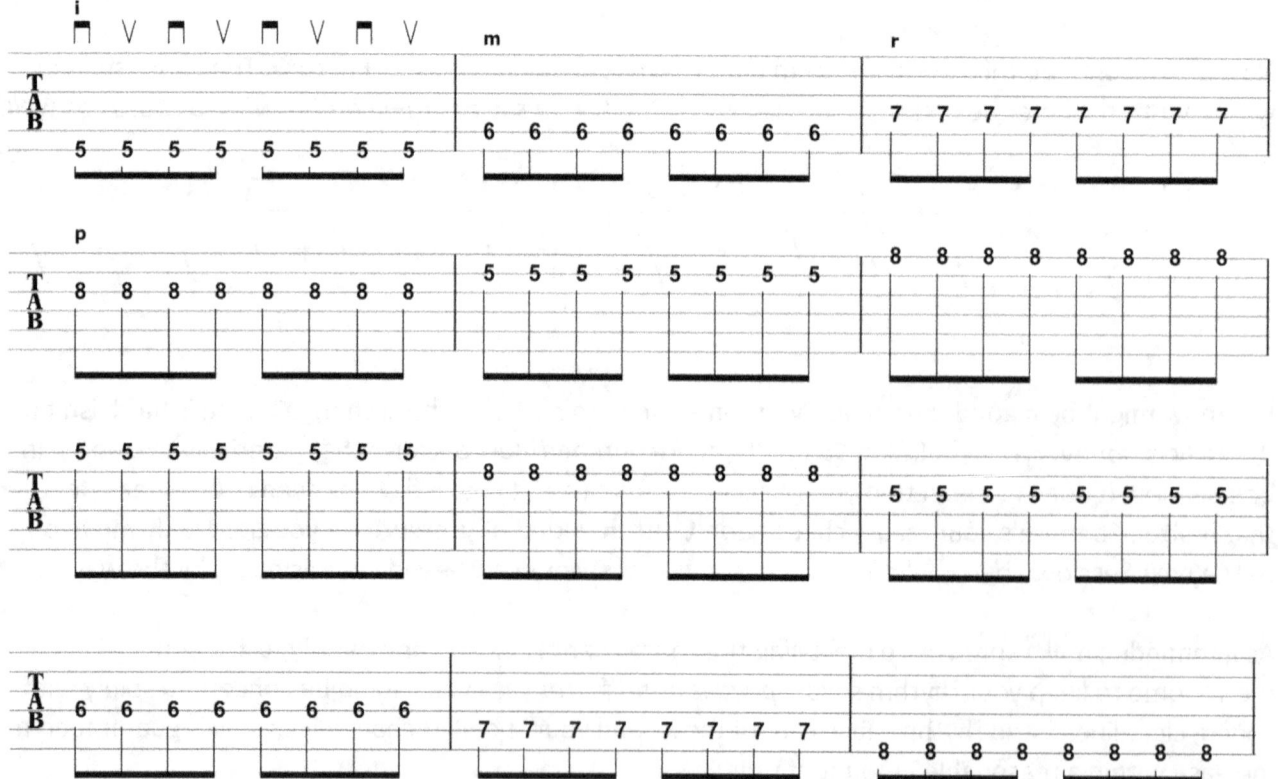

35

MENTAL

You've probably heard other musicians or guitar players talking about **scales**. Scales are very important when it comes to soloing, writing melodies, playing chords, writing songs - just about every aspect of playing the guitar.

Unfortunately, a lot of these guitarists who throw the word around don't really understand, at the most basic level, what a scale really is (let alone, how to really use them!) We're going to make sure that you're *not* one of those players. So, what is a scale?

We'll be getting a bit more in-depth later on, but for now, the most basic definition of a scale is this:

A series of pitches, ascending step-wise, that starts and ends on the same note.

So, this would be one example of a scale:

A B C D E F G A

Notice that this **series** of pitches **starts and ends** on the note "A" (remember that term **octave**? This is a good example. Another way to say "starts and ends on the same note" is to say "spans an octave").

Here's another example of a scale:

G Bb C D F G

What are some of the similarities between these two scales? Well, they both are made of notes that ascend step-wise, or up through the musical alphabet. They both also **span an octave** (start and end on the same note). There's an obvious difference though between these two scales - *they have a different number of notes.* **An important way to identify a type of scale is to count how many different notes it has**.

The first scale has seven notes (we don't count the "A" twice, since it's the same note). The next scale has only five notes, and has a special name because of it. This one is called a **pentatonic scale** (*penta* = five, *tonic* = tone). This type of scale is *very* common in all kinds of contemporary music (rock, blues, Metal, jazz, fusion), and it will be the first type of scale that you'll learn to use!

Believe it or not, there are actually several different types of pentatonic scales - the one you'll be using is more specifically called the **minor pentatonic scale**. Don't worry about why for right now...you'll understand soon enough.

So, let's get you playing this ultra-cool minor pentatonic scale! The first and most important thing to do when learning any type of new scale is to get to know the sound of the scale. The best way to do this is to keep everything as simple as possible for the left hand - that way, you can focus on the *overall sound* of the scale, and not hyper-focus on finding each individual note in a big, complicated fingering pattern.

To facilitate this, you'll be playing only on the **low E string**, climbing up the neck. We're going to be using the same *minor pentatonic scale* from the previous page:

G Bb C D F G

Because the scale starts on the note **G**, we call this the **root note** of the scale. A root note, because it's the first one that you hear, tends to have a dominant sound over the other notes. Your brain keeps relating each new note you hear in the scale *back* to the first one. Makes sense, right? The root note is how we name a scale, too. We know that the *type* of scale here is minor pentatonic. But since the root note is G, we can now be more specific with the name: this is a **G minor pentatonic**. Now, let's find those notes on the low E string:

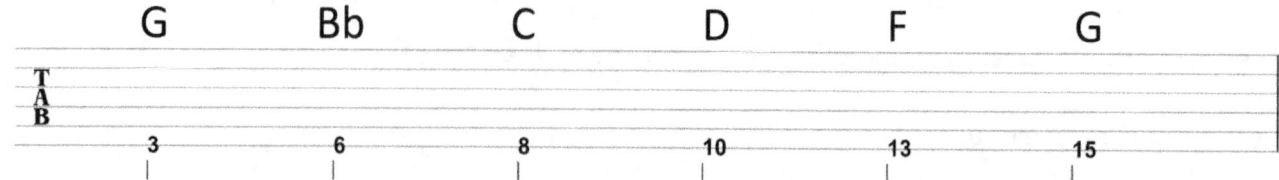

Pretty cool, bluesy sound, isn't it? Now here's the thing: since we know the names of the notes in this G minor pentatonic scale, we don't have to just play it on the low E sting. Anywhere we can find the root note (G), we can do the same thing and play the scale up the fretboard. Here's an example of the scale played on the G string:

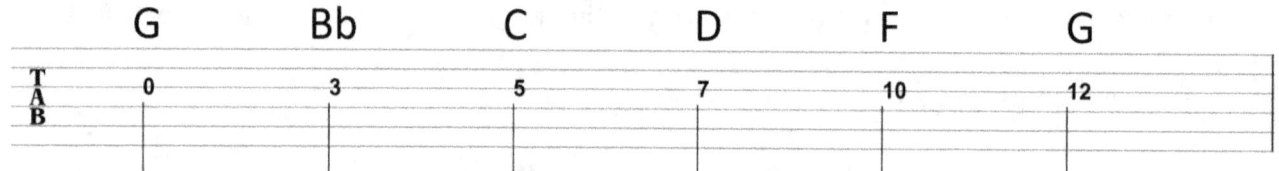

And one more place, this time on the D string:

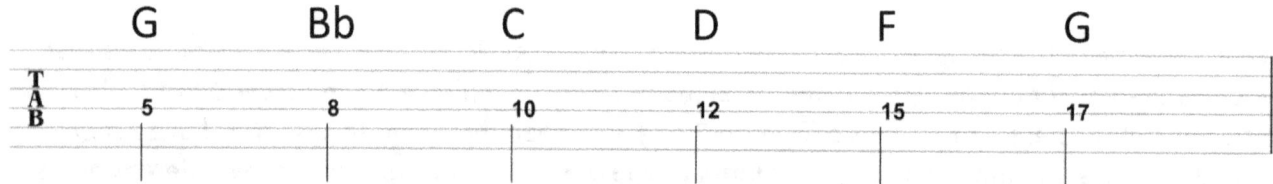

When you see guitar players soloing, flying and jumping all over the neck, it can often look like they're playing a mind-numbingly large amount of notes. As illustrated above though, this is usually *not* the case. What's really going on is, **they're playing a fairly limited number of notes** (only five, in the case of the minor pentatonic scale) but playing those notes *all over the neck, in different places*.

The guitar has a pretty big **range** - which means there are really low notes (like the open low E string) all the way up to very high notes (like the 22nd fret on the high E string). Because of this, there will be **many places to play the same notes in a scale**. It's why those seemingly million-note solos sound coherent, and like all the notes "fit" together - because they do!

SESSION 07

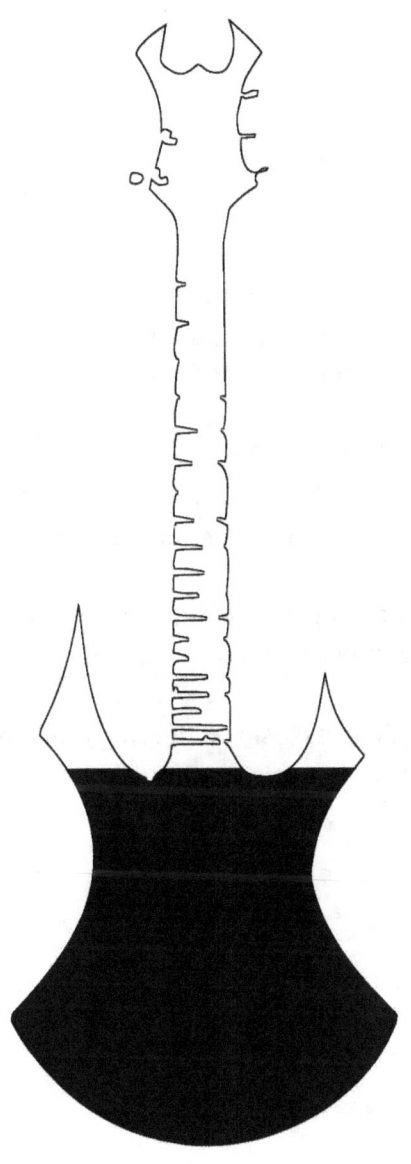

PHYSICAL

Strumming at a slightly faster rate of speed, using both up and down strums, and changing between **four chords at a time** is your next physical challenge. Managing multiple chords like this is *essential* for being able to play songs - and when you can do this comfortably, you'll find that you can easily strum your way through literally hundreds of them!

Here's the first example, using this set of four chords:

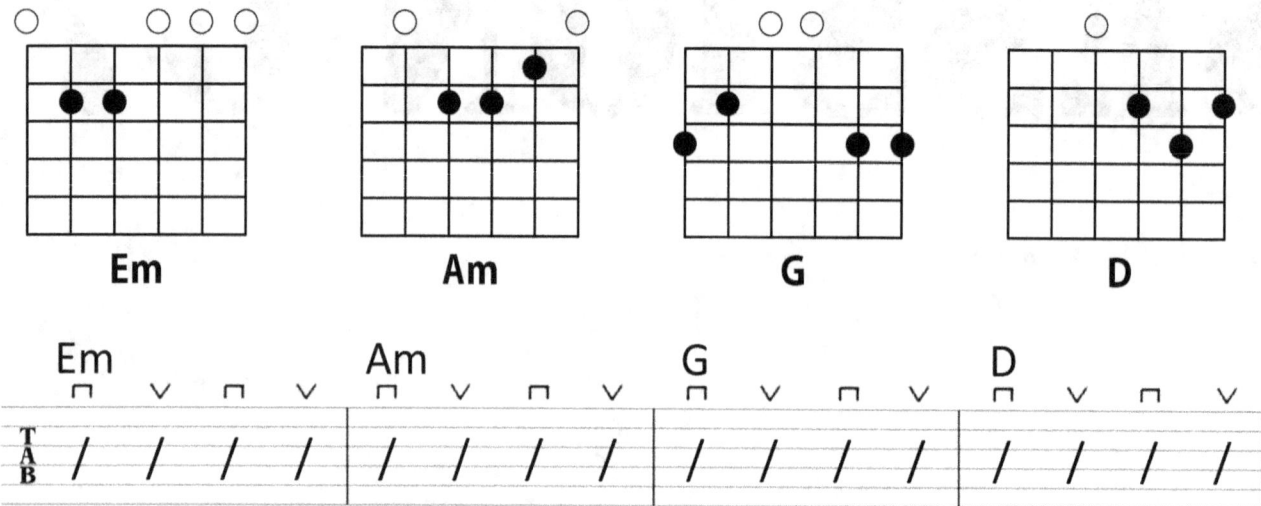

Tricky at first, isn't it? Make sure to play this at a **slow enough tempo** so that there's *no pausing* when it's time to switch chords! Remember, it's better to have a sloppy chord than a sloppy rhythm - you can fix up the chord, but it's hard to get out of the habit of imprecise rhythm.

Here's another tip: *don't fight the thumb motion!* Two of these chords (Em and G) *include* the low E string, so your thumb will be **supporting on the back of the neck**. The other two chords (Am and D) *don't* include the low E string, so your thumb will be **hooked over the neck** in order to mute that string.

As you move from chord to chord, your thumb will be moving as well. Let that motion happen; **don't fight it by locking your thumb in place**. It will be "sliding" up and down a bit, and this is a good thing!

Here are two more examples of chord changes, using different combinations of chords that you know. Heed the aforementioned "rule of thumb" (sorry, couldn't resist!) for these chord changes as well. Continue to play using *down strums* and *up strums*:

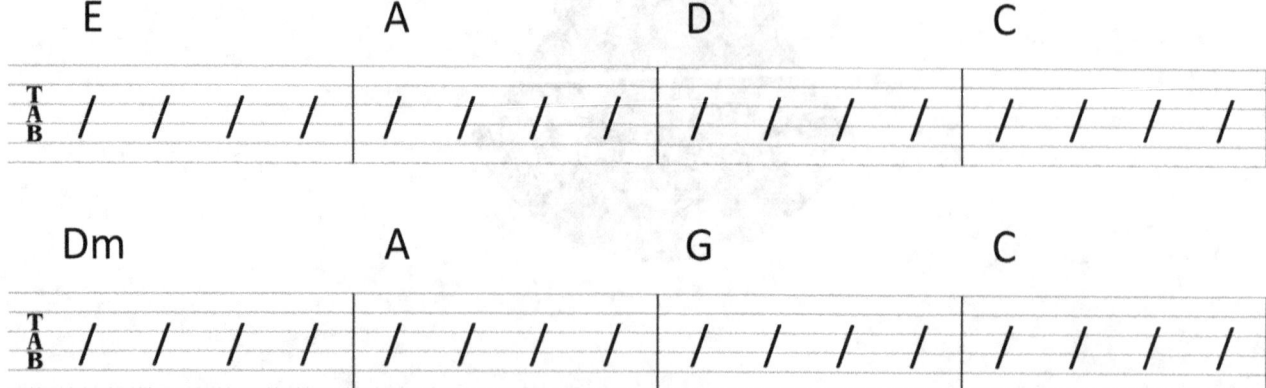

We've learned that scales can be played on one string, ascending up the neck, and starting from different points on the neck. While this way of playing scales is often used when soloing, it's even more common to play a scale using **more than one string**. This way, you can keep your left hand in one area of the neck for a longer amount of time - this increases both *speed* and *efficiency*.

For example, let's revisit that **G minor pentatonic** scale:

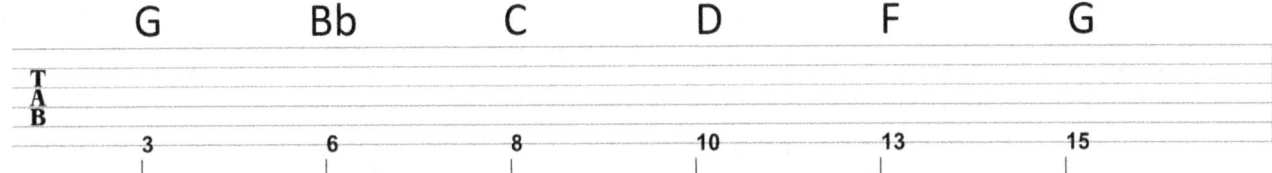

There's a way that we can play the exact same notes, but using all six strings. The hand will stay in one area, and in fact, we'll be able to play through the scale twice - the notes will repeat in a higher **octave**:

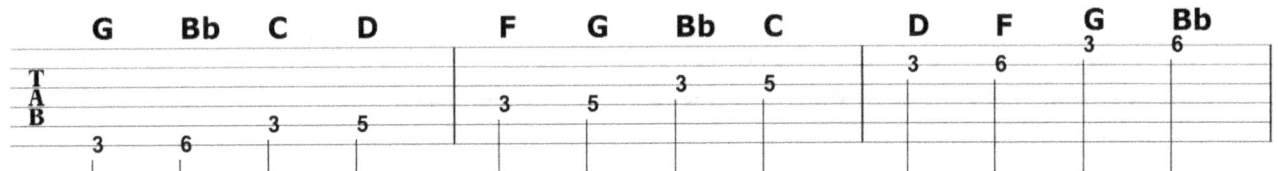

In addition to using TAB to show where the notes for this scale can be played, it's also extremely common to use a **scale diagram**. The "3rd" is written to indicate which fret to start on.

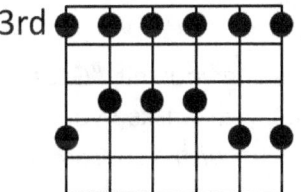

When playing this type of scale (which spans four frets) it's important to use the correct **fingering**. The correct fingering in this case is simply *one finger per fret.* Play through the scale again, and make sure that you're using this specific fingering:

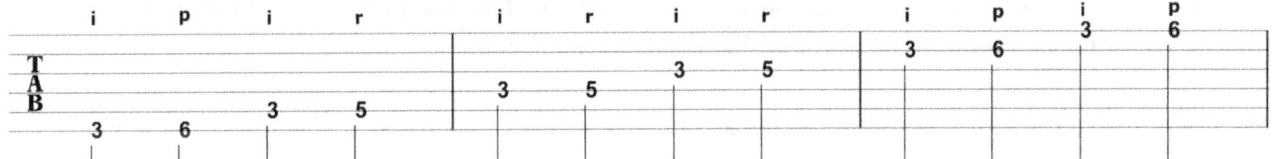

Also, when practicing this scale, it's important to **hover** your fingers over their assigned fret. For example, when pressing down the low E string with your index finger, your pinky should be *hovering right over* the 6th fret, ready to drop down. This may be difficult at first, but be patient and keep trying! This technique will be essential for soloing and building some speed later on. To facilitate this, make sure that your thumb is in the proper position, in the middle of the neck, behind your middle finger.

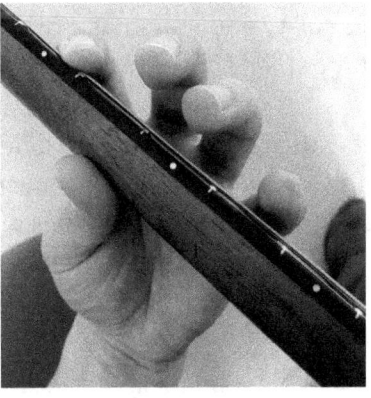

40

Here is an exercise for you to practice which uses the **G minor pentatonic** scale. It's called a **sequence**, which means repeating a specific musical pattern throughout the notes in a scale. Sequences are great technique builders, because they allow you to "get more out of" a scale when practicing - not just playing right up and right back down. Play this example, and remember to *use the correct fingering, to hover your fingers, and to use alternate picking*. Here it is ascending and descending. Go for it!

MENTAL

So by now your might be asking yourself, *"Geez - why all this chord and scale business? I want to play some songs!"* You've probably also asked yourself this next question a lot (maybe even subconsciously): *"How do people even come up with a cool song or a great solo? Is it magic? Is it luck? Do people just slap stuff together through trial and error, and it works? Are they geniuses?"*

The answer to the second question totally ties into the first. To start with, the answer is "no" - it's not magic, luck, trial and error, or inherent genius that makes a cool song, riff, or solo. Yes it takes experience and good old fashioned practice to achieve these results (just like any human endeavor). But there is a set of tools, a knowledge base, without which all the experience and practice would amount to nothing. What are those tools? Why, chords and scales!

See, you need to think of chords and scales as the **vocabulary** of music. Knowing how they work together and relate to each other is akin to understanding **grammar**. For example, what makes a Mark Twain story different from a 3rd grader's story? Well, life experience for one. But a huge difference would be vocabulary and grammar - Twain would just have more vocabulary, *and the knowledge about how to put it together effectively*.

Writing an awesome song or riff is no different. Learning more chords and scales increases your musical vocabulary, and learning about some music theory (which you're doing in this book!) is like learning grammar - how those chords and scales work together. Sure there's creativity involved, just like in writing an article or a book. But, there are certain logical ways that chords and scales "fit" to create a coherent song, riff, or solo. It's not just random - at least not for *good* musicians anyway!

So rest assured - you're building the skills necessary to not only *play* songs, but to write your own too!

SESSION 08

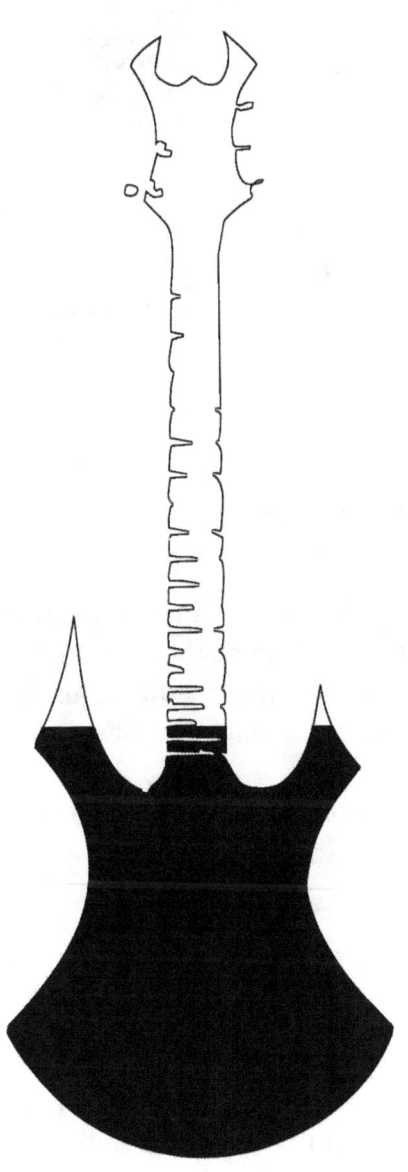

PHYSICAL

Time to delve a bit deeper into **power chords** - those two-string movable shapes that so many great and heavy riffs are comprised of. If you've been practicing, then you can make 'em and move 'em - but now, we're going to increase the speed and try some more advanced movements.

Before we cover anything new, it's a good idea to get warmed up. So, here's a riff that's good to get you going. For the power chord with the open E string, **use your index finger to play the A string** at the second fret. This is a very common power chord; you'll see it all the time!

While that fingering may not *look* like a power chord, it still is. If there was a fret **behind your first fret**, you'd have to put your index finger there - and your ring finger would play the A string, second fret.

But, that would be ridiculous! So, we just use the index finger instead of the ring finger.

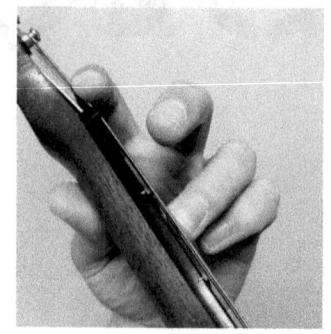
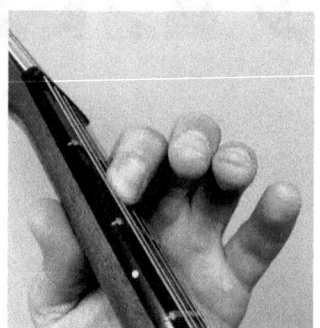

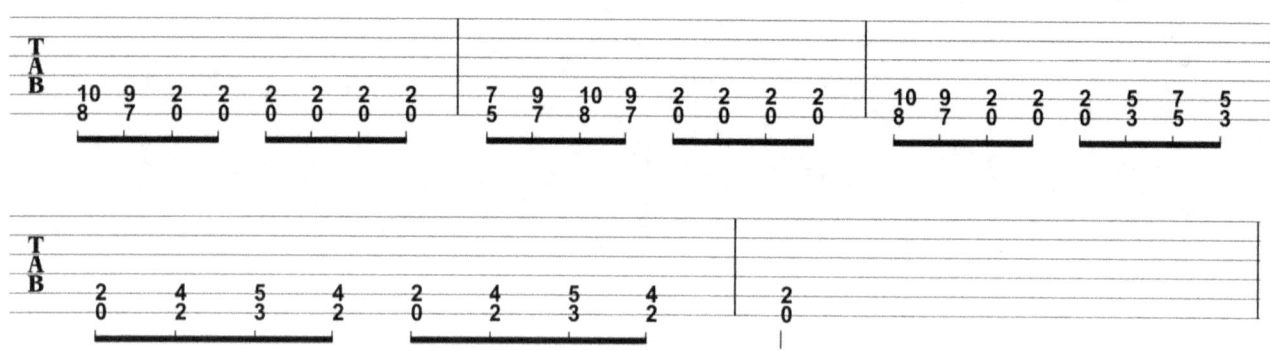

So how fast should you be practicing that riff? Well, there's no single answer for that - everyone's different. *You* should find a tempo on the metronome that challenges *you*. Not so fast that it becomes a train wreck (remember, never sacrifice accuracy for speed), but just fast enough so that you feel like you could lose control at any second. That's your **edge** - and it's the most effective place for practice.

Okay, here's one more for speed work. Try to loop this one over and over again without stopping:

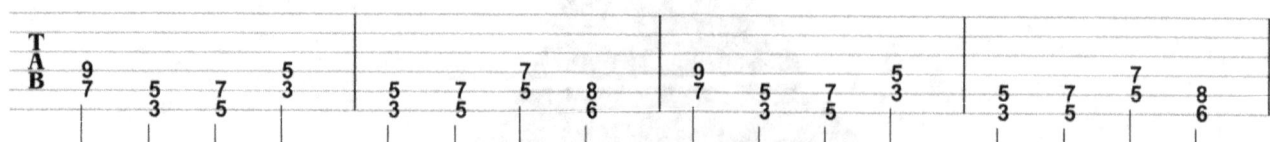

Excellent! Now that you're good and warmed up (or frustrated!), it's time for a new power chord technique: the **slide**. Sometimes, a riff gets going so fast that it becomes *impractical* to pick every single power chord. You won't be practicing this technique at super-speeds yet, but it's just as effective when played slowly. In fact, you'll notice that it even *sounds* a little different. The slide is an example of what's called an **articulation** - a different way to perform the notes (*legato* is an **articulation** as well!)

43

To perform a slide, start by making a power chord on the **5th fret**, using the E and A strings. Play it, and then *while you're still clamping down and the chord is still sounding*, slide both of your fingers three frets higher. *Don't pick the second power chord*. Here's how that move would look in TAB:

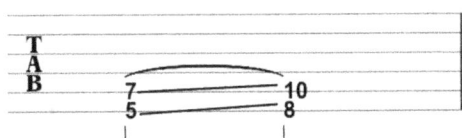

Notice both the **slur** and the **lines** connecting the notes. *This is what you'll see in TAB when the slide technique is called for*. The momentum of your slide is what will cause the second chord to sound.

The most important thing to remember about the slide technique is to *keep clamping down as you move*. For many people, this seems counterintuitive at first - "How can my hand move if I'm clamping my fingers down?" - but just try it, and you'll see! **Make sure your thumb is sliding** right along with your fingers too; *don't* cement it into place! This is especially important when sliding *down* the neck - which can often be more difficult (at first) than sliding *up* the neck. Here's an exercise using **slides up and down the neck**:

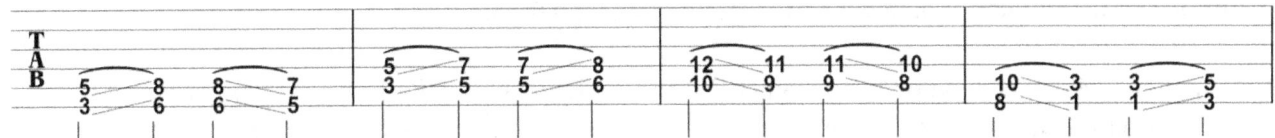

Another important power chord technique that is absolutely *essential* to master is called **palm muting**. You'll hear this technique in all styles of music, but especially in rock and Metal. As soon as you try it, you'll recognize the sound - it gives a *chunk, chunk* feel to the chords.

This technique is all in the **right hand**. Normally, we rest that hand *behind* the strings when playing. For palm muting, you'll actually be resting your hand **on the strings** - right where they meet the bridge. You may need to adjust your hand forward or backward (towards the neck, or towards the body), until you find the "sweet spot" on your guitar.

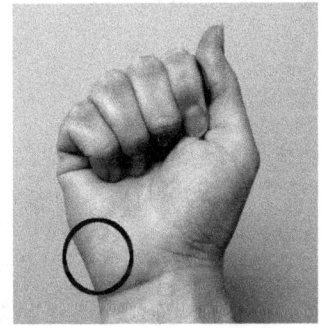 

This is where you can still **hear the pitches** in the chord, but it's got a nice, **chunky sound**.

If your hand is too far forward, then the sound will be too "clicky" (not enough sound of the notes). If your hand is too far back, you won't hear any "chunk" at all. Experiment with this next exercise; the "P.M." stands for palm mute. Let's start by using single notes:

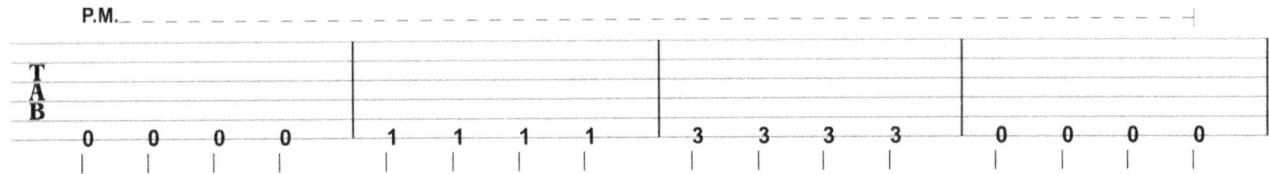

Did you get the perfect mix of **pitch** and **chunk**? If not, then keep practicing! When you're ready, here's the same thing - but this time with full power chords. Make sure to keep your right hand on those strings *while you're picking the chords.* Sometimes people will place their hand correctly, but will *lift just before* connecting with the pick. Don't do this! **Keep touching those strings!**

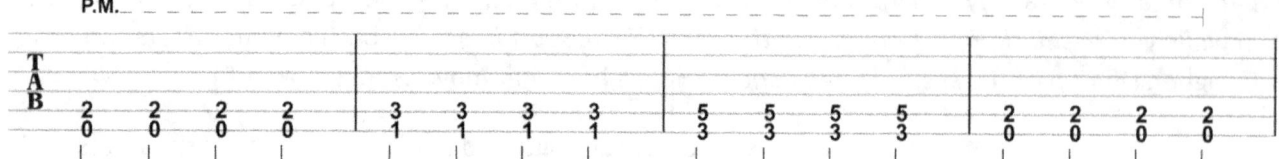

Now try it with one of the previous exercises - switching between power chords on different strings!

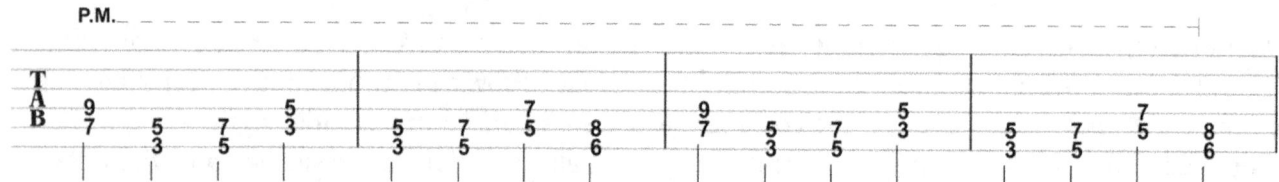

When riffing, it's very common to switch quickly from a palm muted note or power chord, to a non-muted, normal note or power chord. When doing this, you will **not** slide your hand back and forth on the bridge - that would be too awkward to perform at higher speeds.

Instead, you will be **lifting your hand slightly**, so that it floats above the bridge for the non-muted notes. This allows you to quickly drop your hand back into the palm muting position.

It's important to remember that this "floating" above the bridge is *only to be used when transitions between normal and palm muted notes are necessary*. When playing a series of power chords where no palm muting is called for, you'll want to be resting your hand behind the strings at the bridge - just like you learned when first starting to pick.

Here are two photos; the first is the **palm muted hand position**, and the second is the **"floating" position**:

When moving back into a palm mute *after* playing a normal note, make sure that you **pick** at the *exact moment* your hand **mutes** the strings. This should be **one motion** - mute and pick *simultaneously*. Many players can have trouble at first, because they are inadvertently *performing two separate motions* - muting, then picking. Watch out for this! It's a common mistake, but one that's easy to head off if you're looking out for it.

Here's an exercise on the low E string that gets your right hand moving up and down. Watch for the "P.M." symbol and the dotted line; these will tell you which notes to palm mute, and which not to *(hint: the first note of each measure is **not** palm muted!)*

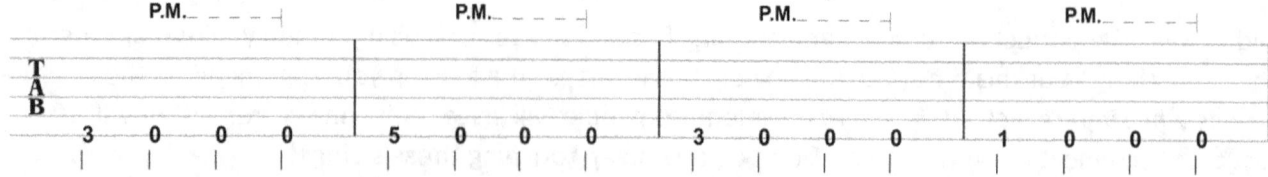

45

This next exercise is similar, but includes power chords played on the **A and D strings**. To eliminate unwanted string noise, when playing the open E string, **stop pressing down the power chord**. Don't lift your fingers off the strings - that would be inefficient motion, and will slow you down - *just stop pressing, and leave them resting on the strings*. This way, you'll be stopping those strings from vibrating.

It's very important to practice those two exercises with a metronome, and start building some speed, just as soon as you've got the mechanics down. Using all down strokes is fine for now; in fact, power chords are often played with *only* down strokes, even at faster tempos.

Your final physical challenge for today involves moving from **open chords** to **power chords**. This occurs quite frequently in songs, and can be difficult at first. Why? **There is more movement of the elbow and forearm**. Many guitarists fight this movement at first, so in order to move naturally and smoothly, it's important to be aware of it.

Open Chord Elbow

Power Chord Elbow

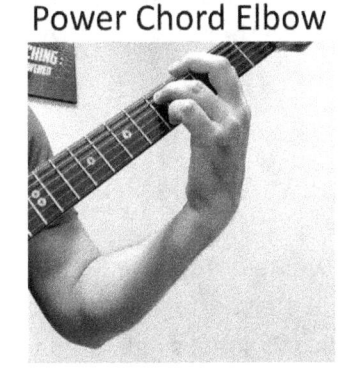

For the following three exercises, just let your elbow move down, where it naturally wants to go, when changing to the power chords. Use **down and up strums** for the open chords, and **all down strokes** for the power chords.

Another part of the practice here is making sure that your right hand changes successfully from *strumming* the open chords, to *resting* on the bridge when playing the power chords:

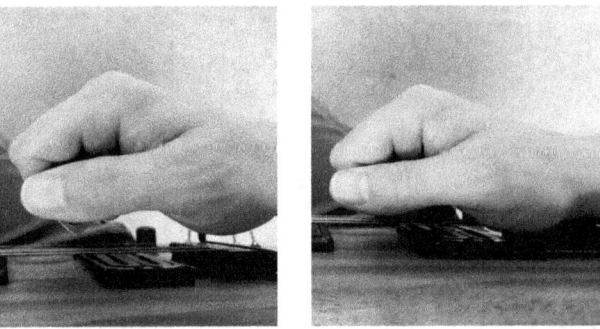

Try to keep all of this in mind, and practice these next exercises slowly:

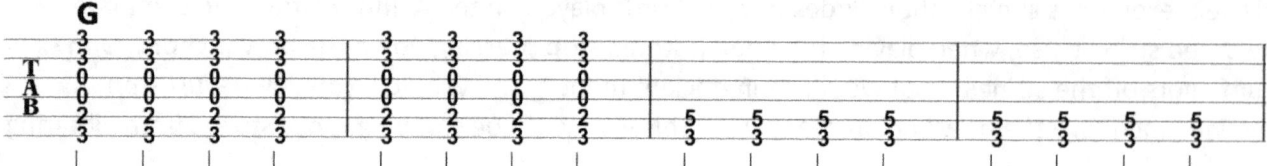

MENTAL

Rhythm in music is all about **duration** - how long one note lasts in relation to another. Different types of notes (or **note values**) will last for longer or shorter amounts of time. *It's extremely important to learn about note values and begin to read rhythm.* It's probably one of the best things you could ever do in order to continually become a better guitarist. Seriously.

Different types of notes have different names, and different shapes. Your first task is to learn to recognize them...so here they are!

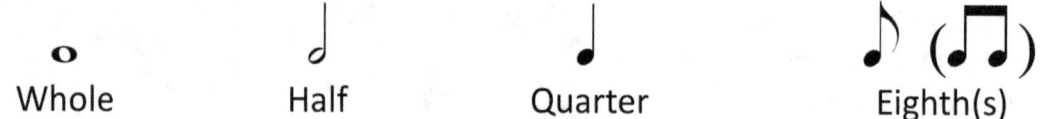

The whole note is the longest lasting note value, and the eighth (or 8th) is the shortest note value (there are shorter notes, but you'll be learning up to the 8th note in this book!) Speaking of 8th notes, when you see a single 8th, it will have a small **flag** attached to the **stem** (as you can see above). If more than one 8th note is written, they will usually be connected by a **beam** at the top.

So how do these notes relate? A great way to find out is to use the **Rhythm Pyramid**:

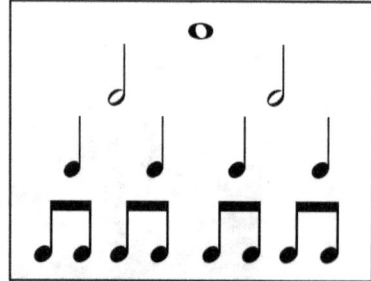

At the apex of the pyramid, we find the **whole note**. Pretend that the whole note rings out for 60 seconds (that would be pretty boring, but just pretend!) A whole note can be split into two half notes, so each of the **half notes** underneath would ring out for 30 seconds.

A half note can be split into two **quarter notes**. So, each of the four quarter notes would last for 15 seconds in our thought experiment. Finally, since a quarter note can be split into two **8th notes**, each 8th note would last for 7.5 seconds.

Remember, the times here are just arbitrary - we're using them because the math is easy. What's important is not the length of time, *but how each note relates to the others*. That's why the rhythm pyramid can be such a useful tool. **These relationships stay the same, no matter how slow or fast the music is.**

Now that you know the names of the notes and how they relate to one another, it's time to see how they look in **TAB**! Since we're using TAB exclusively (and since the best, most accurate reference material, like guitar magazines, does too) this is pretty essential. Here's how each type of note value would look when written in TAB:

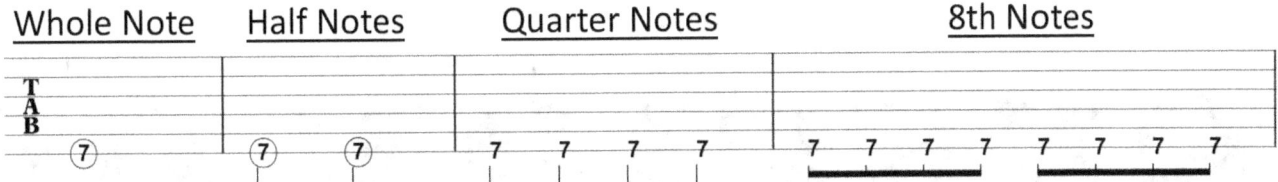

A-ha! So *that's* what those lines have been underneath the numbers! Yes indeed - you've been seeing these notes all along. But now, you know what they're called.

Here's one more thing about these note values - when they're written inside a **measure** (which they will be), they'll always **add up to the same amount of time**.

For instance, check out the above example. The first measure contains only **one note** - the whole note. In other words, since it's the longest type of note value, it's all that the measure can hold. The second measure though contains **two half notes**. *Remember from the Rhythm Pyramid that one whole note can be split up into two half notes.* This means that the second measure contains the same amount of time as the first - just taken up by half notes instead.

Similarly, the third measure contains **four quarter notes**; the result of splitting each of the half notes in two. It adds up to the same amount of time! Finally, if each quarter note is split in two, the result would be **eight 8th notes** - exactly what we see filling up the last measure.

So the take away here? When writing TAB using rhythm, *each measure will last for the same amount of time*. That time can be sliced up many different ways though, **depending upon the types of note values used**. Think of a measure like it's a big fish tank full of Jello. You can slice up that Jello into any amount of slices you want, but it's still going to be the same amount of Jello.

Because of this, you can even mix and match different types of notes within one measure - *as long as the notes add up to the right amount.*

Check out this example, and you'll get the idea. Each measure will contain **four quarter notes worth of time**. In other words, no matter what type of notes there are in the measure, they will add up to that amount - four quarter notes. Count them up, and refer back to the **Rhythm Pyramid** as often as you need to:

SESSION 09

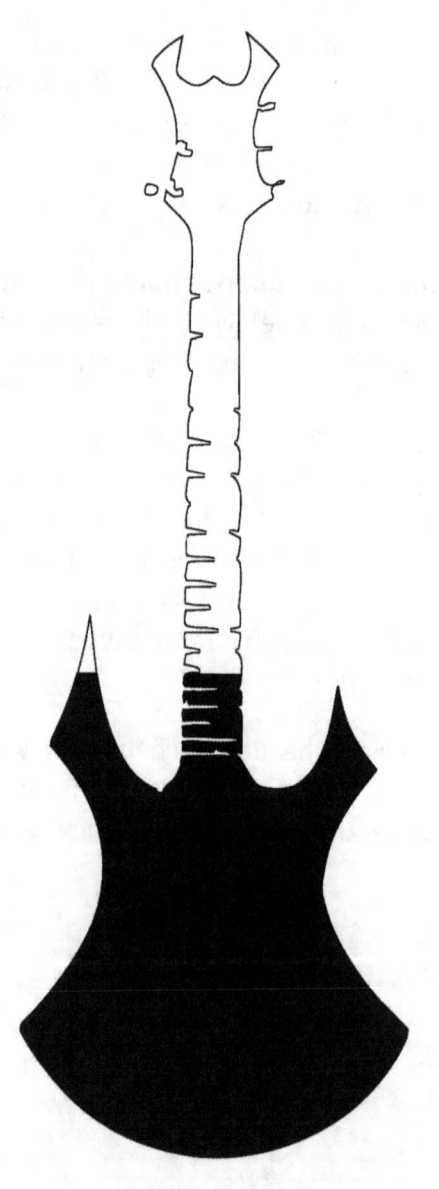

PHYSICAL

Adding in **rhythm** is what turns a plain old chord progression into an actual song. Today, you'll be learning how to strum and **count** a specific rhythm.

If we have a measure that can hold **four quarter notes**, we assign each quarter note a number (or **beat**):

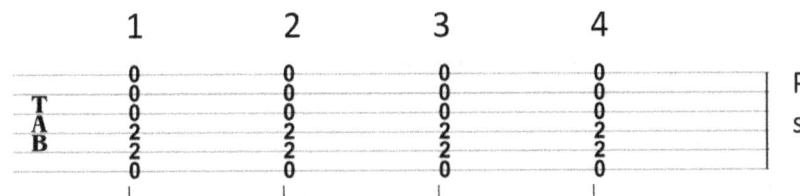

Practice **saying** the beats as you strum the chords. *Do this out loud!*

Since a **half note** takes up the same amount of time as two quarter notes, let it ring for **two beats:**

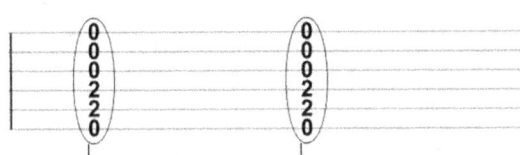

Say all four beats, but **don't** strum on beats 2 and 4 - let the half notes ring out. Beats in parentheses mean "don't strum":

And of course, since a **whole note** takes up the same amount of time as four quarter notes, we have:

Strum *only* on beat 1, and let the chord ring out for the other three beats. Make sure to say all four beats out loud!

What about 8th notes? How do we count those? Well, since we can play **two 8th notes** in the time it takes to play one quarter note, *we need something else to say when we play that extra note* - like a verbal placeholder:

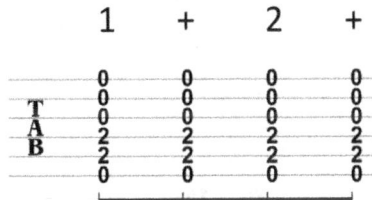

We say the word **"and"** - written as a "+" - when we play the 8th notes that fall *between the beats*.

Since different types of notes can be written within the same measure, counting the beats like this gives your brain something to latch on to - **it's a way to always know exactly where you are within the measure**. Try this two-measure example, counting out loud as you play:

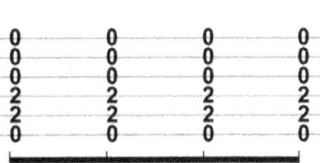

50

Great! Now that you can read rhythm, it's time to practice some chord changes *with* rhythm - and to sound like you're playing a song!

Let's start with that rhythm example you just played, but this time with more chords thrown in:

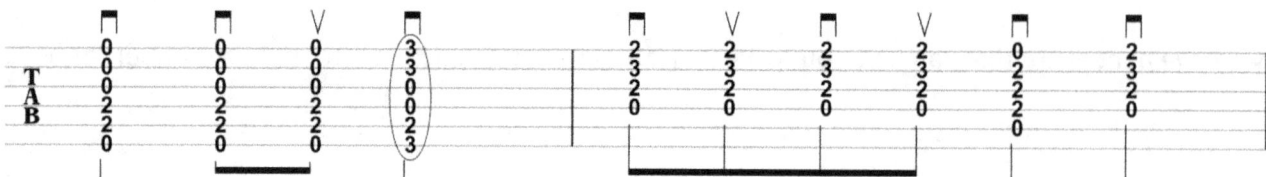

Remember to count this rhythm exactly the same as you did the previous example. Also, notice that whenever you see two or more 8th notes in a row, you should strum with alternate down and up strums. Here's a good rule of thumb (or strum!): **When you see the shortest note value in a measure, that's when you should alternate pick or strum.** For the other notes, it's okay to repeat a down strum.

So for instance, in the above example, the 8th notes are the shortest type of note. It will feel the most natural to strum these with down and up strums. Quarter notes, however, will be played with down strums repeatedly.

Two quick things to remind you of while you practice - first, when strumming, remember that *it's okay to "float" your wrist above the bridge*. **Strumming** is the exception to the "rest your hand on the bridge" rule, because you'll need to hit so many strings at once. Keep your wrist *relaxed* and *loose*.

Second - **always use your metronome when practicing rhythm**! Set it to a slow tempo at first, and decide that each click is a **quarter note.** *You'll be saying two words per click* - like "1 and". If you have trouble, speed up the tempo, and decide that each click is an **8th note** instead. This can help keep you on track, since now *each word you say will be a click* ("1" is a click, "and" is a click, etc.)

Now, let's get back to some **lead playing** practice! You've already learned how to play the **G minor pentatonic scale** across all six strings, starting on the 3rd fret. Here's the thing though: if that was the *only* place that you could play those notes, it would be pretty boring! Luckily, we can play the *same* five notes **a little higher up the neck**. Here they are again, on one string:

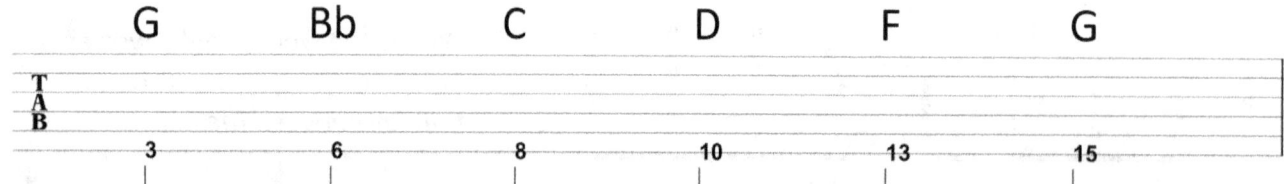

What if, instead of starting on the **root note** of the scale (G), you started with the *2nd note* (Bb)?

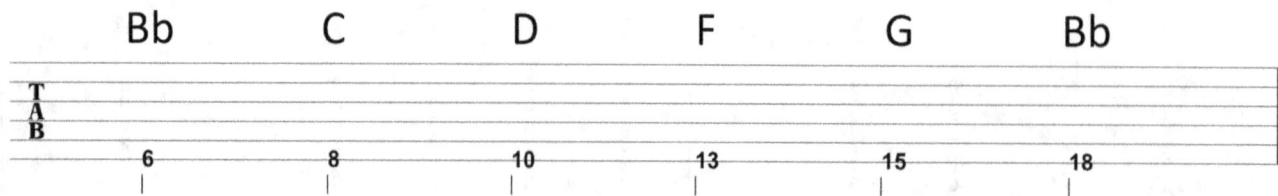

51

Just as you've done before, you can take these notes and **play a two-note per string finger pattern** instead:

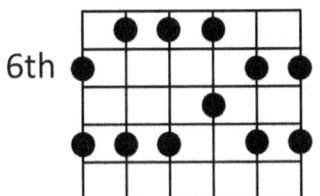
6th

Because this finger pattern, *and* the previous one you've learned are *both* comprised of the same five notes (G Bb C D F), we can think of them as **two different forms** of the same scale. Since the previous pattern started with the *first* note of the scale (G), we call it **Form #1**. This new pattern, because it starts with the *second* note of the scale (Bb), is called **Form #2**.

As you can see in the above **scale diagram**, the fingering of Form #2 is quite different from Form #1:

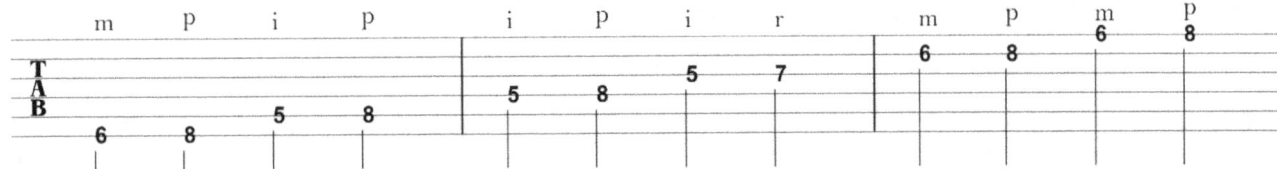

After **memorizing** Form #2 (by playing it over and over again, both *ascending* and *descending*) try this exercise combining **Form #1** and **Form #2**. Now you're really moving!

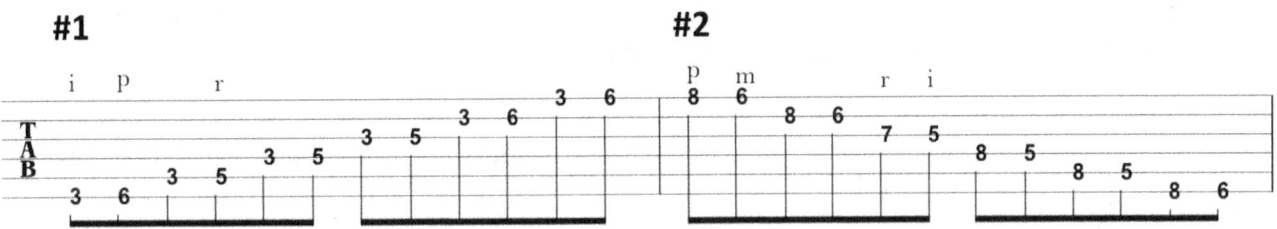

Remember the term **articulation**? It means a *specific* way to play notes. The two types that you've tried are **legato** and **sliding**. Well, here's a really cool technique to add to your repetoire - **string bending**! This is one of the coolest techniques for guitar, and it's a sound that you'll immediately recognize.

Here's how it works: first, place your **ring finger** on the **7th fret**, on the **G string**. Then, place your **middle finger** on the **6th fret** - behind your ring finger, on the *same string*. Next, play the note, and using the strength of both fingers, *push up* so that the string bends. You should hear the pitch get higher when you do so.

The string bending technique is something you'll see often in **TAB** - here's what it looks like:

52

The most important aspect of string bending is your **pitch control**, and a great way to practice this is with **whole step** and **half step** bends. Start by playing two notes, a whole step away from each other. The second note will become your **target note** - the pitch you'll bend the first note to. Next, place your ring finger on the first note (support on the fret behind it with the middle finger!) and bend. Keep bending until you hit that target note:

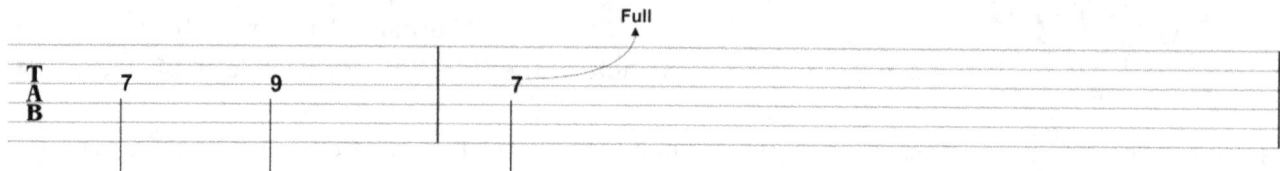

Try it again, this time bending a **half step** instead:

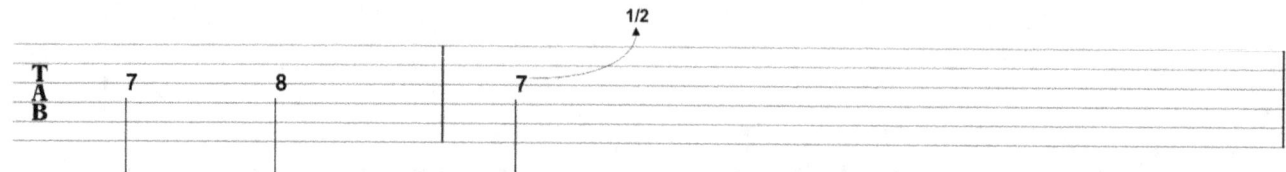

Great! Now, let's tackle the other part of string bending - the **release**. Releasing the bend simply means **letting the string come back to its original position**. During a release, you'll *hear* the note go back down. That's the point! In **TAB**, the release is notated using a down arrow:

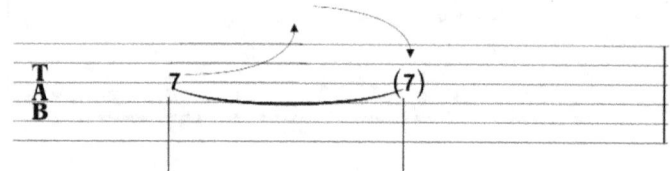

Notice the note underneath the down arrow is in *parentheses*; this means **don't pick it** - just release it while it rings!

There are a couple of problems that players often encounter when first learning to **bend and release**. First, if the string immediately stops ringing when you start to bend it, make sure that you're **pressing down hard enough** with your ring finger. You might be inadvertantly pressing *too much* with the middle finger, and *not enough* with the ring finger (the one actually fretting the note!)

In fact, **letting up on the ring finger pressure** can also cause the sound to stop during the *release* too. So, make sure to press down hard enough to keep that string ringing, but not so much that you're preventing the string from moving at all! It's a balancing act - so take your time, listen, and be patient.

The other issue that you may encounter is **excess string noise**. Look carefullly when you bend the G string, and you'll see that *you're also pushing the D string up a bit as well*. As you start to release the bend, *the D string can begin to vibrate*. This happens to everyone, even pro players. The truth is, it's **physically impossible** to *not* hit a lower string when bending. So, how can we stop that excess noise? Why, with the **right hand**, that's how!

Practice the following: bend that **G string**, but *without your right hand touching the guitar at all*. Quickly **release the bend**, and you'll likely hear that **D string** begin to annoyingly ring out. Now, do the same thing, but this time, put your right hand into its proper position. Try to *mute the D string* as you release the bend - making sure that you *don't* mute the G string.

This can take some practice! At first, you may find yourself muting *both* strings with the right hand. If this happens, try **rolling your hand slightly**, so that the *bottom* of your hand moves outwards.

This will open up just enough space so that the **G string can ring** - but you'll still be *muting* the D string!

Here are a few more examples of string bending for you to try. Remember all the details that were just laid out, and **take your time**!

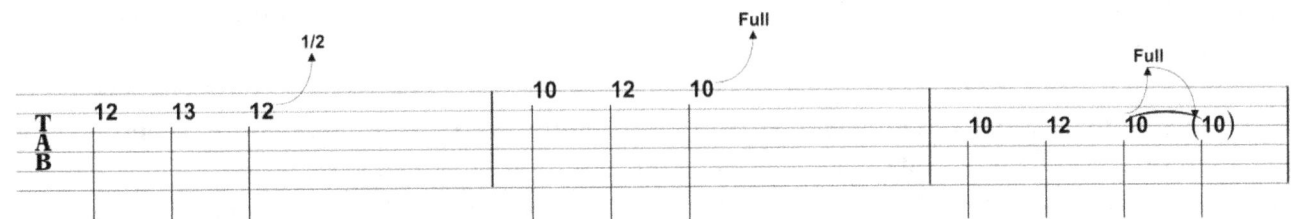

MENTAL

Music - whether it's a song, riff, or solo - rarely features *sound* 100% of the time. In other words, there is also **silence** involved; pauses (whether short, or long) that are thrown in. *Music is an interplay between sound and silence.* Because of this, we also need a way to **notate** silence. You've learned the names of different **note values** so far - quarters, 8ths, etc. - so now it's time to learn about their silent counterparts: **rests**!

For every type of note, there is an *equivalent* rest. Here are their names, and how they look:

Whole   Half   Quarter   8th   16th

Let's take three measures, with each measure containing **four quarter notes** worth of time. You've learned that as long as all the notes *add up* to four quarter notes, each measure could contain **different types of notes**; a mix of halfs, quarters, 8ths, etc.

Adding rests into the mix is simply a matter of **replacing a note** with it's *equivalent rest*. For example, here is the same rhythm, but with some of the **quarter notes** replaced with **quarter rests** (beats with rests will be in *parentheses*). Play this rhythm on your low E string. There are no pitches indicated here, so just using one note is fine for now.

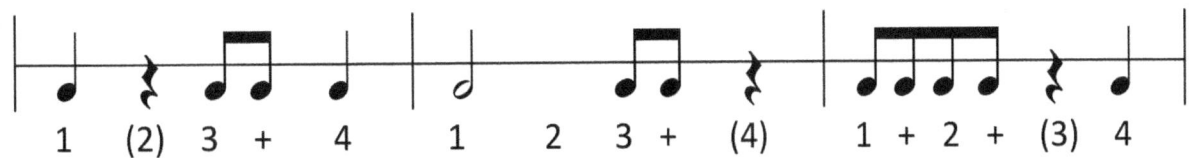

A common mistake that a lot of guitarists make when first learning about rests, is to not **stop the sound**. Not *picking* the note isn't good enough - you've got to actually **cut off the sound** when a rest is indicated. To accomplish this, just *use your right hand to mute the string*. You don't have to do anything weird with your hand or wrist - **just plop on top of the string**! In fact, this can be a great way to "feel" the rhythm. When counting the rhythm out loud, give the strings a good *smack* with the picking hand, right when you **say the beat** where the rest is. This brings something that's purely *mental* (counting) into the *physical realm* (smacking and muting!)

Here's one more example, this time with **8th note rests**. Remember - the 8th note rest can fall on either the **number**, *or* the **"and"**. Count aloud, saying *all* the 8th notes as you go (*1 and, 2 and, 3 and, 4 and*). This will help keep you on track, and help you to **come back in** after a rest, on the appropriate beat.

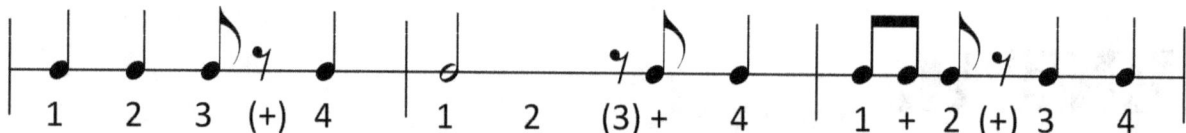

There's one more rhythmic concept to discuss here - the **tie**. The symbol for a *tie* is a curved line - much like the slur that we use for the legato technique. While they look the same, the usage is entirely different. A tie **connects two note values together**. In other words, it causes one note to *ring into* the next note - in effect, making the first note *last longer*. The two notes will **always be the same pitch** - which is how you can tell a *tie* apart from *legato*.

Here is an example of the tie; remember to **count exactly the same as normal**. The only difference is that **you will not pick the tied notes** - they will continue to *ring out* from the previous note:

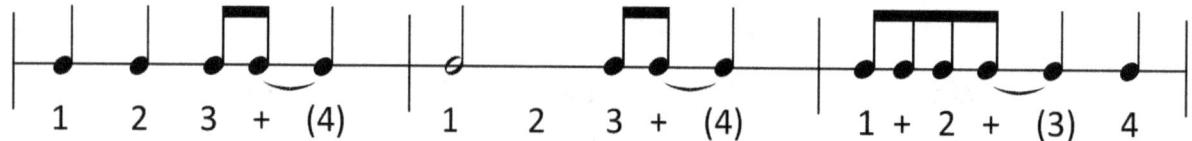

So remember - in the above example, *don't pick beat four* in the first two measures. The "and" of beat three will *ring into* beat four. In the last measure, *don't pick beat three*. Pick the "and" of two, and let it *ring into* beat three.

Once again, it's important for you to **count out loud** while you practice this. Say *all* of the 8th notes (even if you're **not picking** all of them, like during the **"and" of a quarter note**). This will allow you to *always know exactly where you are* in the **beat pattern**, at all times.

Practicing rhythm can certainly seem tedious at first, and the temptation will be there to *skip right over it...*

Don't do it! It may not seem like it right now, but the ability to read rhythm *confidently* and *accurately* is a **secret weapon for guitar greatness**! It will positively affect not only your **technique** (speed, stamina, etc.) but also your ability to **improvise and jam** - not to mention your aptitude for learning difficult **riffs and solos**!

SESSION 10

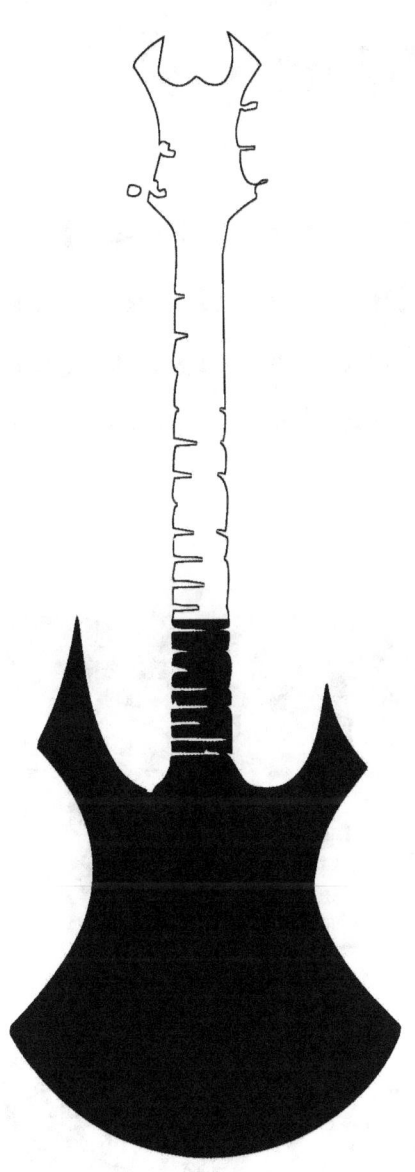

Halfway There! Don't Give Up the Fight! ...
Halfway There! Don't Give Up the Fight! ...
Halfway There! Don't Give Up the Fight! ...
Halfway There! Don't Give Up the Fight! ...

PHYSICAL

So far, you've learned **Form #1** and **Form #2** of the **G minor pentatonic scale**. Form #1 starts on the **root note** of the scale (G), and Form #2 starts on the *second* note of the scale (Bb). Here's a quick refresher, using scale diagrams:

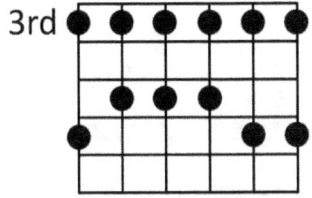
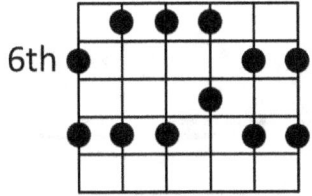

Remember, while it may *look* like there are lots of notes in these two forms, **you are only playing five notes** - G Bb C D F - repeating themselves, and getting higher up the neck.

So what's next? Why **Form #3**, that's what! In keeping with the above logic, Form #3 will start on the *third* note of the scale - **C**, in this case:

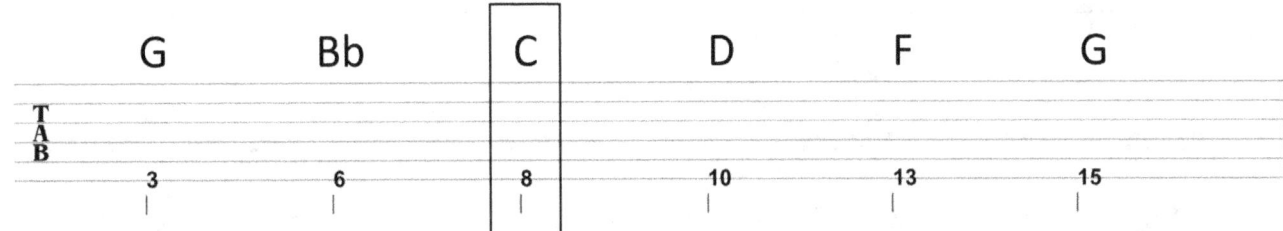

Therefore, the notes that we'll be playing are **C D F G Bb** in a *two note per string* pattern. Here's **Form #3**, in scale diagram format:

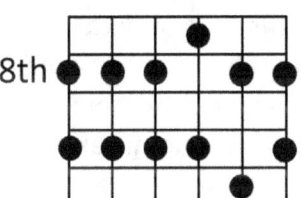

The fingering for **Form #3** is quite different from the previous two forms, and features a slightly larger *stretch* on the B string:

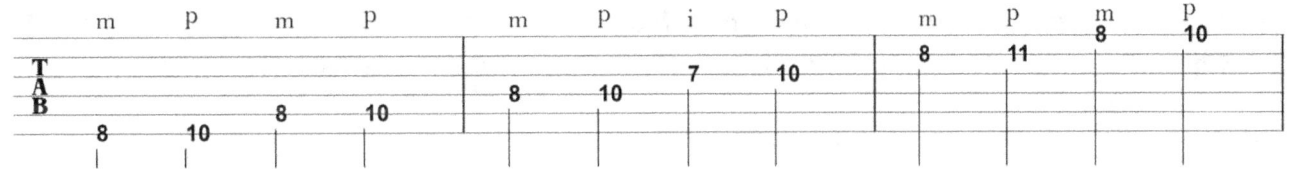

There are two more finger patterns (or forms) to the minor pentatonic scale...but first, let's take the ones you already know and work on your **technique**. Using a scale to come up with licks, patterns, and runs is one of the best ways to increase your accuracy, speed, and stamina - so let's get moving! Here's a cool exercise that uses the **E and A strings** from **all three forms**; make sure to use **alternate picking**!

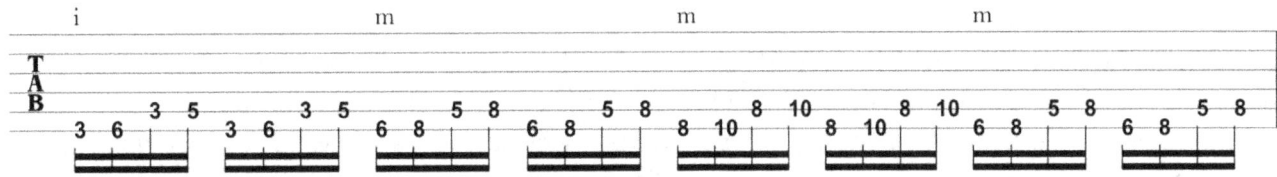

58

Some of these technique exercises will be written using **16th notes**. Don't worry about it - this is simply a **space-saving strategy** for this book (more notes fit in one measure!) Reading and counting 16ths is beyond the scope of this book, so just keep an **even rhythm** for everything, and you'll be in good shape!

Also, unless otherwise indicated, you should use **alternate picking** for all of these exercises. The exception is when practicing **legato** (hammers and pulls). In that case, consecutive downstrokes are usually acceptable. Here's another minor pentatonic exercise, this time using **three strings**:

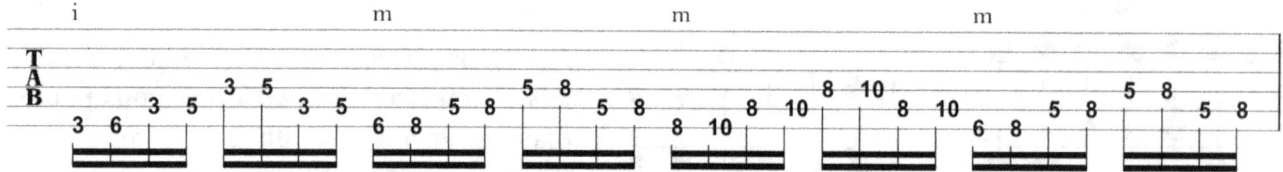

Next, let's get back to some **legato** - this time, combining the technique with the three **minor pentatonic forms** to create a cool rock and Metal lick. Remember to *start* and *end up* with **both fingers down** - and to pick again at the beginning of each new **slur**. You can use all downstrokes when picking:

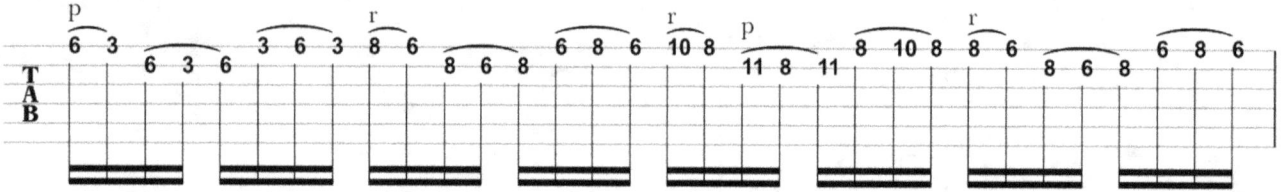

Go slooooowww at first! There isn't a "one-tempo-fits-all" here, which is why there's no suggested speed. **Use your metronome to challenge yourself** - but *not* at the expense of *cleanliness* and *even rhythm*. It's okay to be a bit sloppy when first increasing the speed, but you need to **remain in control mentally** - in other words, you must be *consciously aware* of any mistakes you're making. That way, you can work to fix them during the next go-around. Practice too fast though, and you simply *won't* be able to catch your mistakes...and that means you're wasting your time. Find your *edge* - that's where to be!

Okay, back to some **strumming** and **chord practice**. You get to play some cooler rhythms this time - with **rests** and **ties**! Let's use two chords - **Em** and **G** - for this one. Now, not only are you challenging yourself with the *chord change*, but we've got *counting, up and down strums*...lots to think about! So you know what that means - take it *slow*, and be patient! *Repetition is the key* - slow, accurate, repetition. Each measure in this exercise will have **four quarter notes worth of time**. Remember to say all the 8th notes out loud, and mute the strings with your right hand during the rests:

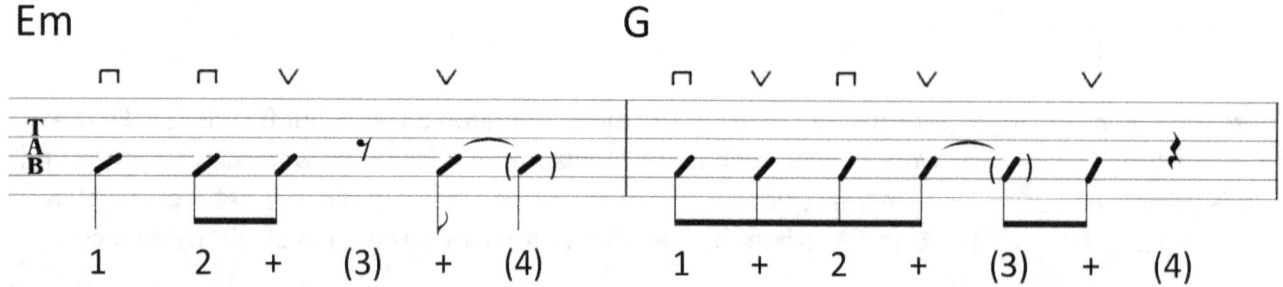

In the second measure, on **beat 3** (the tied note), *let your hand continue to perform a down strum motion*, just without hitting any strings. *Don't* let your hand get "stuck" or "frozen" in the up strum position! If you *were* to play on beat 3, you would naturally perform it as a down strum - so *don't stop the momentum of your hand*. This will make the following up strum feel a lot more natural.

If you find these strumming exercises to be extra-tricky, then don't worry about the **chord change** at first - you can just **hold the Em** for both measures, as you master the strum pattern. Now, try this next example:

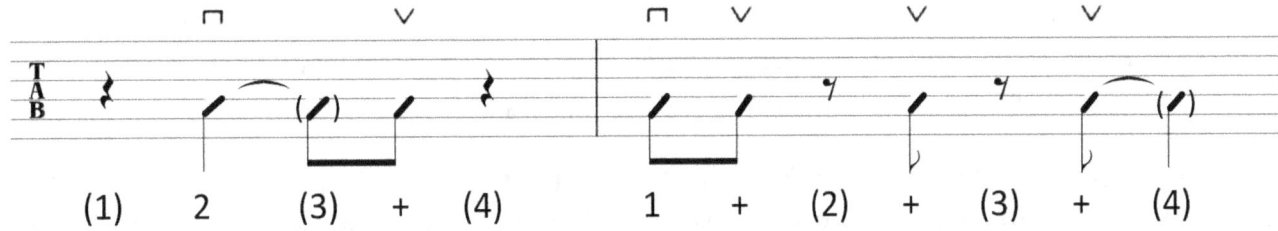

Next, you get to try these rhythms again - this time using **power chords**! Here are the two examples, written in TAB this time, and including **palm mutes**. Use all downstrokes for this riff...go for it!

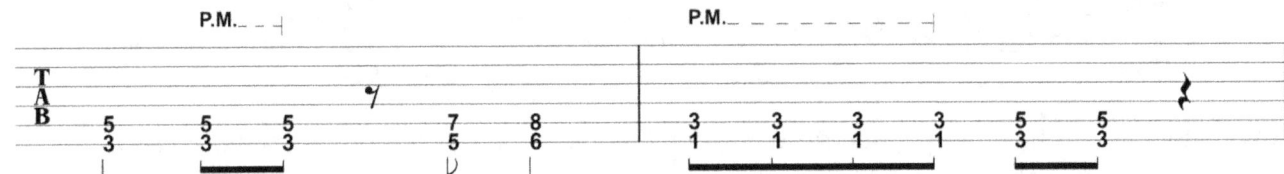

During the rests, **stop pressing the power chord**. *Don't* take your fingers off of the strings; keep touching them. This will ensure **total silence**, without any unwanted string noise. Try this next riff:

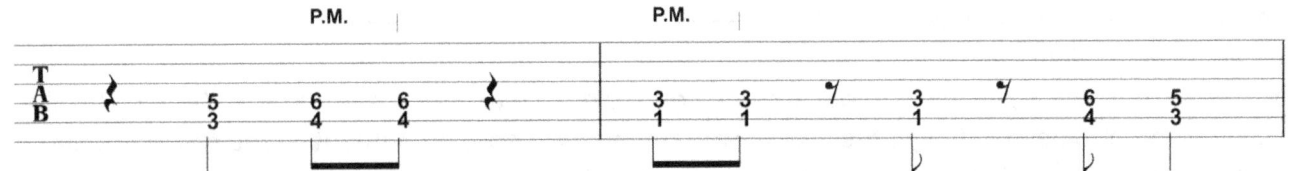

MENTAL

Now that you're reading rhythm, it's time to learn about an important concept: the **time signature**. We've described a *measure* as **a box that contains a certain amount of time** - like four quarter notes. A time signature tells us *exactly how many notes a measure can hold* - and this is important, because not every song will be alike! There are two components to a time signature: the **top number**, and the **bottom number**. The top number tells us how many *beats* or *counts* are in the measure - in other words, the **pulse** you feel when listening to a song (like "One, two, three, four / One, two, three, four").

Time Signature

4
4

Now, here's why the top number alone doesn't give us enough information. Pretend $1,000 cash is at stake - someone *claps five beats*, and you get the money if you tell them what kind of notes they clapped (half notes, *8th* notes, etc.) Ready?

"Clap, clap, clap, clap, clap"

Would you ever win? No way! Think about it - *a beat is just a beat*. It's an amorphous concept. What if those claps were five **really fast half notes**? Or five **really slow 8th notes**? Without any additional context, there's just no way to know - you'd always just be guessing.

That's where the **bottom number** of a time signature comes in - it's like a code breaker, telling you the *type* of note that you're counting!

The **top number** can theoretically be *any* number at all - you could put 312 on the top, and have 312 beats in your measure (it'd be a mile long, but certainly possible!) The **bottom number**, though, *can't* be any old number. Since it tells you the *type* of note you're counting, it can only be the following: 1 (whole notes), 2 (half notes), 4 (quarter notes), 8 (eighth notes), and 16 (sixteenth notes).

So - when you see a **4/4** time signature, it means **the measure can hold four quarter notes**. No more, no less. If you see a **3/8** time signature, it means **the measure can hold three eighth notes**. Here are a few sample time signatures that tell you *how much time one measure can hold*:

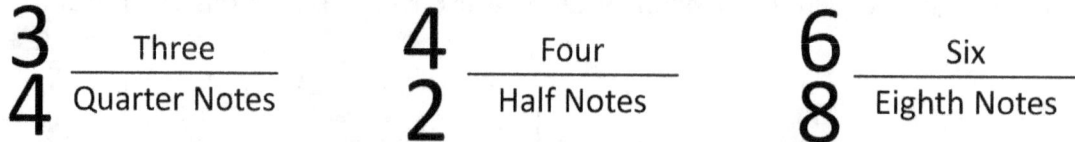

Now that you know how time signatures work, don't worry - **4/4** is by far the *most common one*, and we'll be sticking to it for the rest of the book!

When beginning to learn guitar, it's easy for concepts like **scales**, **rhythm**, **articulations** (legato, bends, slides) to seem unrelated. You might be asking yourself, *"How does all of this stuff fit together, and what do people actually do with it?"*

That's a valid question, and here's your answer: *you use all of it to create riffs and solos!* Think of it like baking bread. You need a **dough**, the basic raw material of your bread. Without it, you can forget about a fancy finished product. The **minor pentatonic scale** is like the flour, water, and yeast for your dough - absolutely *essential*, but pretty flavorless on it's own. For example, this would be a pretty boring solo:

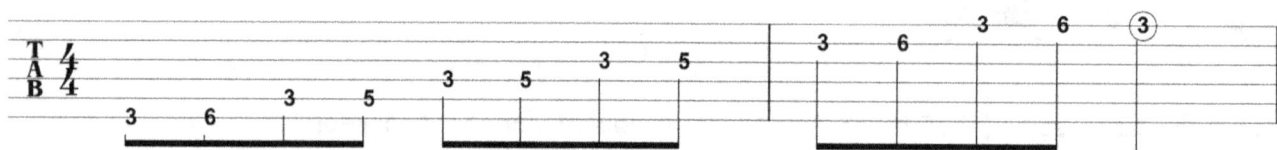

It's got the notes - but it sounds like someone is just running up a scale! Not very exciting. Let's fix it by adding some **sugar and salt** to our dough - in the form of some *rhythm!*

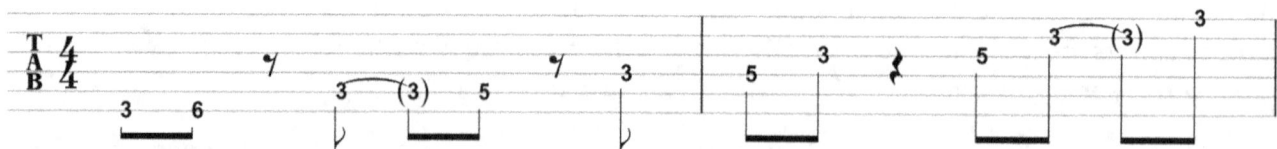

Notice that the notes are still basically **ascending** (no different from the boring example). Now though, it *doesn't* just sound like you're running a scale. By adding in some **unexpected rhythm**, we've created a world of difference. The "cool factor" for this solo just went up dramatically!

Hey, why don't *you* try it! When practicing this short solo, take it slow at first, and **say the rhythm out loud**. Count *all* of the **8th notes** (*"one, and, two, and, three, and, four, and"*) to keep yourself on track!

Finally, let's add some **bananas and strawberries** to this bread - by throwing in the flavor of **articulations**! *Legato*, *slides*, and *string bends* take this lick over the top:

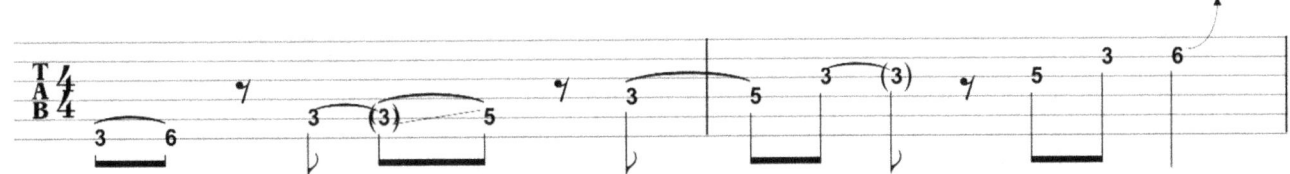

As you can see (and hear!), the point of learning things like scales, rhythms, and articulations is to give you **creative control**. The ability to **make music** out of this raw material is the coveted skill that *all* dedicated guitarists should strive for. Don't ever forget - *that's the whole point.* You increase your knowledge and technical ability in order to *serve the music*. Not the other way around!

SESSION 11

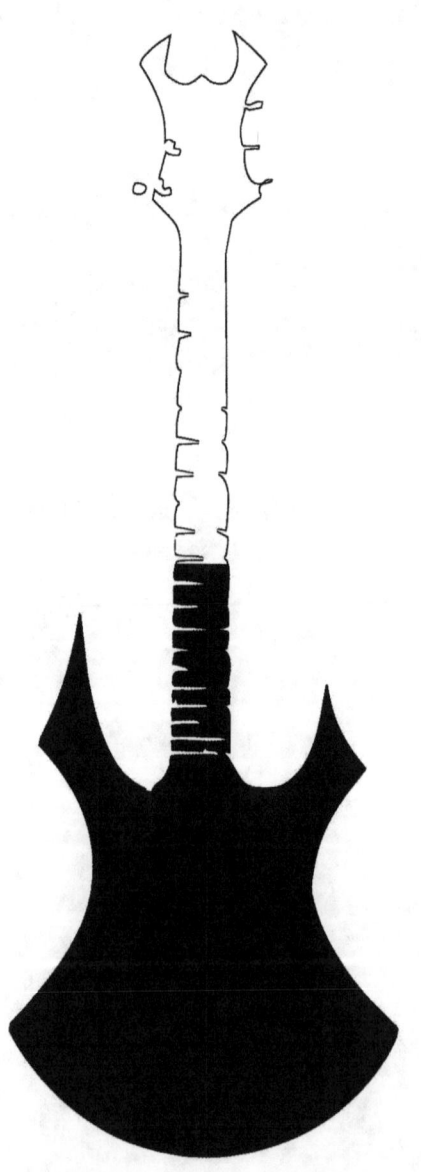

PHYSICAL

"Barre Chords! That name alone can chill the blood! Barre Chords!
Was it they who brought the plague to Bremen in 1838?"

Just like the eponymous character from the 1922 silent film classic *Nosferatu*, barre chords have been known to strike fear into the hearts of advancing guitarists such as yourself. But despair not! With the proper guidance, you'll find that barre chords aren't that big of a deal. Frustrating, yes - but certainly within your ability to master, and within a reasonable time frame.

What's a barre chord, you ask? The *barre* technique involves **pressing down more than one string, with only one finger**. There are some very useful chord shapes that utilize this technique, so it's an absolutely *indispensable* skill to master. Because you'll be using a *single finger* to press down several strings, you'll find barre chords to be **more physically demanding** at first than the other chords you've learned. That's why we're starting small! Here's a **minor chord**, played using only your index finger:

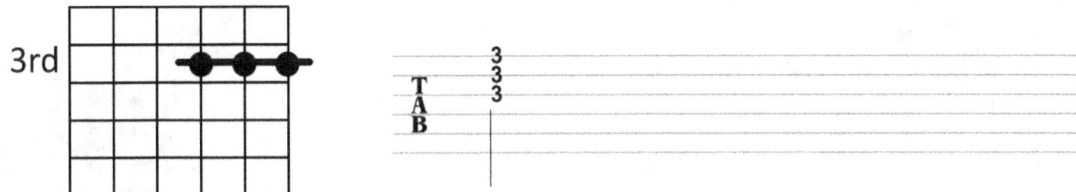

When playing a barre chord, especially on the lower frets, it's important to employ two strategies:
1. **Don't** stick your finger joint out. Curve your finger **around the neck**.
2. **Roll** your finger slightly towards the headstock of the guitar. *Don't* try to lay it perfectly flat.

Once you've got everything looking good, go ahead and play the chord. Pick one string at a time, to make sure that **all three strings are ringing out**. Once you're confident that you can hear all three, go ahead and strum!

Here's an exercise that gets you moving this chord up the neck. One of the great advantages of barre chords is that they're **movable** - and you'll soon understand why!

64

As you perform that exercise, notice how the **roll angle** of your index finger changes. When playing a barre chord on the lower frets, your finger was **rolling back**. As you climb the neck, your finger will start to **roll forward** and end up **flatter** against the frets:

Don't fight this motion! It occurs naturally, and you should just go with it.

Next, you'll be playing the **major** barre chord. This variation has you barring two strings (the B and high E), and using your **middle finger** to play a note on the G string. Like the minor chord diagram, this one also has a *line* indicating the *barred* notes.

When playing this chord, your index finger should look just like it did for the minor barre...except now only pressing the two strings.

If you find your middle finger is **muting** the B string, then you've got to straighten it out *even more than you think you need to*. Again, use your *finger itself* to achieve this, not your wrist! Sliding your thumb a bit lower (towards the floor) is also an effective strategy. The best strategy? Slow, patient practice!

As soon as you've got all three strings ringing out clearly, try moving this major chord around. Moving a barre chord is similar to moving a power chord - relax your fingers, stop pressing, but *don't* take your fingers off the strings. Slide across the strings, like ice skating, then press down again when you're ready.

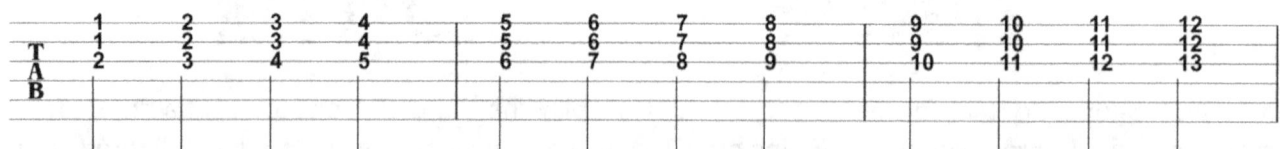

Since these barre chords are **movable**, let's find out how you can take advantage of it. You've learned that scales have a root note - the very first note, the one you hear as the "main note", or "home base". The root note **names the scale** - for example *G* minor pentatonic. Well, **chords have root notes too**, and they also give a **specific name** to a type of chord. You've probably noticed that we've been using the generic terms "major" and "minor", not *A* major, or *B* minor, for example.

In the two barre chords you've been playing, **the root note is always found on the E string**. Because of this, all you need to do is find a *specific* note on the high E string, and then form the chord around it.

Voila! You can auto-magically play *any major or minor chord you want*. Here are a few examples, to make sure this important concept is understood. Let's say that you want to play a **Bb minor chord**. What's the **root note** of that chord? Why, **Bb** of course. So, you simply locate the Bb on the high E string:

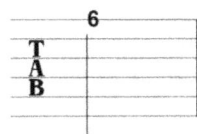   Then, just form the minor barre chord at that location: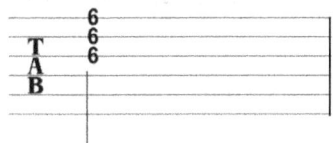

Hey - that chord's the Antichrist! Anyway, it really is that easy to find chords. Let's do one more. How about an **A major chord**? First, find an **A** on the high E string:

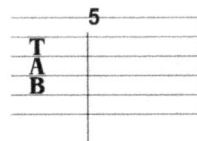   Then, just form the major barre chord at that location: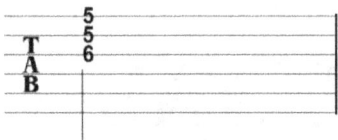

That's all it is! You can use this method to play *any* major or minor chord, using these movable barre chord shapes. One last thing - how would you know that the root note is found on the E string? **The chord diagram will tell you!** Going forward, any movable chord shape in the book will feature a *circled note*. This specially marked note will tell you **on which string you can find the root note** for that chord:

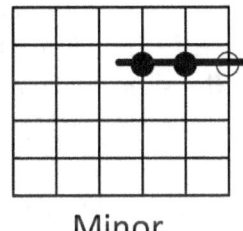   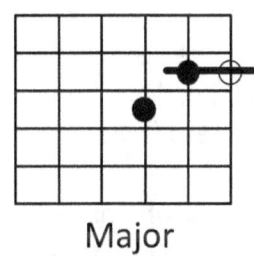

Minor   Major

Now, back to the minor pentatonic scale - consummating your ability to play it across the **entire neck**! You'll be starting on the *fourth* and *fifth* notes, respectively, of the **G minor pentatonic scale**:

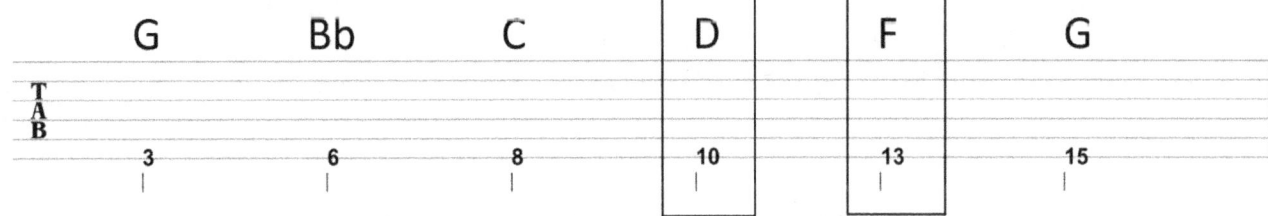

Form #4 of the G minor pentatonic scale contains the notes **D F G Bb C** - the same five notes as the other three forms, but this time starting with the note **D**. Here is the *two note per string pattern,* in both scale diagram and TAB form:

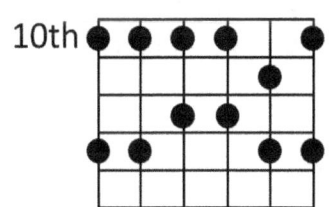

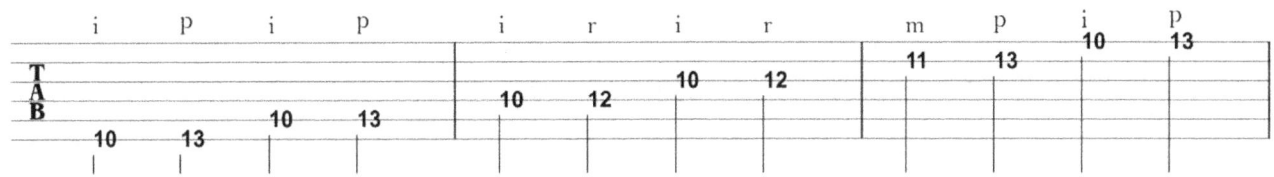

66

Form #5 of the **G minor pentatonic scale** contains the notes
F G Bb C D - the *same* five notes found in the other forms.
This fingering pattern will, however, start on the *fifth note* of
the scale - **F**.

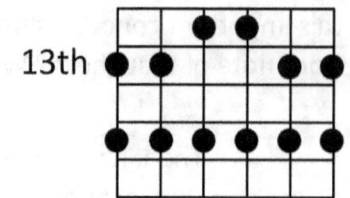

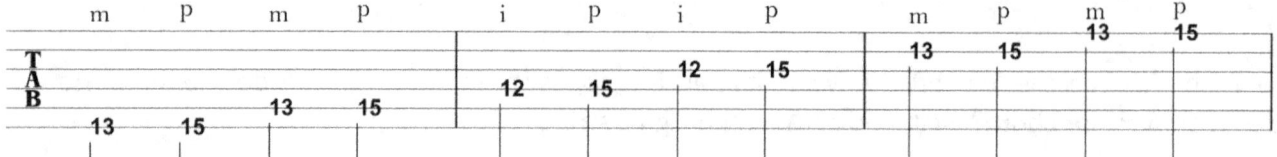

MENTAL

So far, you've learned a number of **chords** that are used in literally *millions* of songs. So what *is* a chord anyway? Since they're the building blocks for songs of all styles, wouldn't it make sense to know more about them? Of course it would!

Chords need to have at least **three notes, in a specific relationship to each other**, to truly be considered a chord. Remember the term **interval**? You learned about it when you began finding notes on the guitar. An interval is the **distance in pitch between two notes**. There is a certain interval that is *extremely* important when building chords. It's called a **3rd**, and there are two different types: **major 3rd (M3)**, and **minor 3rd (m3)**.

Every type of interval has it's own unique sound that you can learn to recognize - so what's the sound of a major 3rd? When you jump the **distance of two whole steps**, the resulting sound is what we call the major 3rd. For example, **C to D** is a whole step, and **D to E** is another whole step. Therefore, if you just **leap from C to E**, that's the sound of a major 3rd:

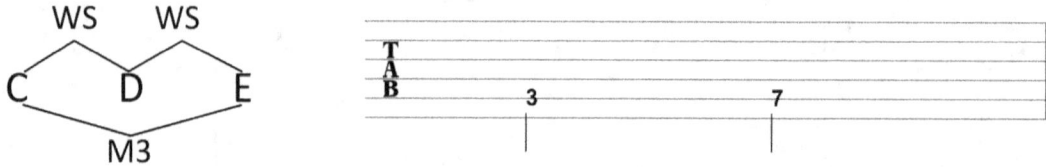

When you jump the distance of a **whole step and a half step**, the resulting sound is what we call the minor 3rd. For example, **C to D** is a whole step, and **D to Eb** is a half step. Therefore, if you just **leap from C to Eb**, that's the sound of a minor 3rd:

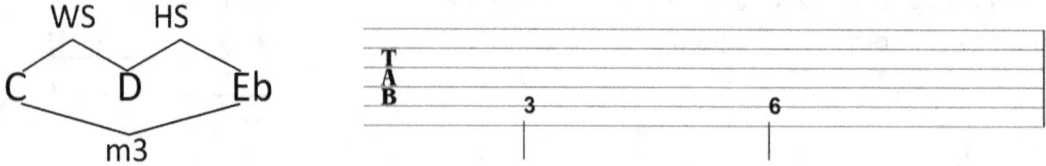

So, how does all this relate to finding the **three notes in a chord**?

Well, by **stacking up two 3rds in a row**, we end up with three notes. These are the three notes that *make up a chord!* For example, let's say we start with **C** and jump a **M3** - bringing us to **E**. If we then jump a **m3** from E, that would bring us to the note **G**:

Play those three notes in a row, and *you'll hear the sound of a major chord!* In fact, here's a simple formula you can follow to figure out the notes in *any* major chord:

M3 + m3 = Major Chord

What if we reverse it? Let's play the **m3** first, and then the **M3**...and *hear the sound of a minor chord!*

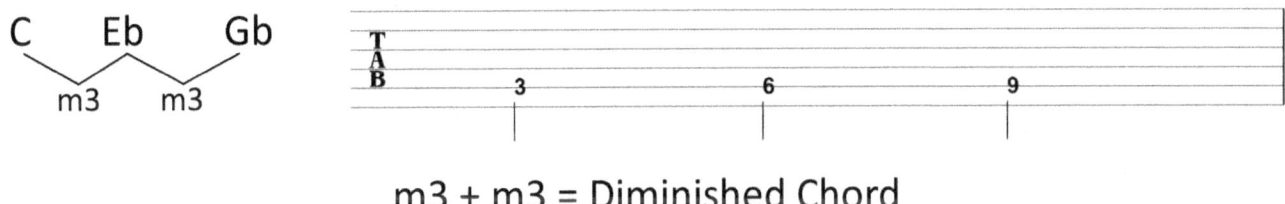

m3 + M3 = Minor Chord

Now, let's stack up **two minor thirds in a row** - this formula will result in a chord called **diminished**:

m3 + m3 = Diminished Chord

Try choosing some **different starting notes**, and play these "formulas" on one string (like the above examples). You'll hear the sounds of the major, minor, and diminished chords coming to life on the fretboard! *Memorizing* these formulas will also allow you to begin **building chords in your head** - even when away from the guitar.

For example, let's figure out the notes in an **A major chord**. Start with **A**, and ascend by a **M3** - this brings you to **C#** (*two whole steps* higher than the A). Then, ascend a **m3** from the C# - this brings you to **E** (a *half step* and *whole step* higher than the C#). So, **an A major chord contains the notes A C# E!**

Let's figure out one more chord - an **E minor**. Start with **E**, and ascend by a **m3** - this brings you to **G** (a *whole step* and *half step* higher than the E). Then, ascend a **M3** from the G - this brings you to **B** (*two whole steps* higher than the G). So, **an E minor chord contains the notes E G B!**

SESSION 12

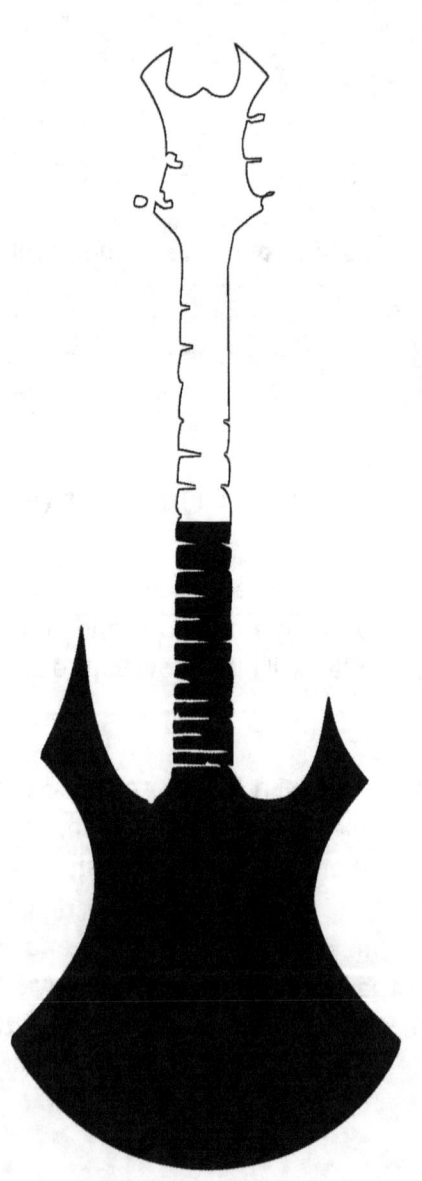

PHYSICAL

Time for you to begin construction on another *pillar of guitar power* - **triads**! We've learned that chords are constructed of *three notes*, and we can create them by stacking up **major 3rds** and **minor 3rds**. For example, want to build an **E minor chord**?

m3 + M3 = Minor Chord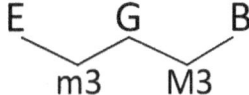

According to one of our easily memorizable formulas, an **Em** chord contains the notes **E G B**. Now, you might be asking yourself, *"Wait a minute, when I play the Em with all the open strings, it's got six notes, not three!"* Here's how that whole thing computes - let's use your note finding ability to figure out what you're **actually playing** when using the big Em shape:

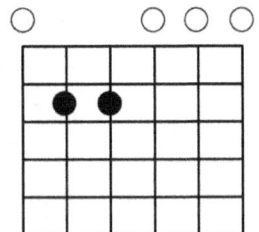 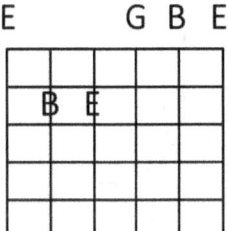

Well, cover me in chainmail and call me Metal - *it's the notes E G B!* In fact, if you figure out the notes for *any* of the open chords you've learned, you'll see that **there's only three** - with some of them *doubled* or *tripled*. The **triad**, however, is very important because of its *compactness*. **It's like a bare-bones chord**, a small and movable one that can be played all over the neck. In fact, you've already learned two of them: the minor and major barre chords!

An important feature of those two triads (and all of the following triad shapes) is the **circled root note location**. By knowing *on which string* to find the root note, you can use the triad to play *any* specific major, minor, or diminished chord you want. So, if we want to play a **Dm chord**, and the triad we're using has the **root note on the G string**, you'd simply *find a D on the G string*, and then apply the shape:

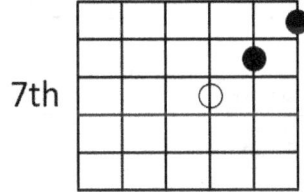 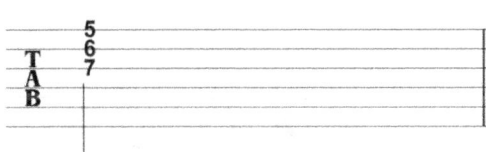

Because these triad shapes will be utilizing the **G**, **B**, and **E** strings, *each* of these strings can be the potential location of the root note. In other words, we *could have* found the **D** on the B or high E strings in our previous example - **not just on the G string**. If we had, the resulting triad shape would've been *different*. Therefore, **you'll learn three different shapes for each type of triad** - three shapes for major, three for minor, and three for diminished. *Each of the three will have a different circled note*, indicating which string contains the root note for that shape. Your job is to **memorize** the shapes *and* which string is circled for that shape. Ready? *Go!*

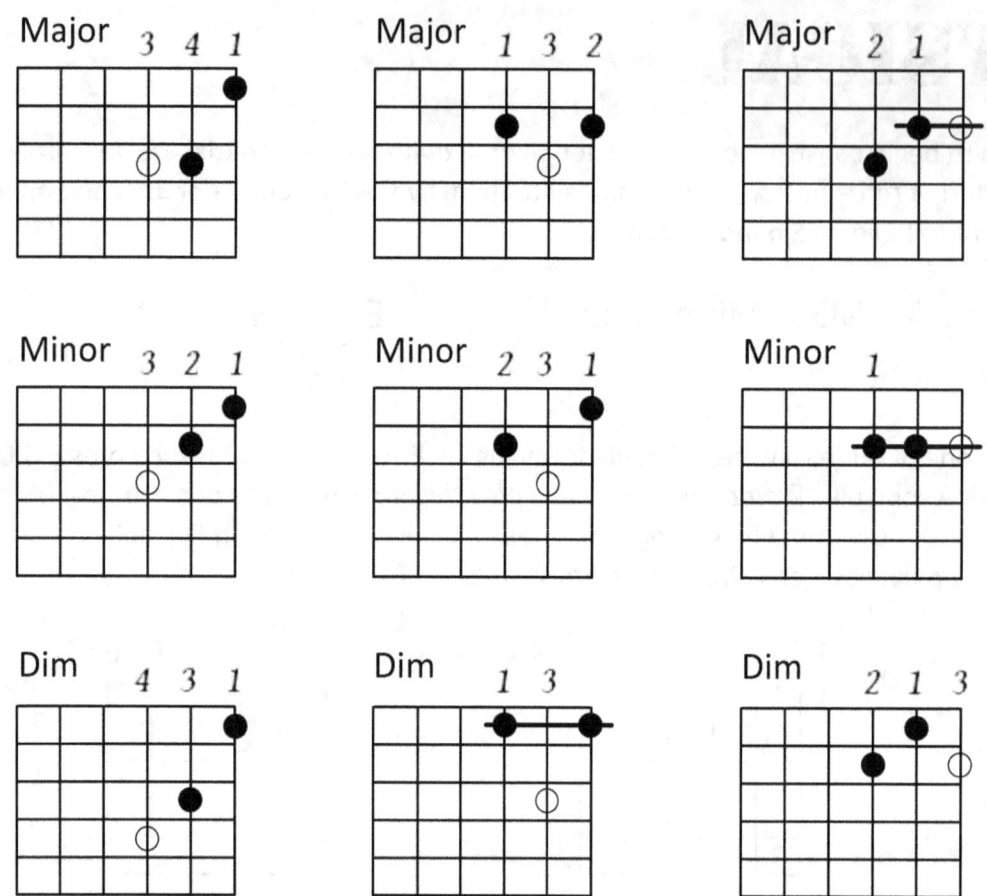

Okay, enough chord stuff for now - it's time to shred! One of the great things about knowing all five forms of the minor pentatonic scale is that you can use them for technique exercises. The following exercise will focus on your **picking**, developing *control*, *speed*, and *stamina*. **Tremolo picking** is a technique where you **pick multiple times on a single note**. You're about to do this - and across the entire neck! First though, here's a reminder for you: *all five forms* of the **G minor pentatonic scale**!

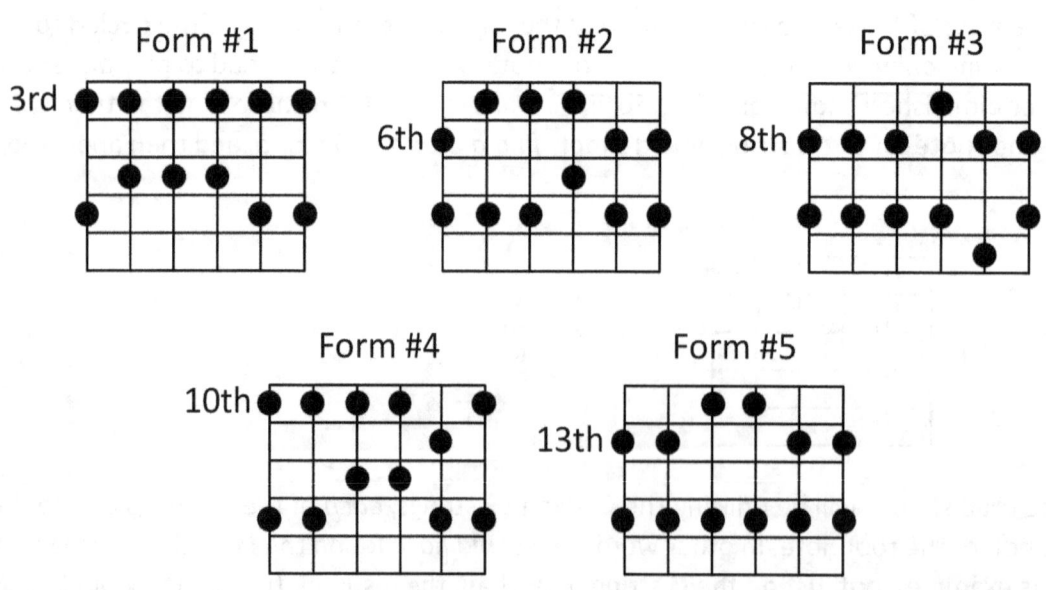

Review these patterns before getting too heavily into the following tremolo picking exercise. *Memorization is key here* - when focusing on technique, you don't want to be using brain power to think *"Does my finger go here, or there?"* That gets too distracting from the matter at hand - faster and more powerful picking!

The following exercise will be written in TAB, but *only* for **Form #1**. Going forward, it's important to be able to **apply a technique or sequence** from *one* finger pattern, to *another* finger pattern. You'll be picking each note **four times**, being careful to use **alternate picking** throughout, *especially when moving to the next string!* When finished with Form #1, continue with the rest of the forms. Go for it!

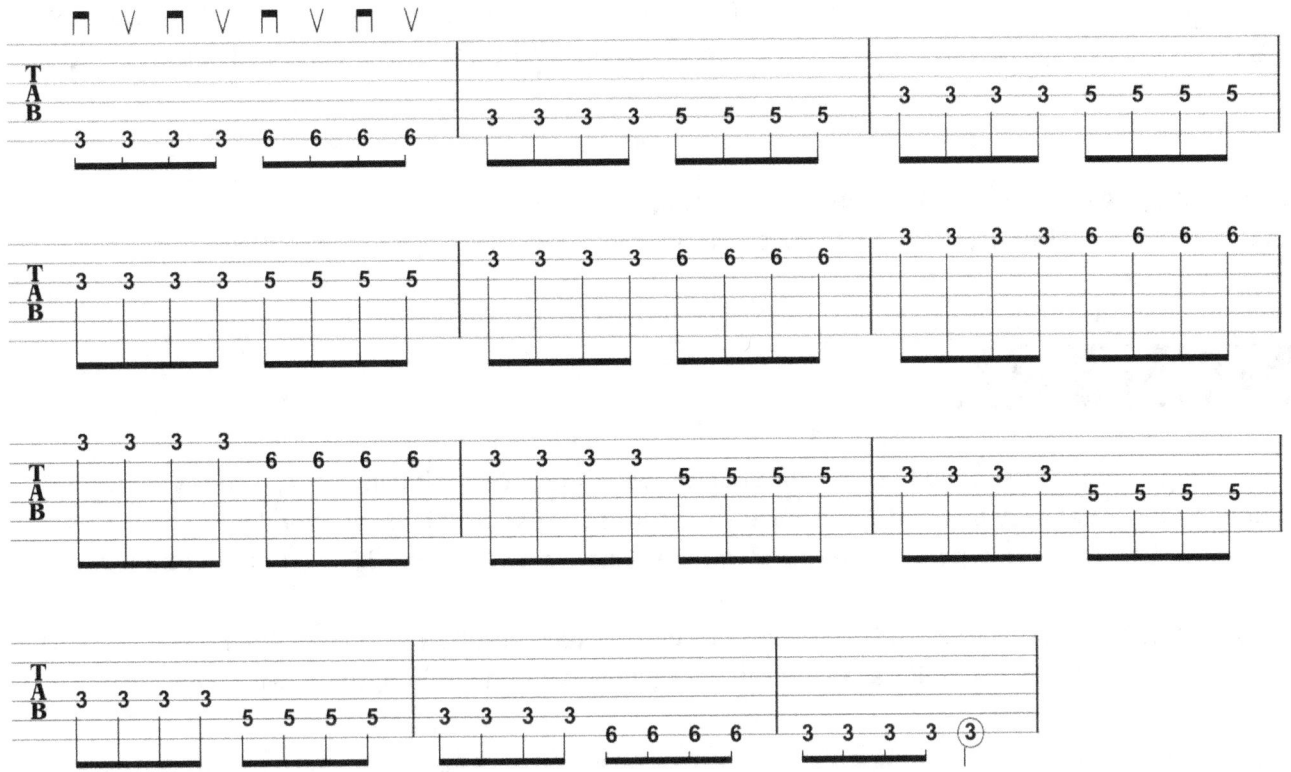

There's no specific tempo or metronome setting indicated here - it's up to you to **find your edge**! Push yourself so that you're right on the edge of messing it up, but still in control mentally. **Repetition is key!**

Now, let's get a bit more into string bends with a special technique called a **unison bend**. You've heard this technique a million times in guitar solos; it's a cool, screaming-sort-of effect. Here's how to do it:

First, put your ring finger on the **G string**, at the **14th fret**. While keeping it there, *also* place your index finger on the **B string**, at the **12th fret**. Play *both strings*, and make sure you can hear them ringing out *at the same time*. You may have to keep that ring finger extra straight-up-and-down.

Once you can hear them both, **bend the G string up one whole step**. Bend *only* the G string - the B string note should *stay put*, and you should **continue to hear it ring** while you bend the G string.

Remember the techniques you've been practicing for string bends: keep that **ring finger** pressing the whole time (now your index finger too!) and use your right hand to **mute the lower strings** that you don't want to hear!

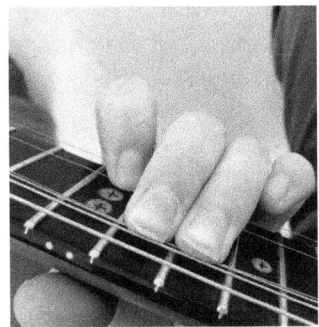

Your index finger is holding a **B**, and your ring finger is holding an **A**. The awesome sound you hear is the result of the A note being bent **until it becomes a B as well**. This brings the notes into **unison** - hence the name! Here's how a unison bend looks when written in TAB:

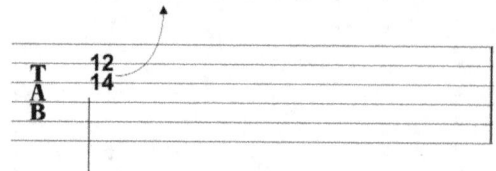

Notice the arrow is *only* coming out from the **lower note**; this is a sure sign that you're dealing with a unison bend.

Now, try playing a unison bend on the **B and E strings**. Your ring finger is a fret *higher* when using these two:

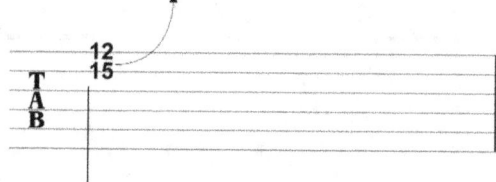

MENTAL

Since **scales** can be considered the raw material for just about everything in music, it's very important to understand what they are, and what makes different scales *sound* the way they do. By the way, what is it exactly that makes a **type of scale** sound unique? Like *major* vs. *minor*? Ever thought about it?

Every type of scale is simply an **unique pattern of whole steps and half steps**. For example, if we start with the note **C**, and play a **major scale** up the neck (staying on one string), this is what we'll get:

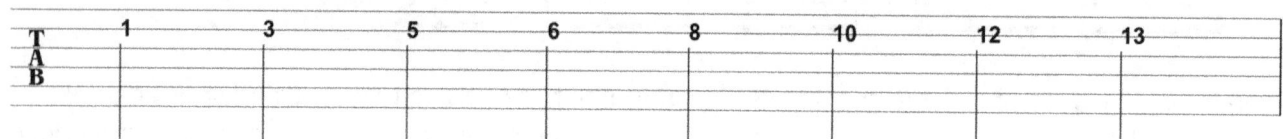

If we take a closer look at the pattern of whole steps and half steps, here's what you've just played:

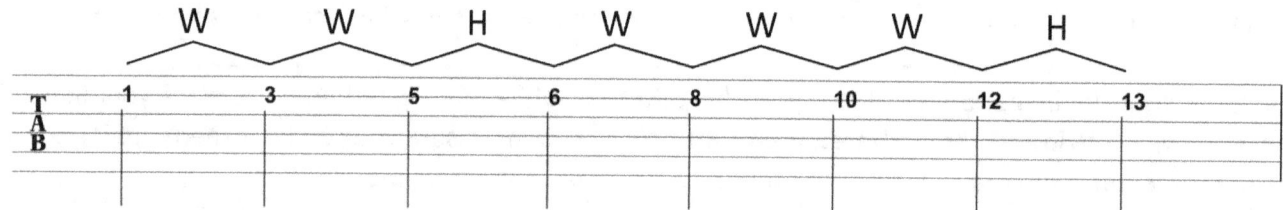

That sound pattern - **W W H W W W H** - *is* a major scale. At the most basic level, *that's what your brain interprets as the sound of a major scale*. If you start on *any* note, and follow that pattern up one string, it will **always** come out sounding like a **major scale**. Try it out and see!

By contrast, if we **change the pattern** - if we put the half steps in a *different* place - we'll end up with an entirely *different* scale. Let's try it with another very common scale, the **minor scale**:

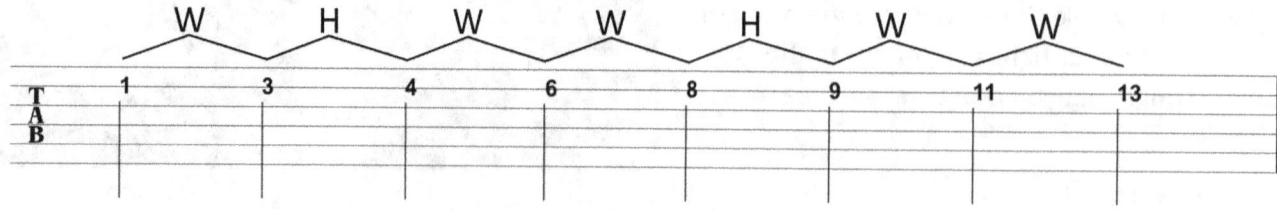

73

That sound pattern - **W H W W H W W** - *is* a minor scale. Follow that pattern, starting on any note, and you'll get a minor scale! There are *lots* of scales out there, but the most important one for you to begin learning (other than the minor pentatonic!) is the **major scale** - so we'll be focusing on it quite a bit.

The great thing about knowing the **whole step / half step pattern** for the major scale, is that you can use it to **build any major scale you want**. Being able to figure out *which* specific notes are in *which* specific major scale is a *huge deal* for becoming a great guitarist! Let's try some out - start with **G**:

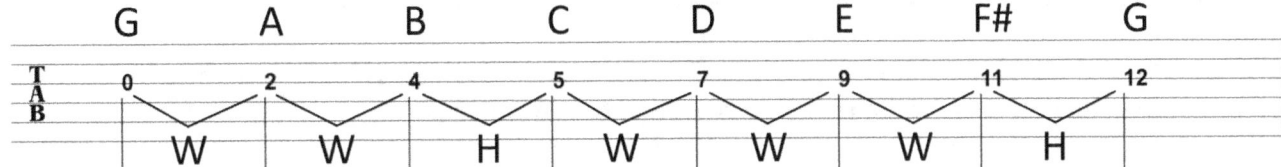

Notice the **F#** - why is it there? Remember, it's the *pattern of sound* that is most important. Your brain is *expecting* to hear a whole step *between the sixth and seventh note*, for the scale to **sound** major. Putting a plain **F** in that "slot" would not match the expected pattern. Therefore, we *have* to put an F# there - because **only an F# is a whole step away from E**. This is the reason we have sharps and flats in the first place; to make a series of notes **conform to an existing sound pattern**. Let's try another one:

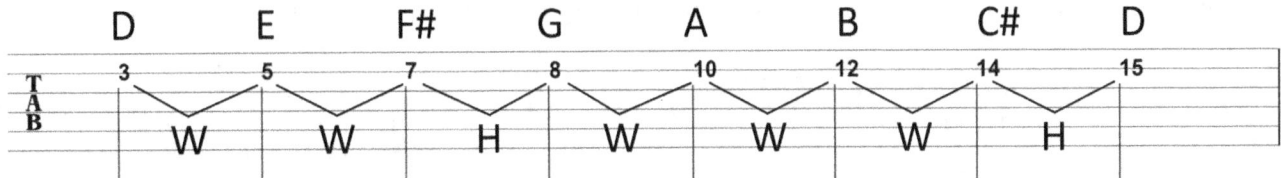

For the **D major scale**, we have to throw in another sharp - **C#** - in order to conform to the pattern. In fact, the **C major scale** is the *only* major scale in which there are no sharps or flats. Every other major scale will have an **unique amount of sharps or flats**, to make the notes fit the pattern. Here's one more:

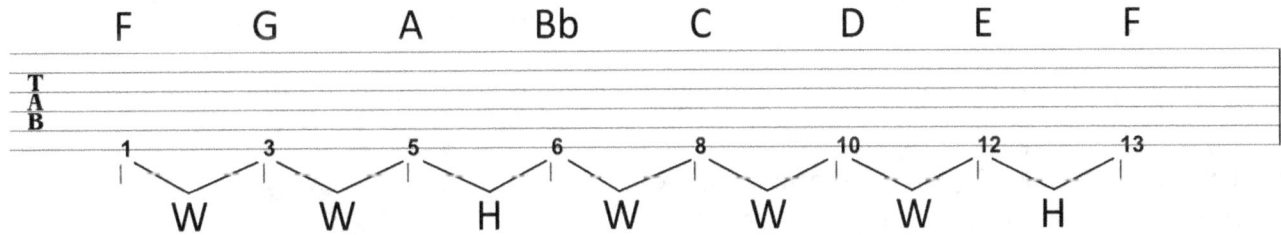

An **F major scale** has a **Bb**, in order to make it fit the pattern. Why Bb, and not **A#**? After all, they sound the same, so what's the difference? If we wrote A# instead of Bb, the scale would have *two kinds of A (A and A#), and no B's at all* - **it would skip right to C**. That wouldn't make any logical sense; it's important to maintain the "letter to letter" sequence when building a scale. When building a major scale, always choose the **accidental** (sharp or flat) that facilitates this sequence.

Playing a major scale up and down a single string is cool, but it's not always practical. So, just like for the minor pentatonic scale, it makes sense to play the notes **across different strings, in one area of the neck**. Because there are *seven* notes in the major scale (compared to *five* in the minor pentatonic), the finger patterns for the major scale are slightly more involved. They feature **three notes per string**.

Another difference between the major scale patterns and the minor pentatonic patterns, is that the major scale patterns **will always start on the root note of the scale**. For example, let's use a C major scale to start:

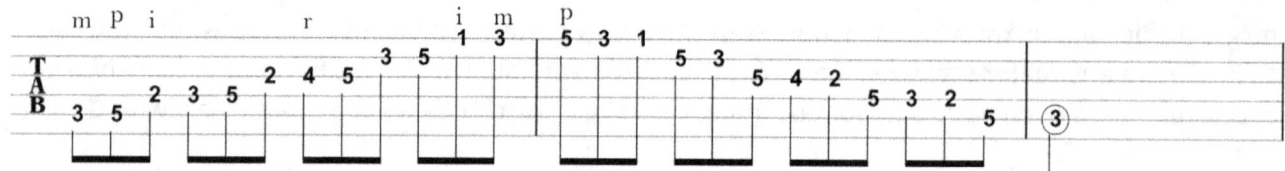

Notice that the scale fingering is in **two octaves** - meaning, you play through all seven notes in the scale, and then have enough room to **start the seven notes over again**:

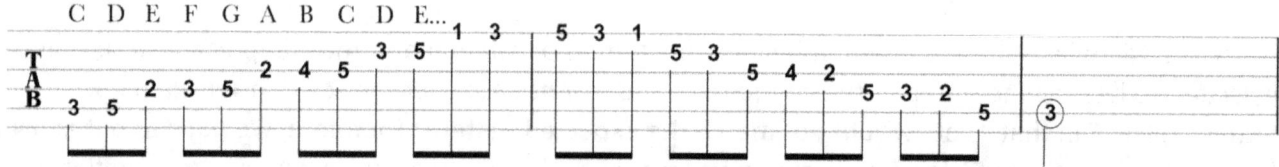

Even though you'll be *starting* and *ending* the finger pattern on the **root note**, we don't want to neglect the notes on the **low E string**. After all, you can play notes from the C major scale on that string too:

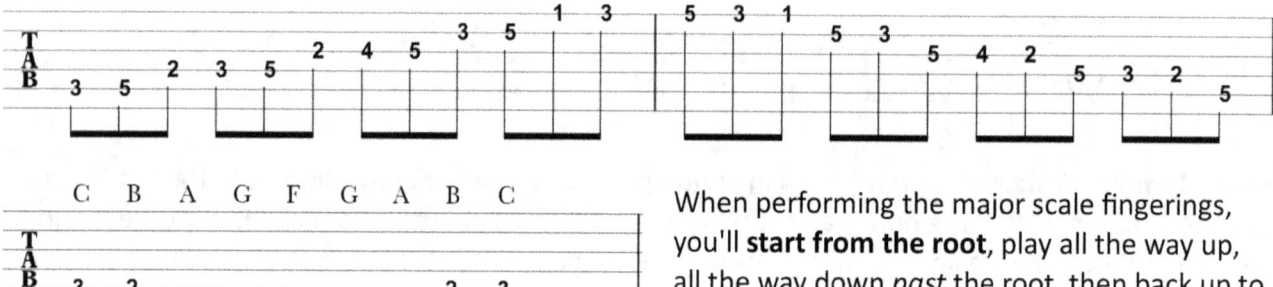

When performing the major scale fingerings, you'll **start from the root**, play all the way up, all the way down *past* the root, then back up to **end on the root**, where you started.

Here is the fingering pattern you just played, this time written as a **scale diagram**. The location of the root note (on the *A string*) is indicated by a circle; this is where you'll **start** and **end** the scale:

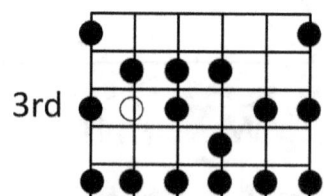

75

SESSION 13

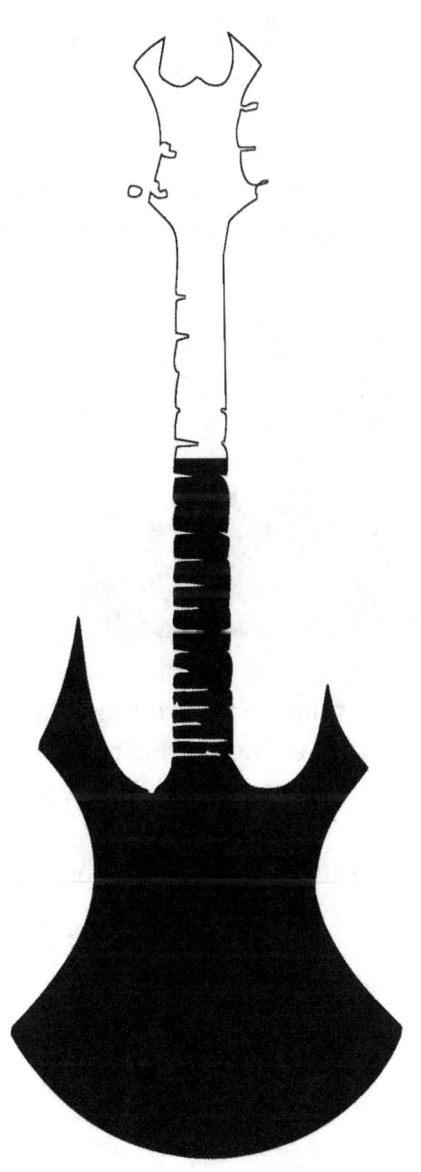

PHYSICAL

Remember these?

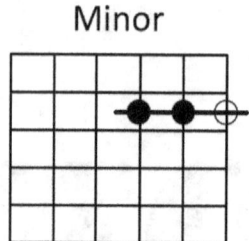
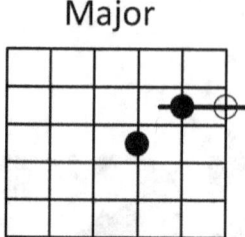

Well, now we're **adding a string**! By *doubling* one of the notes (the **root note**, in this case) on the **D string**, you'll turn these triads into two other, extremely useful (and well used) **barre chord** shapes:

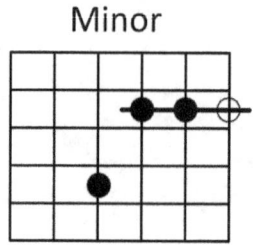
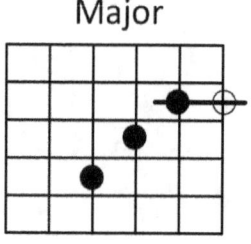
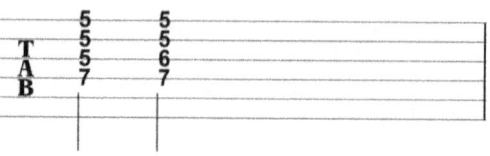

Use your **ring finger** to play the D string note; remember to keep your index finger **slightly rolled out** (having your elbow nearer your body will help with this). Keep your thumb **fairly low** on the neck:

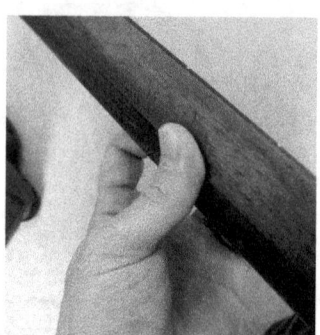

When you're ready, pick the notes **one at a time**, so that you can make sure they're all ringing together. Notice that the D string note sounds the *same* as the E string note - just **one octave lower**. These are major and minor chords, so they still only have **three notes**. We've simply *doubled* one of them!

Just like you did with the triads, this next exercise gets you moving these shapes up the neck. Your finger will start to **flatten**, and then **roll the other way** as you get higher up the neck. Don't fight it!

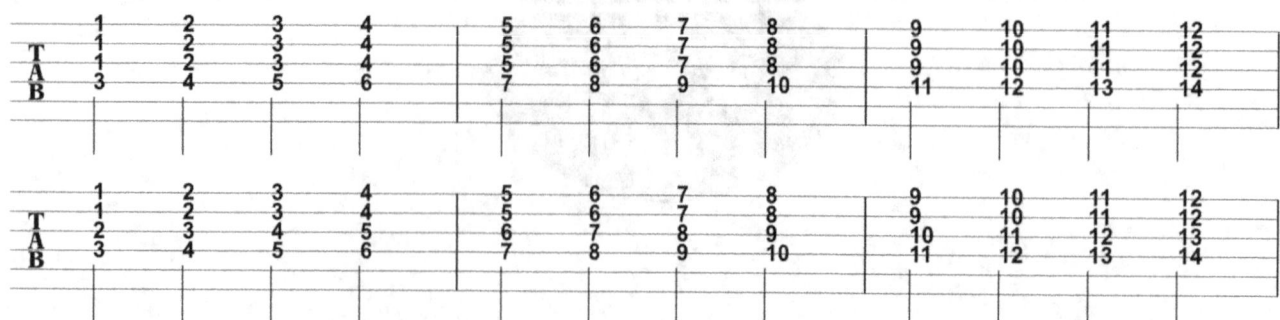

77

You've learned how to play a **major scale** fingering across all six strings - however, we're about to revisit the **one string** major scale pattern. Why? Because it's fantastic raw material for *building your technique!*

Let's use the **C major scale** for the following exercises. First, here's the scale played on the **A string**:

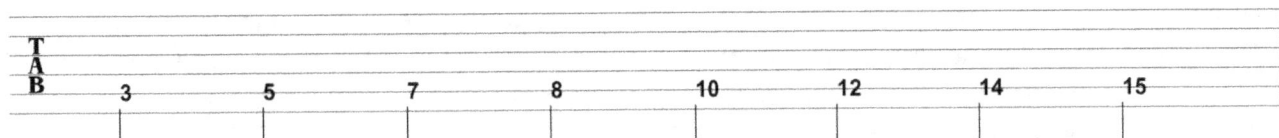

To make the scale more manageable, let's break it down into **groups of three notes**. That way, we can use specific **fingerings** - allowing us to shift up the neck more efficiently. Use *alternate picking* for these!

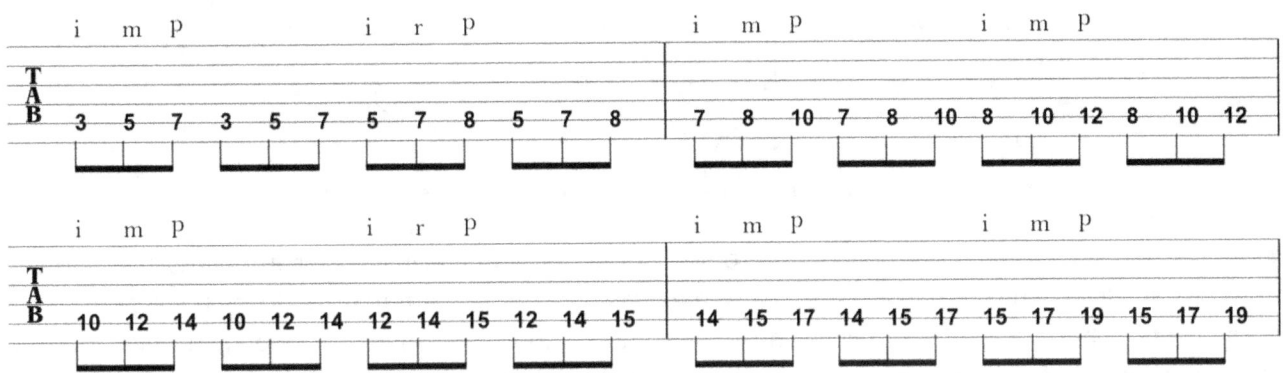

Here's the same thing, this time played on the **B string**:

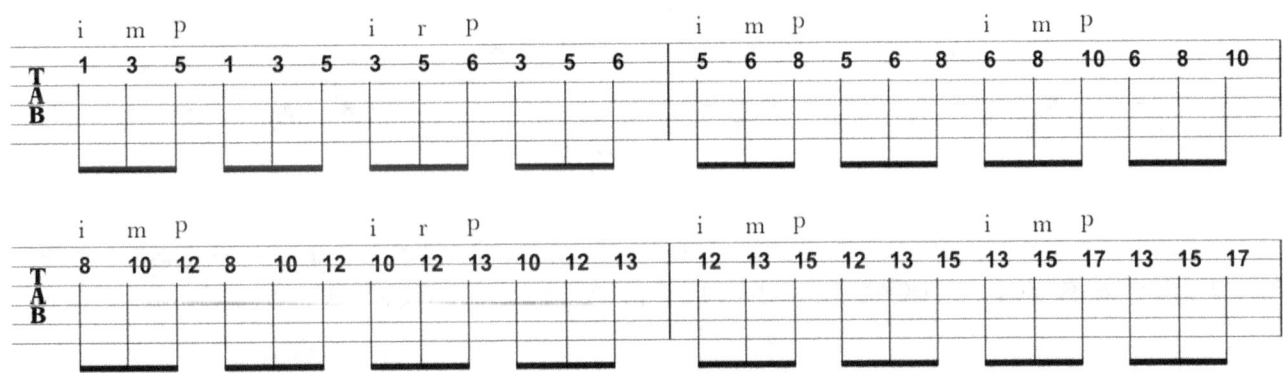

It's important to practice **technique exercises** like this on multiple strings; it can feel a little different to play on the lower strings (like A), than it does to play on the higher strings (like B!) Here's one more to try - a *variation* on the above. It's written on the **B string**, but you should play it on the **A string** too:

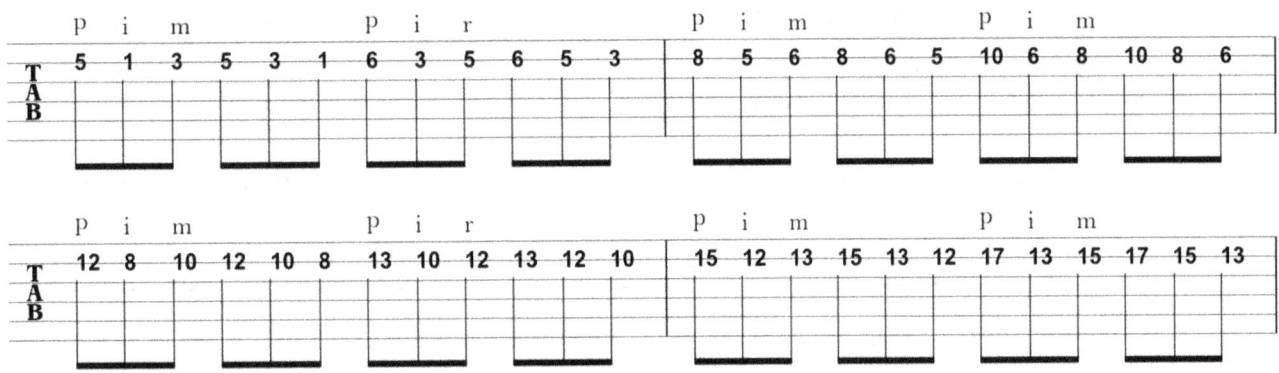

MENTAL

Rhythmic variety is the essential element *most missing* in a boring riff or solo. It stands to reason then, that the more ways you know of to *create* this variety, the better. We've learned that combining different types of **notes** and **rests**, and using the **tie** to connect notes, goes a long way towards that end. When it comes to creating rhythmic variety, the more options the better - so let's take a look at another important concept called **dotted notes**.

Adding a **dot** next to a note will *increase that note's length by one-half of its original value*. Yes, that definition sounds like some sort of algebra - so here's an example to make it simple:

See how it works? A **quarter note** divides into *two* 8th notes...but a **dotted quarter** divides into *three* 8th notes. It's length has been **increased by one extra 8th**. Likewise, a **half note** divides into *two* quarter notes...but a dotted half divides into *three* quarter notes. Its length has been **increased by one extra quarter note**. When it comes to dotted notes, just think "this lasts for *three* of something": three *quarters* for a dotted half note, three *8ths* for a dotted quarter note. Let's look at a few measures, with the **beat pattern** written underneath.

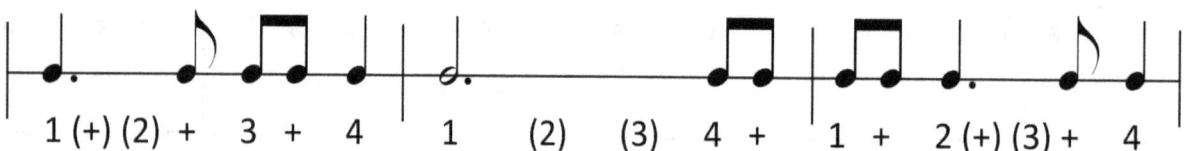

Play any open string you want, count *all* of the 8th notes out loud, and during the beats in parentheses **let the dotted note ring out!** Now, here's another example, this time with rests:

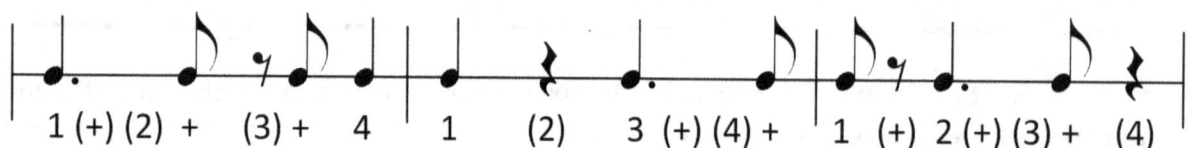

If you're having some trouble, keep a couple of things in mind: *1.* This stuff isn't easy! But, it isn't *complicated* either. If you go sloooow (which you should), there *is* a logic to it. Line up the notes and rests with the 8th notes you're counting, and you'll succeed. *2.* Just because you "get it" mentally, it doesn't mean your hands will automatically cooperate. There is still repetition needed, so be patient.

Here's one last example...the ultimate rhythm challenge, combining rests, ties, *and* dotted notes!

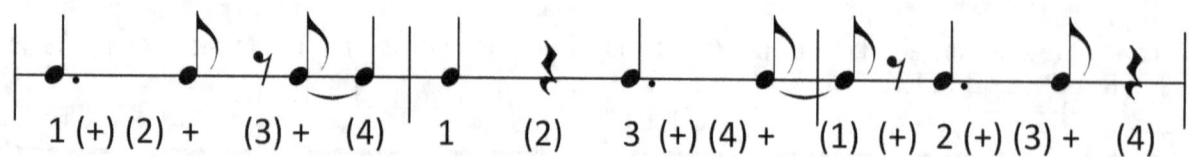

SESSION 14

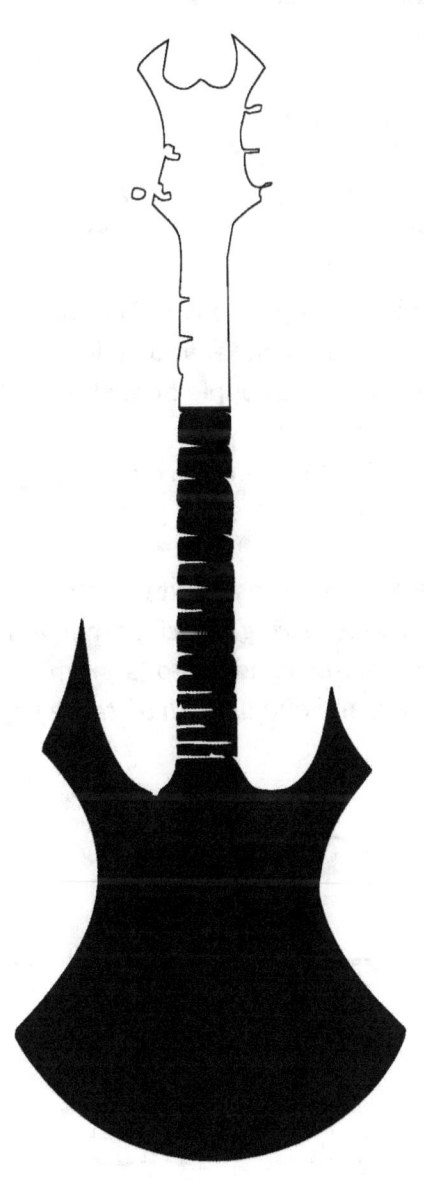

PHYSICAL

Minor pentatonic scale. Rhythms. Hammers and pulls. Bends. Slides. Looks like you're armed and ready for action - **time to start shredding a solo**! There's an eight measure guitar solo with your name on it, and you're going to master it:

Wait!!! No video to show you exactly how to play it, so you don't have to think???? That's right! Sweating yet? Good! The challenge here is to **use what you've learned so far**. Get confident - if you break it all down, practicing a measure (or even a couple of beats) at a time, you can figure it out completely on your own. Even if it takes longer at first than just passively watching a video, **you're getting a ton more value from the time**. Trust me on this, *over-relying on YouTube videos* is a failing proposition when it comes to your long-term success as a guitarist. Take your time, and use your head!

Now, let's get back to some technique building. These next three exercises are performed on the **B string**, and are based on the **three-note-per-string** exercises that you'd worked on previously. The difference is, you'll be using legato (hammer-ons and pull-offs!) Here's the first one - remember to only pick the **first note** in every group of three, and *end up with all three fingers down*:

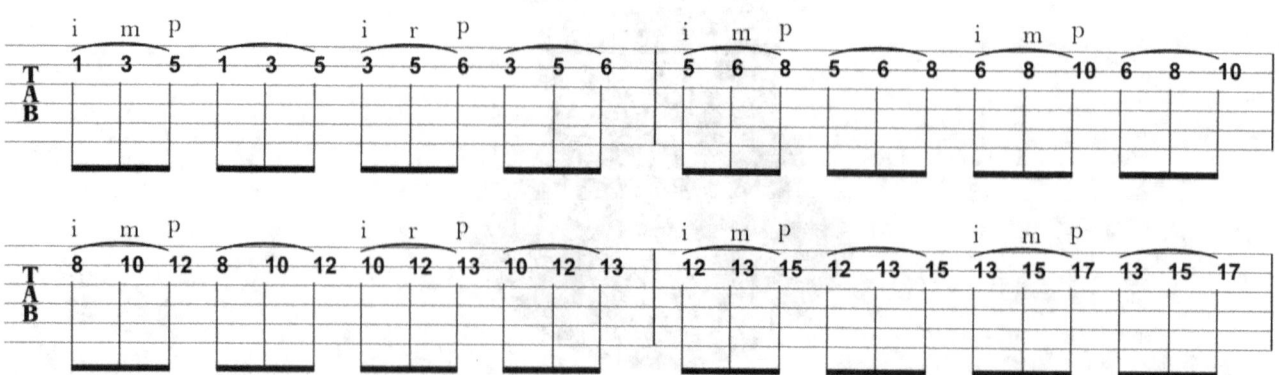

This next exercise is made up wholly of pull-offs. Remember to **start with all three fingers down**, and maintain an even rhythm throughout. Don't gyp the index finger notes, in your haste to shift your hand!

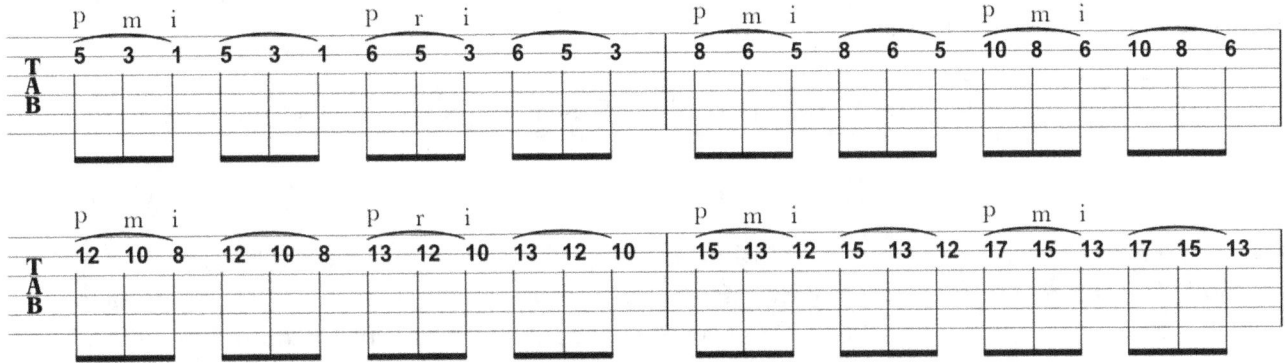

Finally, **let's combine the hammer-ons and pull-offs**. Only pick the first note for each group of six!

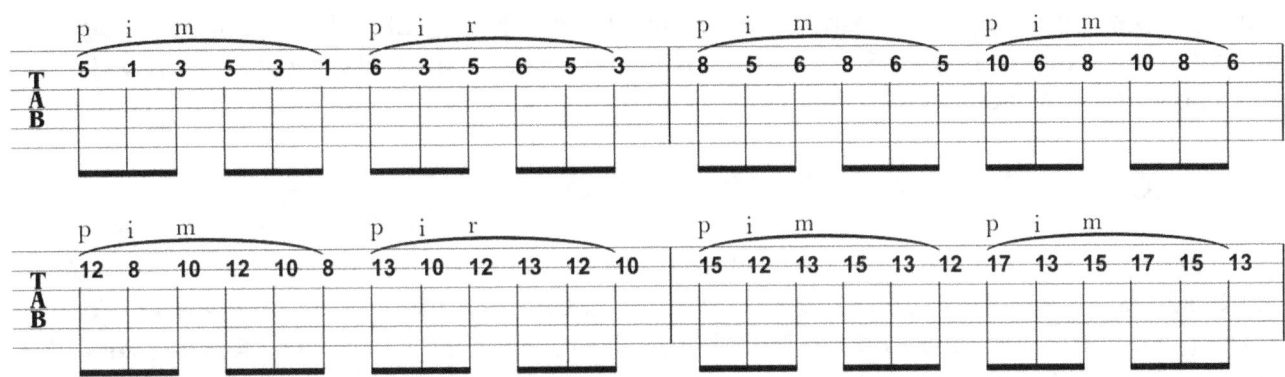

MENTAL

Have you been practicing **building chords** in your head? Let's hope so, because now it's time to figure out how *chords* relate to *scales*. You're about to see how chords and scales are really just **two sides of the same coin**! Remember how chords are constructed using the **interval of a 3rd**?

Well, if we write out a **major scale**, we can see all the 3rds **at a glance**; in fact, *every other note* is a 3rd:

C D E F G A B C
    3rd   3rd

Because of this, you could choose any starting note and quickly **stack up the 3rds**. In other words, you can quickly see *which three notes* are in the chord. For example, start with the note **D**:

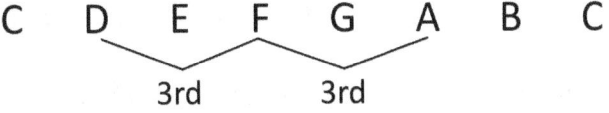

82

This gives us the notes **D F A**, and since these notes are *two 3rds stacked up in a row*, we know that it *has to be* some type of chord. Furthermore, there are seven notes in the scale, right? That means that there are *seven possible root notes* from which to build a chord. The bottom line is, **we can get seven different chords from the notes in one scale:**

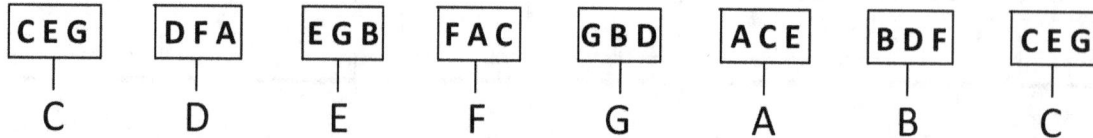

Awesome! Now we can look at the D, for instance, and quickly say to ourselves "D F A are the notes in a D chord". Or, we could look at the F and say "F A C are the notes in the F chord". Only one problem though - what *type* of chords are they? We know they have to be *some* type of chord...but *which* type?

That's where our **formulas** come in. For example, C to E is a **major 3rd**, and E to G is a **minor 3rd**. Since we know that **M3 + m3 = Major Chord**, the first chord in this scale **must be major**. Now, here's something pretty interesting: in music, we use **Roman Numerals** to identify the type of chord. **Big roman numerals mean "major"**. So, since C E G is the *first* chord in the scale, *and* it's major, we label it with a **big Roman Numeral**:

    C   D   E   F   G   A   B   C
    I

Let's build a chord from **D**, the *second* note in the scale. D to F is a **minor 3rd**, and F to A is a **major 3rd**. What's the formula? Since **m3 + M3 = Minor Chord**, the second chord in this scale **must be minor**. We label it with a **small Roman Numeral**:

    C   D   E   F   G   A   B   C
           ii

If we continue in this fashion, figuring out the types of chords (major, minor, diminished) and labeling them with Roman Numerals, this is what we get (small with a circle means *diminished chord*):

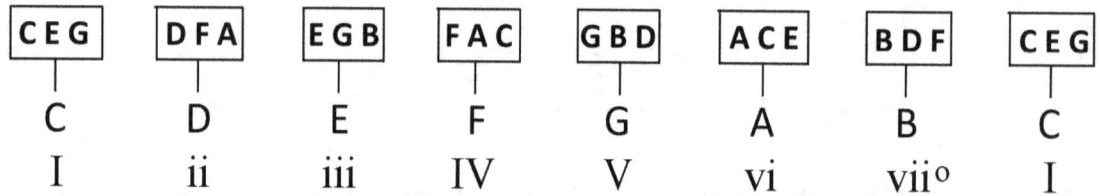

"Boy, that's a lot of busywork," you're probably saying. *"What the hell good is any of this?"* Well, just think about what we've done. **You can now look at a C major scale, and immediately see all the chords it generates**. What's the fifth chord from the scale? Well, it's a big five - must be **G major**. What's the third chord from the scale? It's a small three - must be **E minor**.

There's a word for all of these chords - they're **diatonic**. Diatonic simply means *"of, or from, a scale"*. The great thing about diatonic chords is, since they all come from the same scale, **they will all sound good together in a chord progression**. In a nutshell - *this is where songs come from*.

For now, study all of the above, and memorize the order of diatonic chords: **I ii iii IV V vi vii°**.

SESSION 15

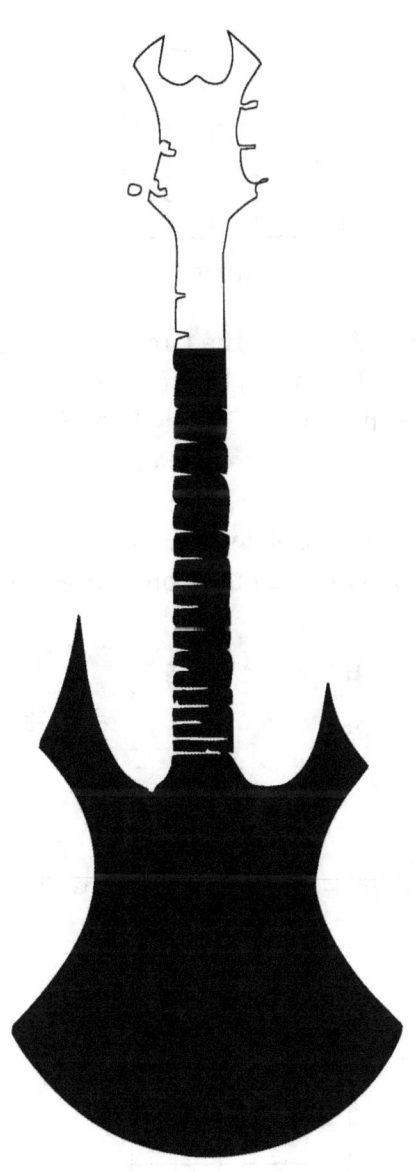

PHYSICAL

Wouldn't it be great to have a **ready-made system** for practicing your **triad shapes** all across the neck? And not just one chord at a time anymore, but a way to mix and match them up? Sure would be great...

Guess what? *Now you do!* The answer is to play the **diatonic chords** of a scale, using triads. Diatonic chords are the ones that can be built from the major scale; there are seven of them (identified with **Roman Numerals**). Here are the chords that we get from a **C major scale**:

C   Dm   Em   F   G   Am   B°   C
I   ii   iii   IV   V   vi   vii°   I

We're going to play *each* of these chords, *in order*, using the triad **voicings** (another word for "shape"). It'll sound like you're playing a scale - but with chords! Let's use the triads that have the **root note** on the **G string**:

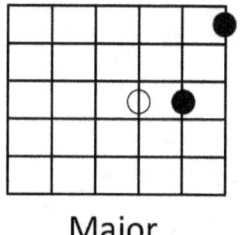
Major

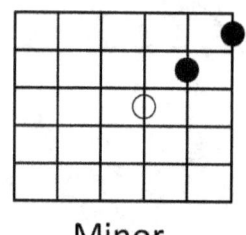
Minor

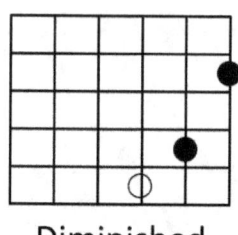
Diminished

The way this works is, you'll be finding each note in the C major scale *on the G string*, and then **building the appropriate triad voicing around it**. The Roman Numerals will tell you which *type* of triad to play on *which* note. For example, if you play an **F** on the G string (10th fret), that will be the root note for the **major triad**. F is the fourth note of the scale, and the *big* Roman Numeral reminds you that it's major.

Here are all the diatonic chords of C major, written in TAB. The first measure maps out the **root notes**, and the second measure shows the **triad voicings** built from those roots:

```
    C   D   E   F   G   A   B   C    I    ii   iii  IV   V    vi   vii° I
                                     3    5    7    8    10   12   13   15
T                                    5    6    8    10   12   13   15   17
A   5   7   9   10  12  14  16  17   5    7    9    10   12   14   16   17
B
```

Now, let's play the diatonic chords from the **G major scale** - and we'll use the triads that have the root note on the **high E string**:

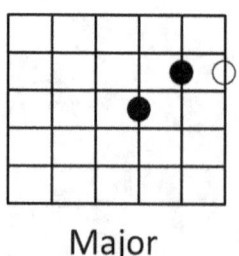
Major

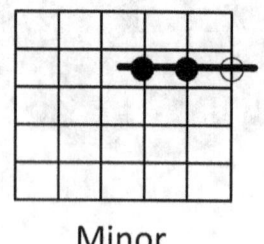
Minor

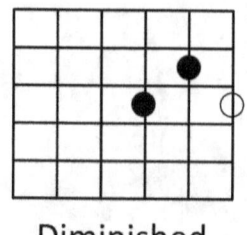
Diminished

85

The great thing about knowing the order of Roman Numerals for the major scale, is that **they will be the same for every major scale**. In other words, now that you've gone through the process of figuring them all out for the C major scale, *all you need to do is plop the Roman Numerals under the notes of any major scale*. You'll be able to see all the chords available from that scale, at a glance!

For example, if we write out a **G major scale**, all we need to do is throw the Roman Numerals in there, and we can immediately see the chords you get to choose from:

```
G    A    B    C    D    E    F#    G
I    ii   iii  IV   V    vi   vii°  I
```

Instead of having to use the **M3/m3 formulas** and figure out each chord, we can just look and see what chords we're dealing with - **G major**, **A minor**, **B minor**, **C major**, **D major**, **E minor**, and **F# diminished**.

Let's play 'em! Here are all the diatonic chords of G major, written in TAB. The first measure maps out the **root notes**, and the second measure shows the **triad voicings** built from those roots:

```
   G    A    B    C    D    E    F#   G     I    ii   iii  IV   V    vi   vii°  I
                                            3    5    7    8    10   12   14    15
                                            3    5    7    8    10   12   13    15
   3    5    7    8    10   12   14   15    4    5    7    9    11   12   14    16
T
A
B
```

Wow, just think about how much amazing practice these **diatonic triads** give you! You get to practice *finding notes on the neck, building scales, memorizing the order of Roman Numerals*, and *memorizing the triad voicings themselves* - all while training your ears to recognize chord progressions! Talk about time well spent! Now, let's play the diatonic triads for one more scale - **D major**:

```
D    E    F#    G    A    B    C#    D
I    ii   iii   IV   V    vi   vii°  I
```

Here are all the diatonic chords of D major, written in TAB. The first measure maps out the **root notes**, and the second measure shows the **triad voicings** built from those roots. We'll use the triad voicings with the root notes on the **B string**:

```
   D    E    F#   G    A    B    C#   D     I    ii   iii  IV   V    vi   vii°  I
                                            2    3    5    7    9    10   12    14
                                            3    5    7    8    10   12   14    15
   3    5    7    8    10   12   14   15    2    4    6    7    9    11   12    14
T
A
B
```

When practicing these diatonic triads, **use the metronome** as soon as you feel comfortable with the order of the chords. One of the goals here is to **increase your speed** while changing chords.

Also, make sure to always **keep your eyes on the string that has the root note**. When moving to the next chord, don't just stare at whatever string is the lowest. Look ahead to the next note in the scale - regardless of which string it's on. This way, your brain and hands will be working together. Your **brain** will be thinking about the next note in the scale, your **eyes** will target it, and your **hand** will move into the correct triad voicing. **Brain / eye / hand coordination** - that's the goal here!

Getting back to some lead playing, it's time to increase your mastery of the **major scale**. Just as the five forms of the **minor pentatonic** allow you to play the same five notes all across the neck, the major scale also has **more than one fingering**. With the major scale patterns, you'll always be **starting from the root note** - on either the low E string or A string.

The pattern you've already learned starts on the **A string**, with your middle finger. Since we're playing the **C major scale**, that note will be C:

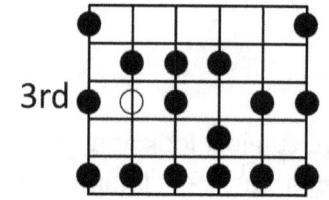

Now that your memory is jogged, let's move onward and upward across the neck. The next major scale pattern will *also* start on the A string, 3rd fret - **the C**. The difference is, you'll shift your hand slightly higher up the neck, and **play that note with your index finger**.

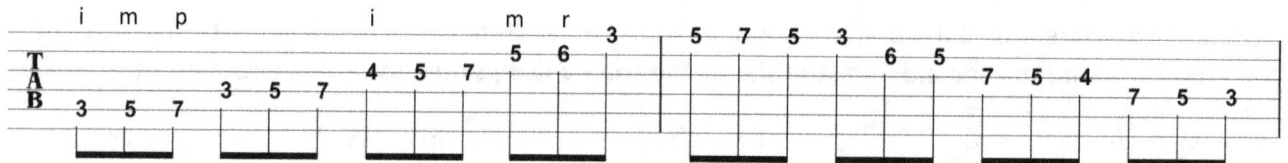

When performing the major scale fingerings, you'll **start from the root**, play all the way up, all the way down *past* the root, then back up to **end on the root**, where you started.

Here is the fingering pattern you just played, this time written as a **scale diagram**. The location of the root note (on the *A string*) is indicated by a circle; this is where you'll **start** and **end** the scale:

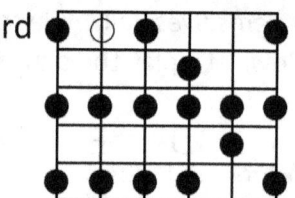

MENTAL

There's a word you've probably heard (a lot of guitarists throw it around), but may not really understand (most of those guitarists throwing it around most likely don't either!) That word is **key**. It's usually heard in the context of something like this: *"Hey, what key is this song in?"*, or *"This song is in the key of G minor."*

A **key** is actually a very simple concept: *key* just means **scale**. So, if a song is in the **key of C major**, it means that everything in the song (the melody, guitar solo, chords, etc.) is *made of notes from the C major scale*. Remember how we built chords from the notes in a C major scale? Those chords (in addition to being called *diatonic* to C major), are in the **key of C major** - because they *only* contain notes from the C major scale.

When you used the Roman Numerals to figure out and play the triads from the **G major scale**, you were playing **in the key of G major**. Likewise for the triads built from the D major scale; you were playing in **the key of D major**. So remember - when talking about a song, solo, or chord progression, *if it's in a certain key, it means the notes come from that scale.*

Each **key** (major scale!) has it's own *unique number* of **sharped notes** or **flatted notes**. This number of sharps or flats can be used to quickly **identify a key**. For example, here are two scales with sharps: G major and D major.

$$G\ A\ B\ C\ D\ E\ F\#\ G$$

$$D\ E\ F\#\ G\ A\ B\ C\#\ D$$

The key of G major has **one sharp**, and the key of D major has two **sharps**. Now, here's a couple of keys that contain flats:

$$F\ G\ A\ Bb\ C\ D\ E\ F$$

$$Bb\ C\ D\ Eb\ F\ G\ A\ Bb$$

The key (scale!) of F major has **one flat**, and the key of Bb major has **two flats**. Hey, here's a question that could stand some review right about now: why do some scales have sharps, and some scales have flats? It isn't as esoteric as you might think - the answer just comes down to *consistency* and *logic*. For example, all of these scales have one thing in common that's pretty obvious: they all go *letter* to *letter* to *letter*. No matter if there are sharps or flats involved, **the letter sequence is preserved**.

What if we take that F major scale, and substitute an A# for the Bb? After all, it's the same pitch (just another way to say it), so nothing would change sound-wise....

$$F\ G\ A\ A\#\ C\ D\ E\ F$$

Uh-oh! Looks kind of weird, doesn't it? Now we've got **two kinds of A** - a regular A, and an A#. No good! We need to **maintain the sequence of letters**! There are some major scales that require sharps to do this, and some that require flats - that's really all there is to it. Now, for reference, here are **all the major scales** - organized according to sharps or flats:

C D E F G A B C	C D E F G A B C
G A B C D E F# G	F G A Bb C D E F
D E F# G A B C# D	Bb C D Eb F G A Bb
A B C# D E F# G# A	Eb F G Ab Bb C D Eb
E F# G# A B C# D# E	Ab Bb C Db Eb F G Ab
B C# D# E F# G# A# B	Db Eb F Gb Ab Bb C Db
F# G# A# B C# D# E# F#	Gb Ab Bb Cb Db Eb F Gb
C# D# E# F# G# A# B# C#	Cb Db Eb Fb Gb Ab Bb Cb

Use this chart as a "cheat sheet" when you practice building major scales in your head. It may not sound like a super-exciting part of playing guitar, but **knowing the notes in each key** is like a **secret weapon for your playing**. It will put you in the top percentile of guitarists if you can quickly rattle off the sharped notes for the key of B major, or the flatted notes for Db major, or...you get the picture. Starting to do this early in your guitar career will pay off in spades later on!

SESSION 16

PHYSICAL

So far, you've got a couple of the major scale fingerings under your belt - one that starts with the **middle finger** on the root, and one that starts with the **index finger** on the root:

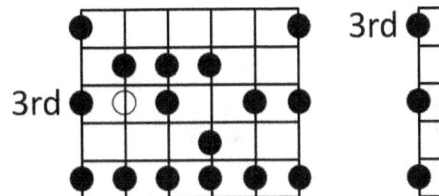
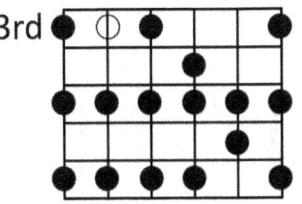

In your quest to shred across the *entire* neck, there's only one thing to do now: move higher up with another major scale fingering! Because the idea here is to **always start with the root note**, we need to find another **C**. Furthermore, you'll always be finding the root note *on either the low E string, or the A string*. That second pattern started with the **index** on the **A string** - looks like we've run out of fingers!

Remember though, for these major scale fingerings, we can find the root note on *either* the A string *or* the low E string. We might have run out of options on the 3rd fret, but what if we **shift the hand higher up the neck** (the whole point of these fingerings anyway)? The root note (C) can be found at the **8th fret on the low E string** - and you can play it, and begin the scale, with your **pinky** this time:

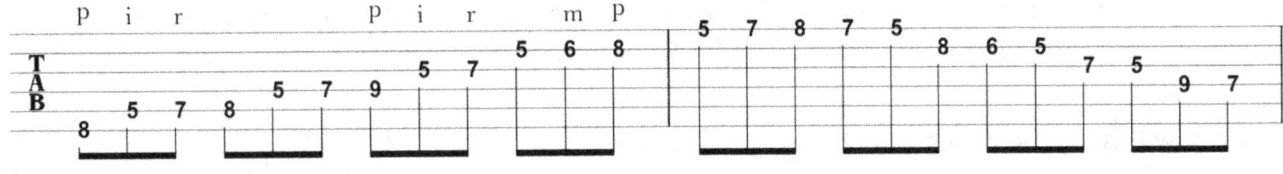

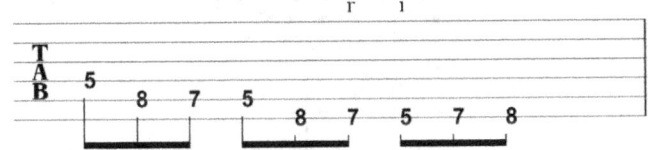

Just like the other major scale fingerings, you'll **start from the root**, play all the way up, all the way down *past* the root, then back up to **end on the root**, where you started.

Here is the fingering pattern you just played, this time written as a **scale diagram**. The location of the root note (on the *E string*) is indicated by a circle; this is where you'll **start** and **end** the scale:

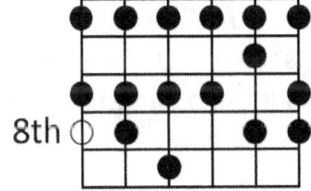

There will be a total of **six finger patterns** that you'll learn for the major scale. You've got half of them now; it's important that you practice them *individually* (to get each pattern down) **and** *one after the other* (to master the art of connecting them). **Continue to use your metronome!**

Now it's time to have some fun with a **technique-building lick** derived from those three major scale fingerings. Remember that solo you played that was based on the **minor pentatonic scale**? Well, the major scale is *also* used as raw material for creating **riffs, solos, and melodic guitar parts**. This lick uses a sequence that moves through the three finger patterns, on the high E and B strings...

Before you start though, just a quick aside about practicing. All the material presented in this book is **cumulative**; in other words, every new lesson or topic *builds on what you've learned before*. It's important to keep working on the material that you've previously learned. The book is written in a 21 Session format...**but by no means should you expect to master each Session in one day, or even one week**. There's a lot of content here, so be patient and review often!

90

Here's that two-string lick; take it slow, and keep your thumb **fairly low on the back of the neck**. This one challenges your finger stretch, and thumb position is key! Once it's memorized, this lick (like any other technique exercise) should be looped over and over again. Remember to use **alternate picking**!

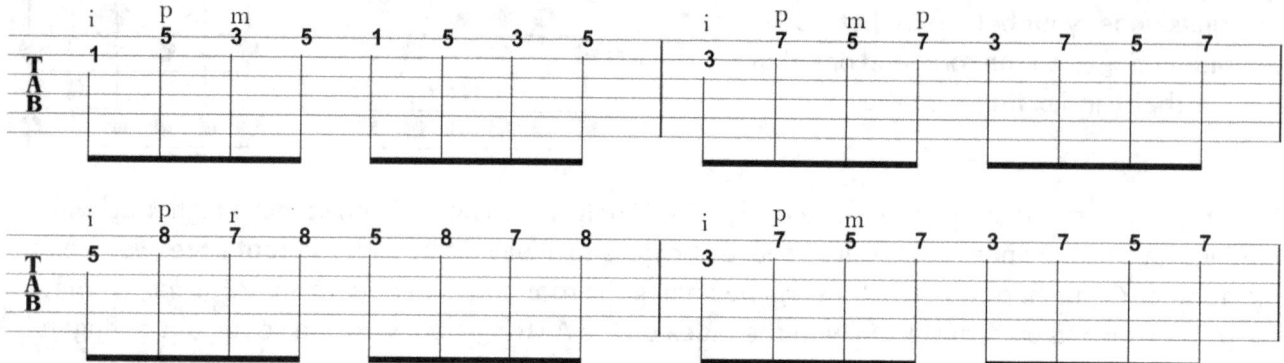

Okay, enough lead playing for now. Time to get back to some **barre chords**! We're about to up the ante on the Barre Chord Brutality - with some *five and six string full barres!* Did you faint just then? Pick yourself up, and once you're fully recovered, we can get started. Yes, you will find these barre chords more **physically demanding** then the other chords you've learned - so here's a tip: *practice these chords frequently, for short bursts of time.* You likely won't have the hand-stamina to sit down and practice these for 20 minutes, so instead **play for 5 minutes and come back later for another 5**. Got it?

Here's how this first beast is going to look - don't play it yet though, because we're going to break it down. But check it out, and visualize how it will look when completed and fingered on the fretboard. We'll be playing it at the **5th fret**.

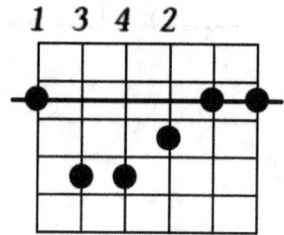

As you can see, this barre chord voicing uses **all four fingers**, and the index finger needs to **plow across all six strings**. Yowza! Definitely challenging, but we've got a way to approach this intelligently. Let's get the ring, middle, and pinky fingers into place first - and then tackle the index finger barre. Ready? Go!

Notice how straight up and down the ring and pinky fingers are. Use as little surface area as possible to press the strings down - **just the tips**. The middle finger is even **slightly over-bent**! Also, the thumb is **low on the neck**. You're setting it up to be in a comfortable place, for when the index finger comes into play.

Pick those three strings, and adjust your fingers until you can hear **all three ringing together**.

Next, you're going to **flatten your index finger** across the entire 5th fret:

Roll your finger outwards slightly, just like you did for the smaller barre chords. *Don't* try to keep your fingertip "flush" with the strings; **push the tip out over the edge of the neck**. This will help keep your finger flat. *Don't* bend your finger at the joint! Your index should feel slightly "wrapped around" the neck.

Pick all six strings, one at a time, and try to get all the notes ringing together. Most people don't get 'em all on the first try (or twentieth!) so be patient. Review all the points above, and make any adjustments necessary - your hand may tire out pretty quickly, so take a lot of breaks!

Here's one more thing to think about. Your other three fingers are already pressing down the A, D, and G strings. So, **the force of your index finger needs to be primarily focused on two points**: the E and B strings, and the low E. Don't waste too much energy trying to power down the middle of your index finger. Focus on clamping down the part of your finger **nearest your hand**, and then independently pressing down the **tip of your finger**.

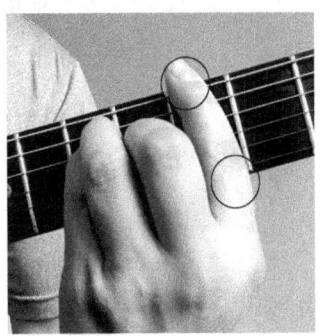

MENTAL

When it comes to rock and Metal, there's a scale that you'll hear way more often than major. It's called the **minor scale**, and it's the progenitor of many a heavy riff and scorching solo. Because the minor scale is just that - a scale - it has its own **unique whole step / half step pattern**:

W H W W H W W

Let's use this pattern to build an **A minor scale**, and then play the notes up the neck on the A string:

 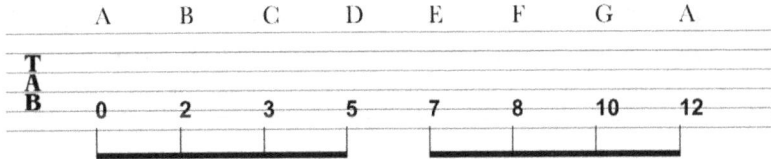

Awesome sound! Let's take a look at something interesting now - compare the notes in the **A minor scale** with the notes in the **C major scale** that you've been learning:

A B C D E F G A | C D E F G A B C
A Minor   C Major

Notice anything interesting? There are **no sharps or flats** in either scale - which means, the C major scale and the A minor scale contain *exactly the same notes*. They are literally *identical!* In music, there's a name for this: it's called **relative minor**. The two scales are related - they have the same seven notes - so **A minor is the relative minor of C major**. This concept will have far-reaching and positive consequences for your playing, so let's reinforce this relative minor business with some more examples.

The easiest way (for now) to identify the relative minor of any major scale is to **find the 6th note of a major scale**. That note will *always* be the root note of a minor scale. For example, **A** is the 6th note of the **C major scale**. Play the notes in C major, but start with A, and you'll automatically generate the *WS/HS pattern* of a minor scale. This will work for *any* major scale - **start with the 6th note, and it becomes a minor scale**. Let's try it with a Bb major scale; here are the notes:

Bb C D Eb F G A Bb

Now, let's start with the **G** instead - *the 6th note* of the Bb major scale:

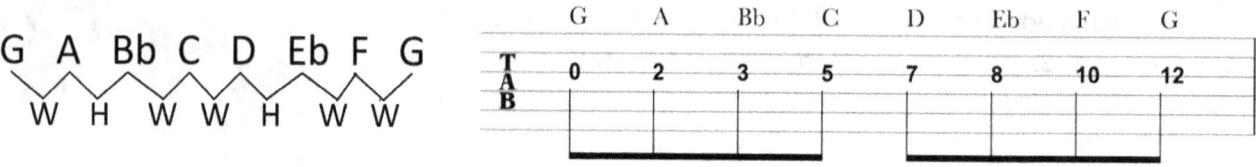

Sure sounds minor! Okay, one more just to seal the deal - here's the F major scale:

F G A Bb C D E F

Now, let's start with the **D** instead - *the 6th note* of the F major scale:

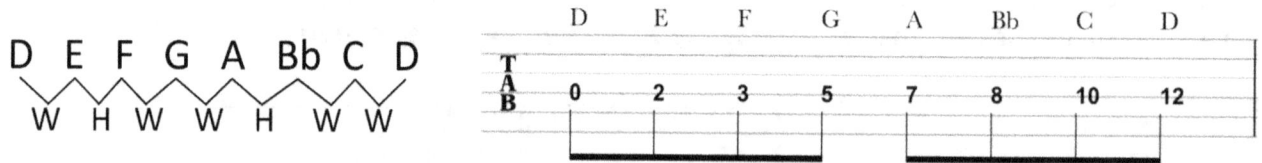

As you continue to practice **building major scales in your head**, a great little addition to the process is to **memorize the 6th note** - the relative minor - of each scale. Pairing them up this way, *thinking of the major and relative minor scales as two sides of the same coin*, will pay off big time later on.

SESSION 17

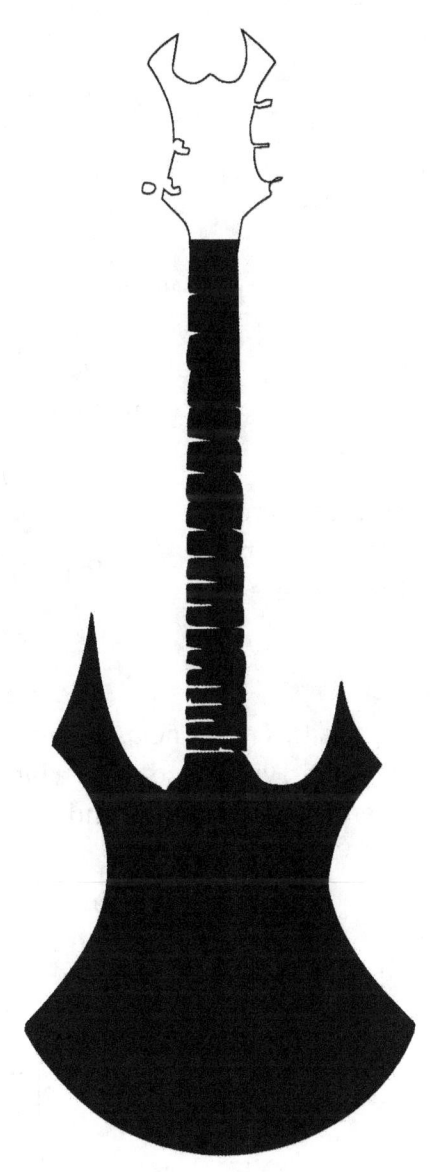

PHYSICAL

So far, you've been able to cover about half of the neck with those three major scale fingerings - you know, the ones where you **always start with the root note, on either the A string or low E string**? Here's a quick refresher - your three fingerings for the **C major scale**:

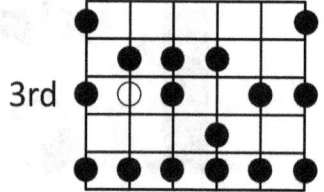
3rd

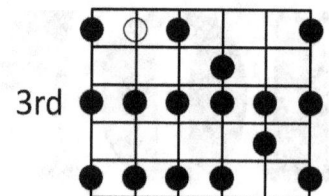
3rd

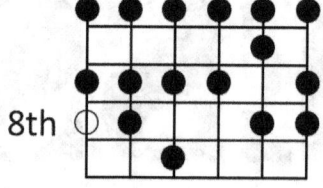
8th

So far, you've ended up on the low **E string** at the **8th fret**, playing the root note with your **pinky**. Since each of these fingerings *always starts on the root note* (can't really say that enough!) you can still use that **C on the 8th fret** to start the next pattern - only this time, you'll use your **middle finger**:

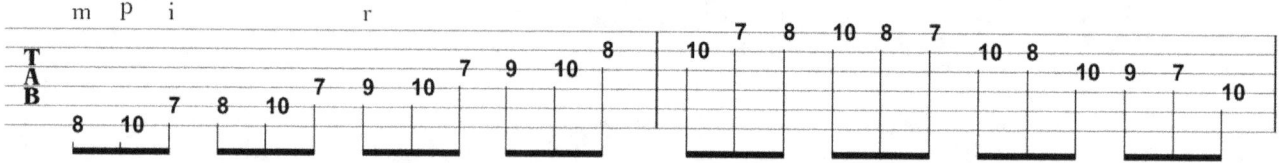

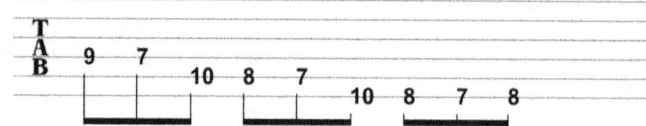

When performing the major scale fingerings, you'll **start from the root**, play all the way up, all the way down *past* the root, then back up to **end on the root**, where you started.

Here is the fingering pattern you just played, this time written as a **scale diagram**. The location of the root note (on the *E string*) is indicated by a circle; this is where you'll **start** and **end** the scale:

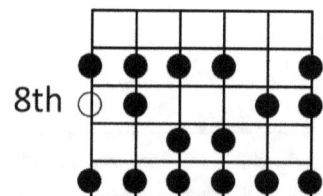
8th

Two more major scale fingerings to learn - and this next one *also* starts with the **root note on the E string**. By putting the **index finger** on the 8th fret, your hand shifts a bit higher, covering more neck. You know the drill by now; here's the next fingering pattern, in TAB and scale diagram form:

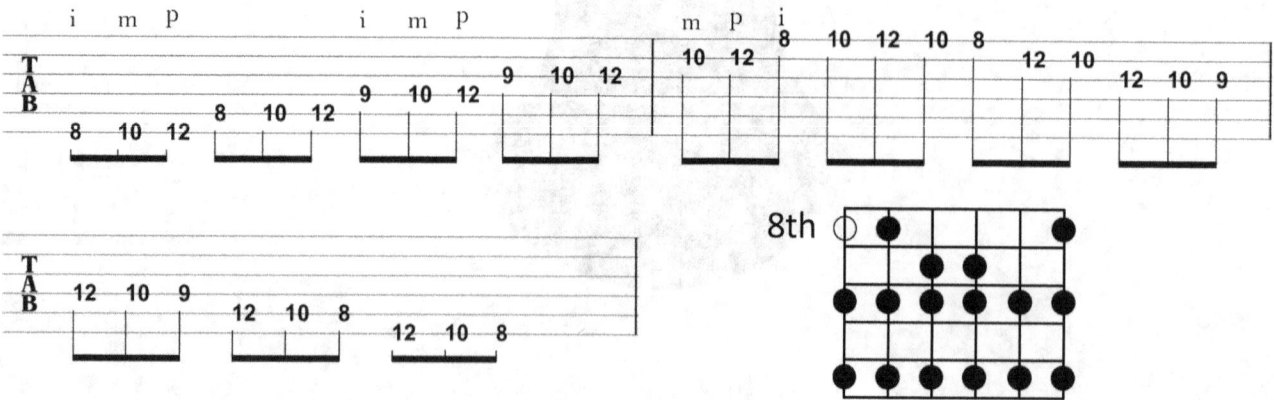

8th

95

Well, looks like we've run out of fingers again - can't go any higher on the low E string. There's **one more C** that we can access though, on the **A string** again. Place your **pinky** on the 15th fret, and behold the sixth and final major scale fingering:

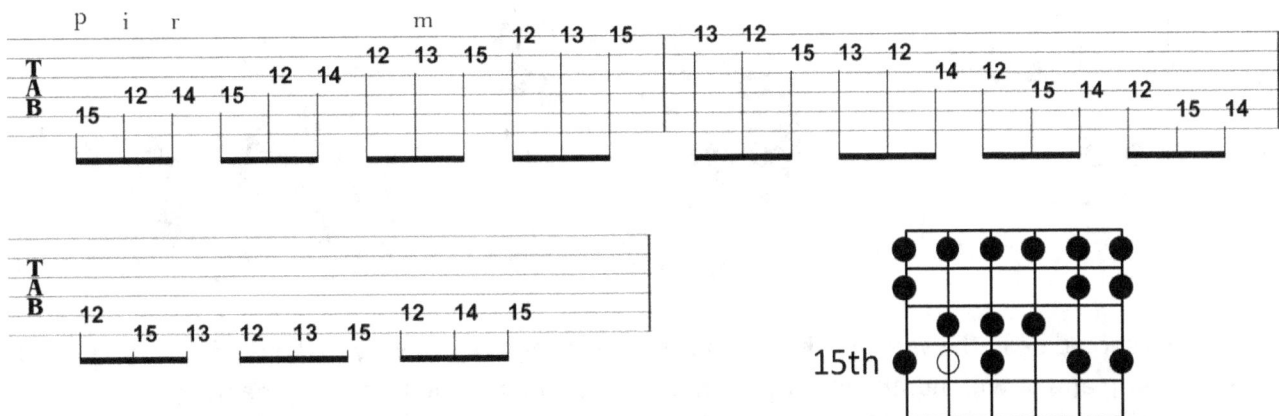

Excellent! Hey, what happens though if you want to keep climbing up the neck? After all, there are some frets left. Well, simply **repeat the fingering that starts with middle finger, A string** - the first one you played. But this time play it an **octave up**, at the 15th fret. The patterns all repeat! Here are all the major scale fingerings - try practicing them all at once, climbing the neck:

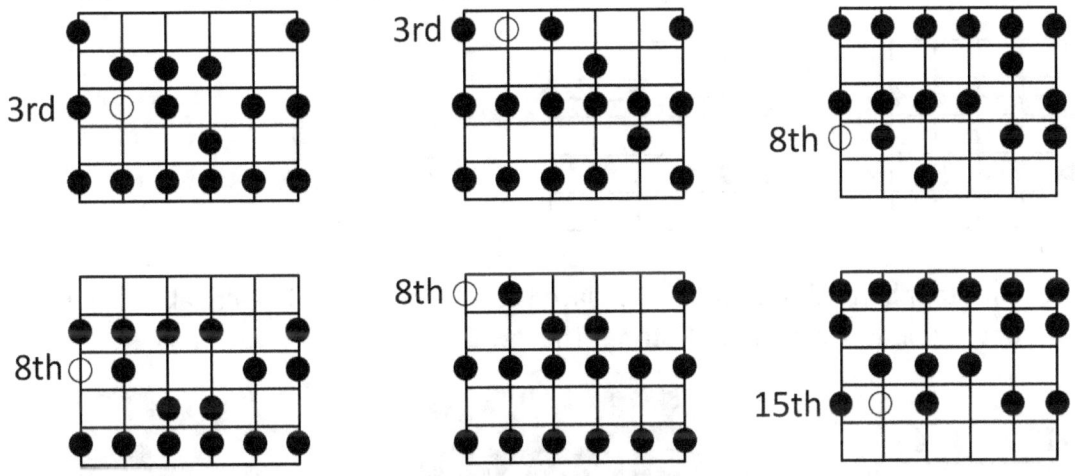

The "standard" (and not very well thought out!) way of presenting major scale fingerings - the way that you'll often see in other books - involves seven fingerings, each starting on a different note of the scale. Rest assured, the manner presented above (starting on the **root note** each time) will serve you much, much better when it comes to jamming, improvising, and navigating your way around the neck.

Sick of single notes this Session? Then back to barre chords it is! You've been tackling the major barre chord (the one with all six strings) :

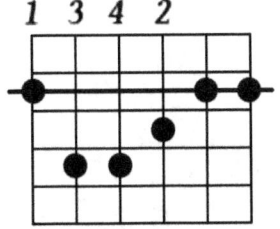

The logical question then is: what about **minor**? Well, we can turn this **full major barre chord** into a **full minor barre chord**. In addition, there is *another* major barre shape, and *another* minor barre shape that are very useful to know.

Let's start with transforming this six-string *major* barre chord into a *minor* barre chord. **Just lift your middle finger!**

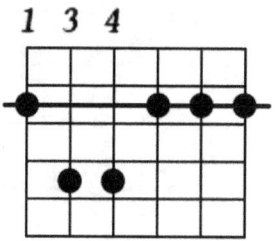

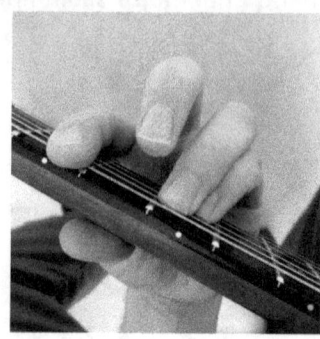

Your fingers should be in the same positions that they were before - slightly rolled out index, pinky and ring straight up and down, thumb fairly low on neck. While the **middle finger** is gone now, and won't interfere with any other strings ringing, the challenge now is for your **index finger**. It needs to press down an extra string, which is pretty demanding at first. Take your time with it, and you will prevail!

Now that you can play these two full barre chords, there's one extra piece of information you'll need - **the location of the root note**. In both of these shapes, the root note is always on the **low E string**. If you want to play a **B major** or **B minor**, using these two shapes, you'd **find a B on the E string**:

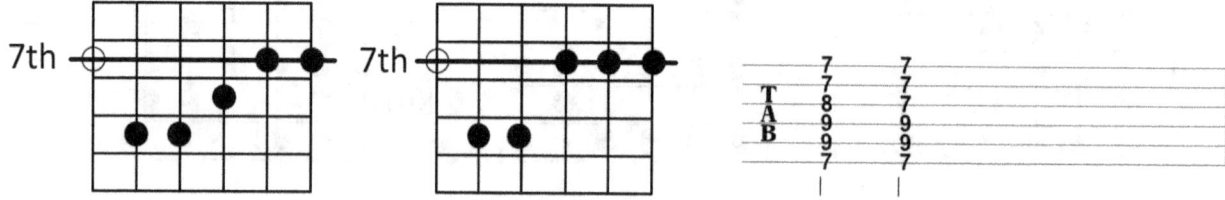

The other two important barre chord shapes are played using **five strings**. They're also major and minor, but the root note is located on the **A string**. The low E string is not played at all:

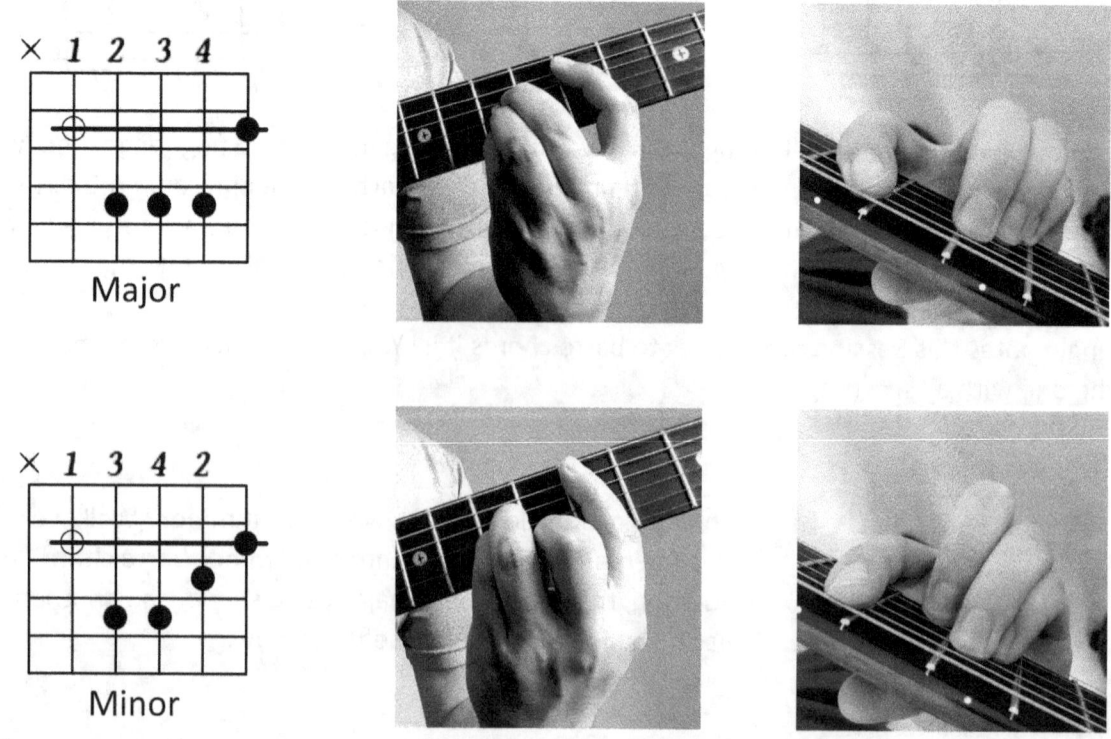

97

For the major shape, it's important to *keep the thumb low on the neck*. Place your middle, ring and pinky fingers on the fret *first*. After they're firmly anchored in place, then **reach back with your index finger** to fret the A string note. It's easier at first to reach back with your index, than it is to reach forward with your other fingers!

The minor barre chord looks similar to the six-string major barre chord. Keep the index slightly rolled out, and the other fingers straight up and down. Since the root note is located on the **A string** for both of these barre chords, to play a **B major** or **B minor chord** using these shapes, **find a B on the A string**:

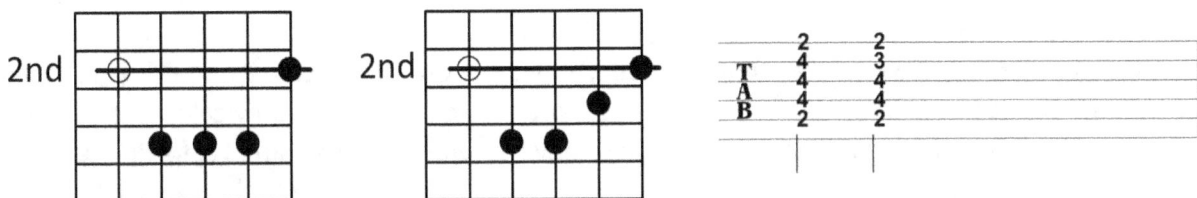

MENTAL

Metal and rock is usually in a **minor key**, not a major key (and it's a good thing, too!) So how can we start playing the minor scale **all across the neck**? Do we have to learn a whole new set of fingerings?

Luckily, the answer is *"No"*! We've already learned that any major scale can be *transformed* into a minor scale, simply by **starting on the 6th note**. This gives us the **relative minor** - the minor scale with *exactly the same notes* as the major scale. So, if the C major scale has exactly the same notes as the A minor scale *(C D E F G A B C /// A B C D E F G A)*...

This means we can use the six C major fingerings to play the A minor scale too!

Actually, this is a pretty big deal. It means you *already know* how to play the minor scale across the entire neck, whether you realized it or not. The only difference is *which* note you **hear** as the root note - either **C or A**. And, the biggest thing that affects which note you hear as the root is *context*.

Context is all about *what* you're playing the scale *over*. For example, if you're soloing with the **C major scale fingerings**, and the riff you're soloing over has **A as the main note**, then that A in the riff will *pull your ear* towards hearing A as the **root note** of the scale. It will sound like you're playing an **A minor scale**, *not* a C major scale.

However, if the song you're soloing over happens to have a **C major chord** as the main chord, then your licks will sound like they're coming from a C major scale instead. The **context** will have changed - and that's enough to make the same licks sound like **C major** instead of A minor.

If you wrote each of the seven notes of the C major scale on a separate index card, then put those seven cards in a hat, shook them up, dumped them on the floor, and asked someone *"Are those notes from the key of A minor, or the key of C major?"*, there wouldn't really be a correct answer would there? They'd have to say *"Well, it depends on the context..."* And, they'd be right!

Context is most often provided by **chord progressions**. Remember the diatonic chords from the key of C major?

                C   D   E   F   G   A   B   C
                I   ii   iii IV   V   vi vii° I

If we played a **I IV V** progression (C major, F major, G major), the **I chord** - C major - will have a *dominant* sound over the other two chords. It becomes the *center of gravity*, so to speak. Therefore, you'll hear the **C in your scale** as the **root note** as well. The context is a *chord progression in the key of C major*.

What happens though if we take an **A minor scale**, and figure out the **Roman Numerals** (the available chords) that we get from it? Well, since all the notes are the *same* as a C major scale, common sense tells us that we'd get the *same* chords...but would they be *numbered* the same? Let's find out:

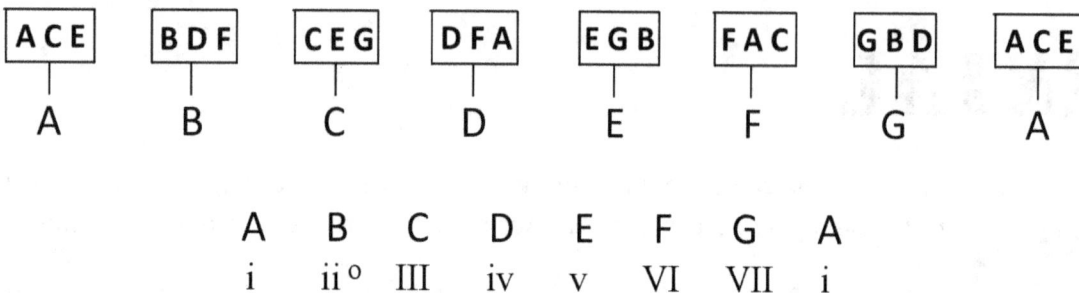

The new numbering reflects the fact that **A is now the first note in the scale** - so, the A minor chord is now labeled "i". The rest of the chords follow suit, reflecting their new position in the scale (A minor, B diminished, C major, D minor, E minor, F major, G major).

If we play a **i VI VII** progression in the **key of A minor** (A minor, F major, G major), two of the chords are the *same* as in our **I IV V** progression from the **key of C major**. But, because the A minor chord is now **functioning as the i chord**, it will have a *dominant* sound over the other two chords. Therefore, you'll hear the **A in your scale** as the **root note** this time. The context is now a *chord progression in the key of A minor*.

What if you're just **noodling around** with the *six C major / A minor scale fingerings,* with nothing playing behind you? How would you play "A minor" licks, versus "C major" licks? The answer is: **emphasis**. If you *emphasize* the C note more as you solo, then your licks will sound *major*. If, however, you *emphasize* the A more, then your licks will sound *minor*. Here's a short example:

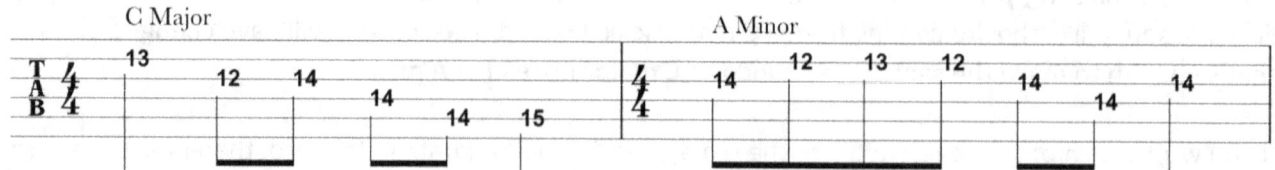

SESSION 18

PHYSICAL

Going to the gym and working out isn't something you do for a limited portion of your life, and then you're healthy forever. It's an *ongoing activity* that's part of staying strong for a lifetime, and should be a part of your *life's* routine.

When it comes to **technique-building** on guitar (getting faster, more accurate, more powerful) you need to approach it the same way. It's not an *end goal* you'll someday reach - **it's an ongoing, neverending part of being a guitarist.** You will continually raise the bar for what you can perform on the guitar, and then raise it again and again until you're 120 years old. So, let's get started!

One of the best technique-building routines that you can get into is using *scale patterns* to play **sequences**. Remember that a sequence is a *rhythmic pattern or melodic phrase* that **repeats itself and spreads through the scale fingering** like a wave. Presented here are two of 'em: a *3-note sequence*, and a *4-note sequence*. You'll get to apply these sequences to your six **C major scale patterns**.

For the first sequence, you'll play an *ascending group of three notes*, starting from each note in the scale. It feels like playing something, then doubling back, playing it again, then doubling back - **throughout the entire scale fingering**. Give it a shot, using this major scale fingering:

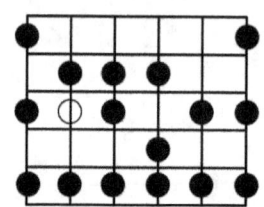

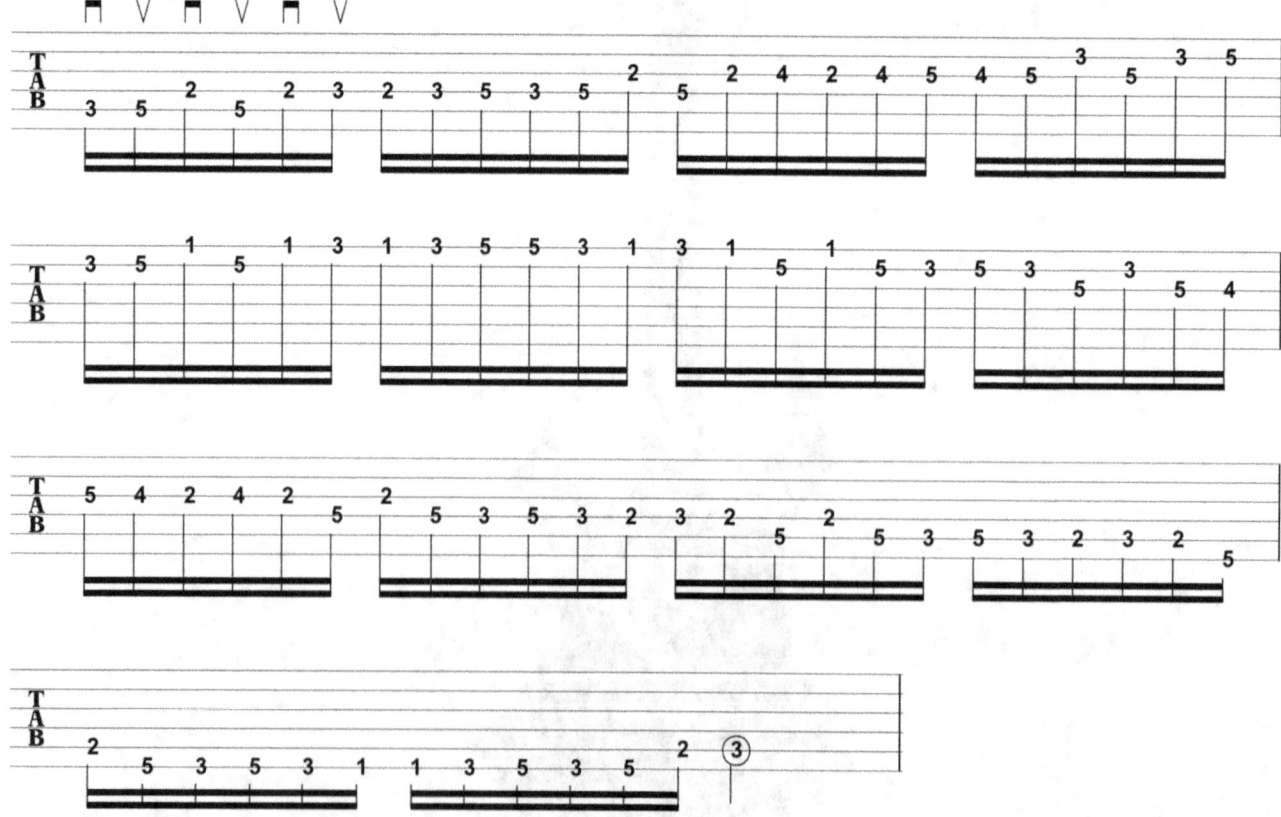

Now, give this *4-note sequence* a shot. Use the **same** major scale pattern, but this time, ascend by groups of four notes. Double back, then ascend again. Go for it!

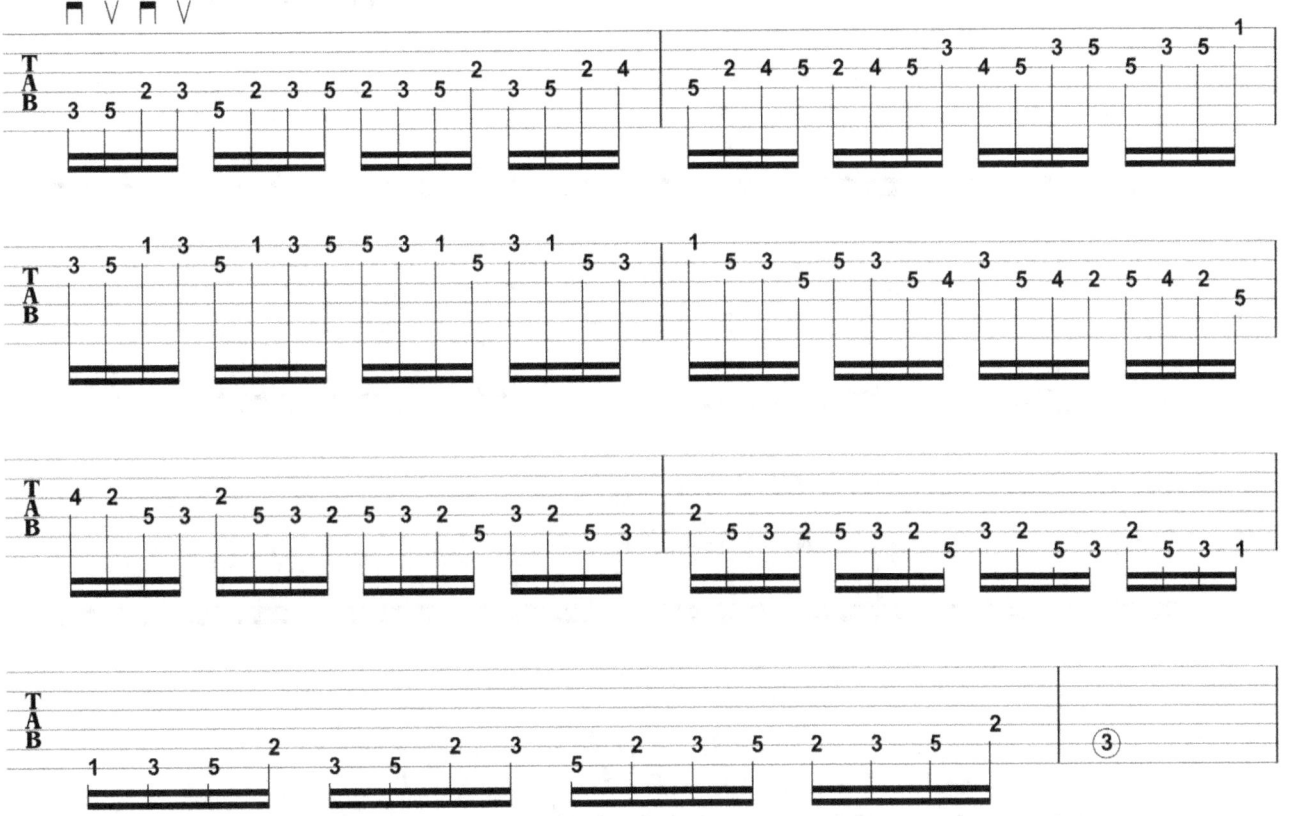

That's quite a workout! Not only do **sequences** improve your *picking technique* and *right/left hand coordination*, they're also great for helping you *memorize* a scale pattern. Having to continually double back and re-start from different notes within the scale means you've got to **really know that fingering** forwards and backwards! Let's blast into the same two sequences, but with the next major scale fingering. **Alternate picking** throughout!

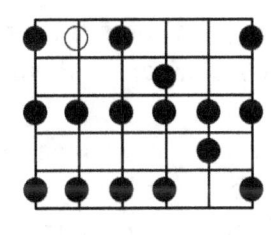

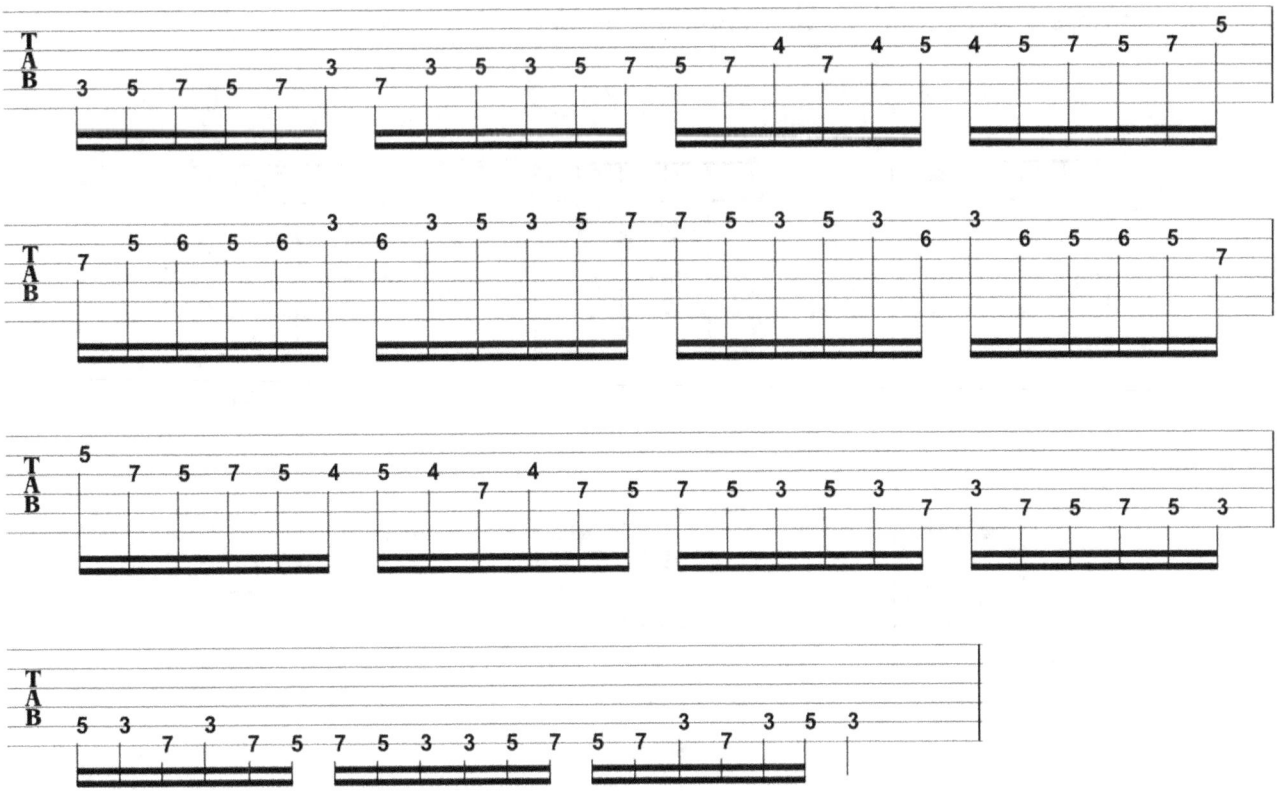

Here's the *4-note sequence* for the same major scale pattern; keep that **alternate picking** going!

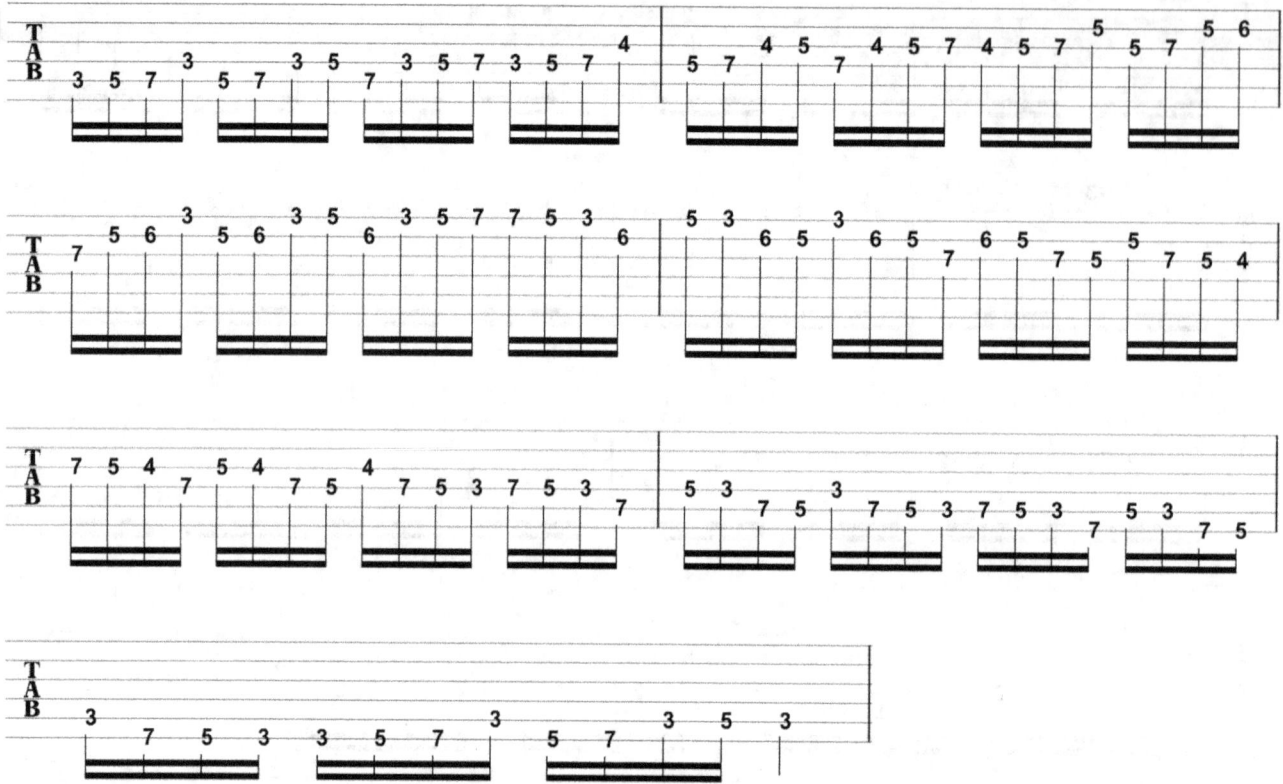

Try applying both the 3-note and 4-note sequence to the **other four major scale patterns** on your own. Take it slow, and remember - the great thing about a sequence is that it can be applied to *any* scale!

Now that you've appeased your inner speed-demon for this Session, it's time for **triads**. You've been memorizing the major, minor, and diminished triads on the G, B, and E string set - but this time, you'll be playing them on the **D**, **G**, and **B** strings! Just like before, the **root note** can be located on each of those three strings, resulting in **three voicings** for *each type* of triad. Here they are:

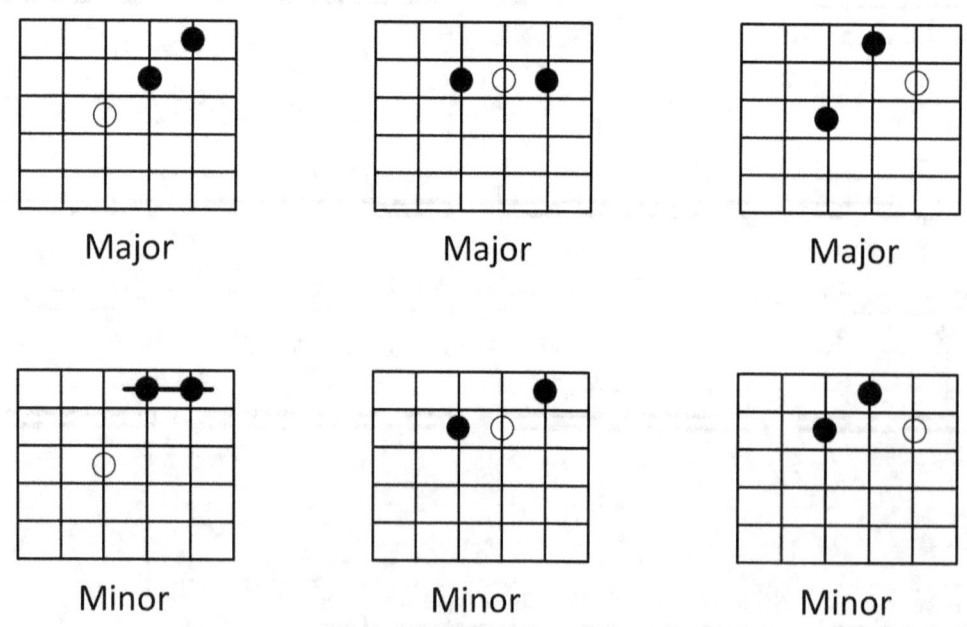

103

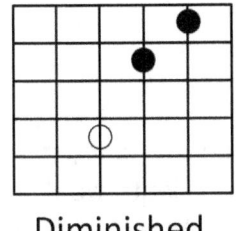
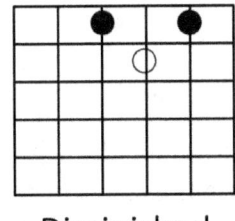
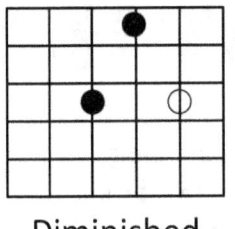

Diminished   Diminished   Diminished

Using these triad voicings to play the **diatonic chords** of a scale is a great way to practice them. We'd used the chords in the **key of C major** before - so, let's start with the **key of A minor** for these new ones:

A	B	C	D	E	F	G	A
i	ii°	III	iv	v	VI	VII	i

Here are the above seven triads, using the voicings with the root note on the **G string**:

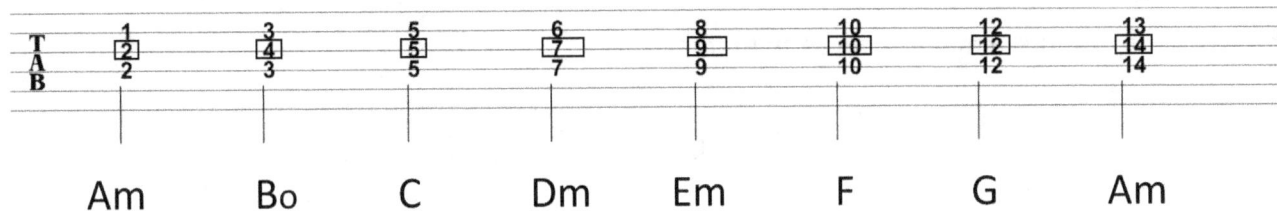

Am   Bo   C   Dm   Em   F   G   Am

Next, the **key of E minor** - using the voicings with the root note on the **B string**:

E	F#	G	A	B	C	D	E
i	ii°	III	iv	v	VI	VII	i

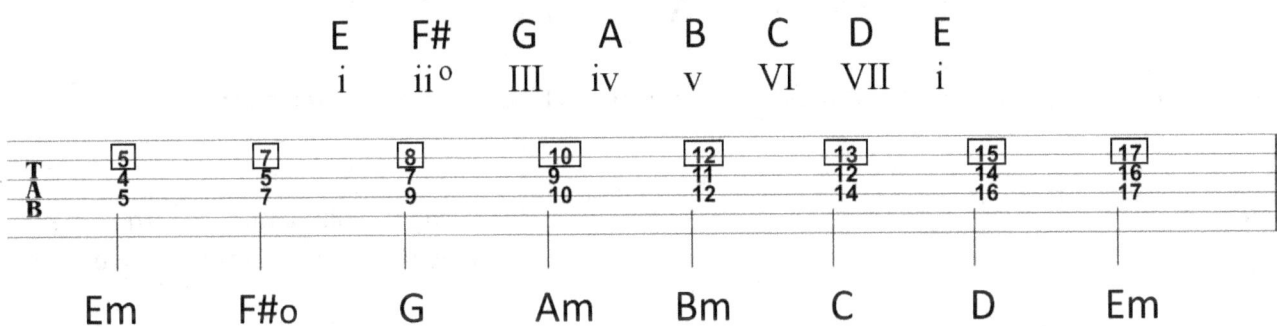

Em   F#o   G   Am   Bm   C   D   Em

Lastly, let's use the **key of G minor**, and the voicings with the root note on the **D string**:

G	A	Bb	C	D	Eb	F	G
i	ii°	III	iv	v	VI	VII	i

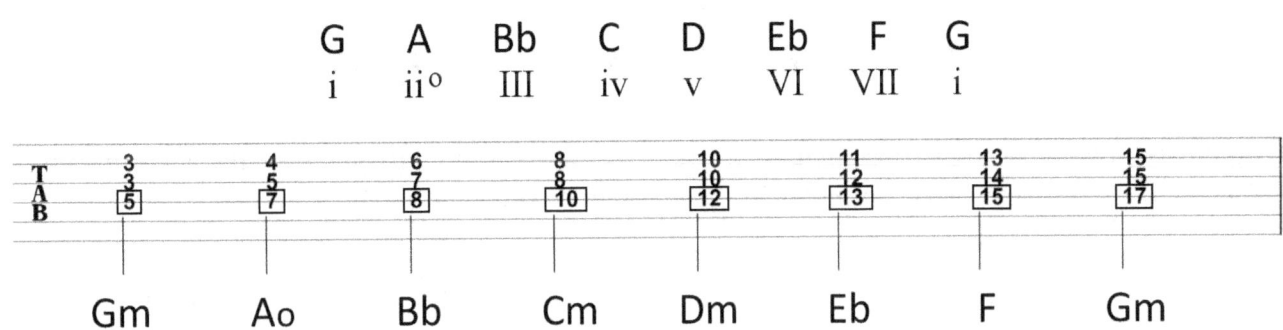

Gm   Ao   Bb   Cm   Dm   Eb   F   Gm

MENTAL

A continually expanding, comprehensive knowledge of the guitar neck (and the ability to shred it!) requires a detective's mind. In the Sherlock Holmes stories, the eponymous sleuth would be brought into a case to tackle a seemingly random crime that had baffled the police. His ability to see **patterns**, to see **related factors** when others saw only disconnected and disparate objects and events, was the key to his success.

It's your job to approach the guitar neck in the same fashion, and you're well on your way. We've discovered that the **major scale** fingerings are *exactly the same* as the **minor scale** fingerings - no need to learn an entirely separate set of patterns. If you can identify the **relative minor** of a major scale, then you can use the major scale fingerings for **both keys**. Find the *sixth note* of any major scale, and you've found its relative minor - but is there a faster, easier way?

There is! Let's take the **G major scale** as an example:

G A B C D (E) F# G

E is the sixth note of the scale, so **E minor** is the relative minor of the G major scale:

(E) F# G A B C D E

Now, let's look at the relationship of those two notes to each other on the **guitar neck**:

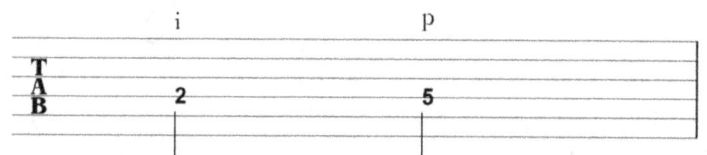

By placing the **pinky** on the G, the **index** naturally falls on the E - the relative minor!

Could figuring out the relative minor relationship be as easy as thinking *"pinky is major, index is minor"*? Let's try another example and find out. How about **D major**?

D E F# G A (B) C# D

B is the sixth note of the scale, so **B minor** is the relative minor of the D major scale. If you place your **pinky** on a D somewhere, does your **index finger** automatically fall onto a B?

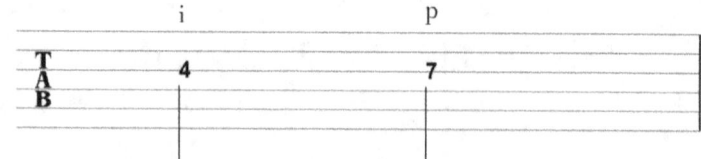

It certainly does! You could place the pinky on *any* D, on *any* string, and this would still happen.

When looking for the **relative minor of any major scale**, just think *"pinky is major, index is minor"*. This easy strategy will allow you to use the **major scale fingerings** to play any **minor scale** you want.

105

Now, here's another relationship that's hidden in plain view - this time, between the **minor scale** and the **minor pentatonic scale**. While on one level, these scales are quite a bit different (one contains *seven notes*, the other *five*), on another level they are **practically the same**. In fact, we can consider the minor pentatonic scale to be a **sub-set** of the minor scale. Let's use **G minor** as an example:

G A Bb C D Eb F G

G minor is the *relative minor* of **Bb major**. So, we'll use one of our Bb major scale fingerings, and simply **start on the G note** instead:

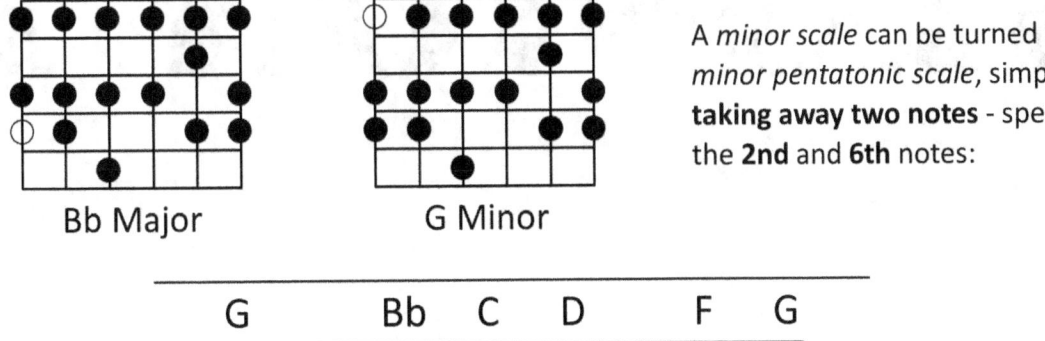

Bb Major   G Minor

A *minor scale* can be turned into a *minor pentatonic scale*, simply by **taking away two notes** - specifically, the **2nd** and **6th** notes:

G Bb C D F G

Removing the **A's** and **Eb's** from the G minor / Bb major scale fingering leaves us with a *very familiar pattern* - **Form #1** of the **minor pentatonic scale**!

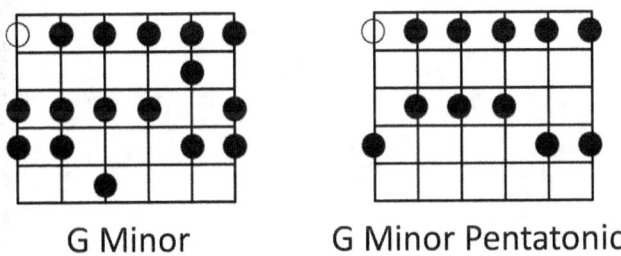

G Minor   G Minor Pentatonic

Because of this relationship, you can always **substitute or add in the minor pentatonic scale** whenever the minor scale is called for (like when playing over a **chord progression** in a minor key). This leads to more variety when soloing and improvising - and that's never a bad thing! Try out this solo, combining the G minor scale fingering with the G minor pentatonic scale fingering:

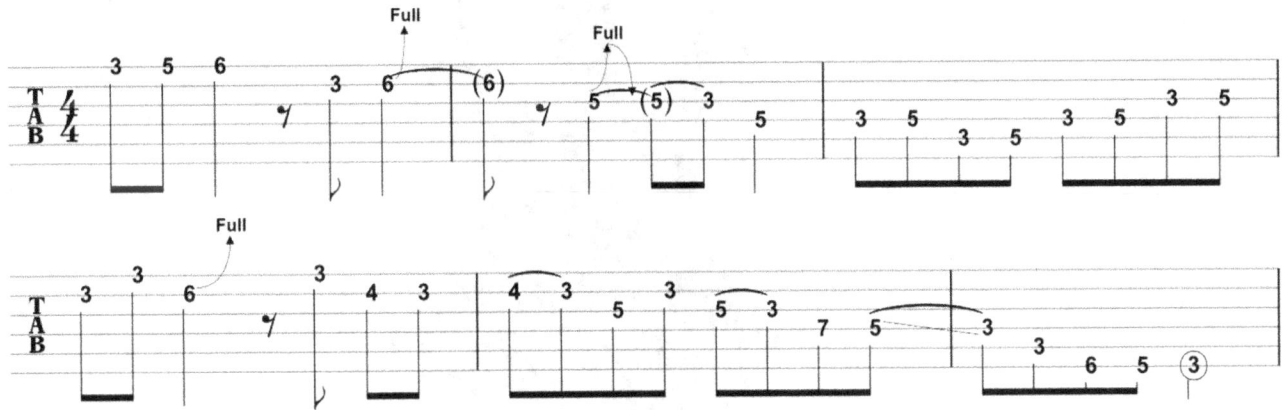

SESSION 19

PHYSICAL

You've been developing **terrifyingly totalitarian technique**, using *3-note* and *4-note sequences* with the major scale fingerings. Now, it's time to apply these sequences to the **minor pentatonic fingerings**. Even though there are *less notes* in these patterns, it can actually be *more difficult* to pick through a two-note per string fingering. Why? The pick has to **cross the strings more frequently**, that's why!

The following sequences will be applied to **Form #1** and **Form #5** of the **G minor pentatonic scale**. Your task is to also apply them to the other three forms, on your own. Here's a cool **3-note sequence** to start:

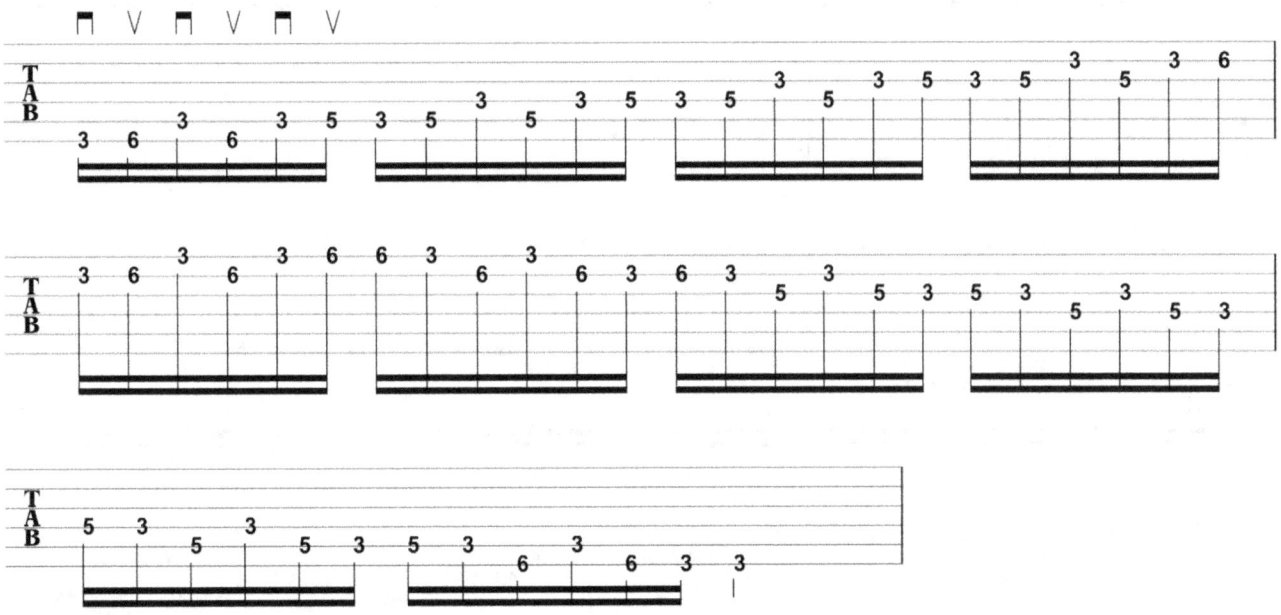

Now the same sequence, using the **5th form**:

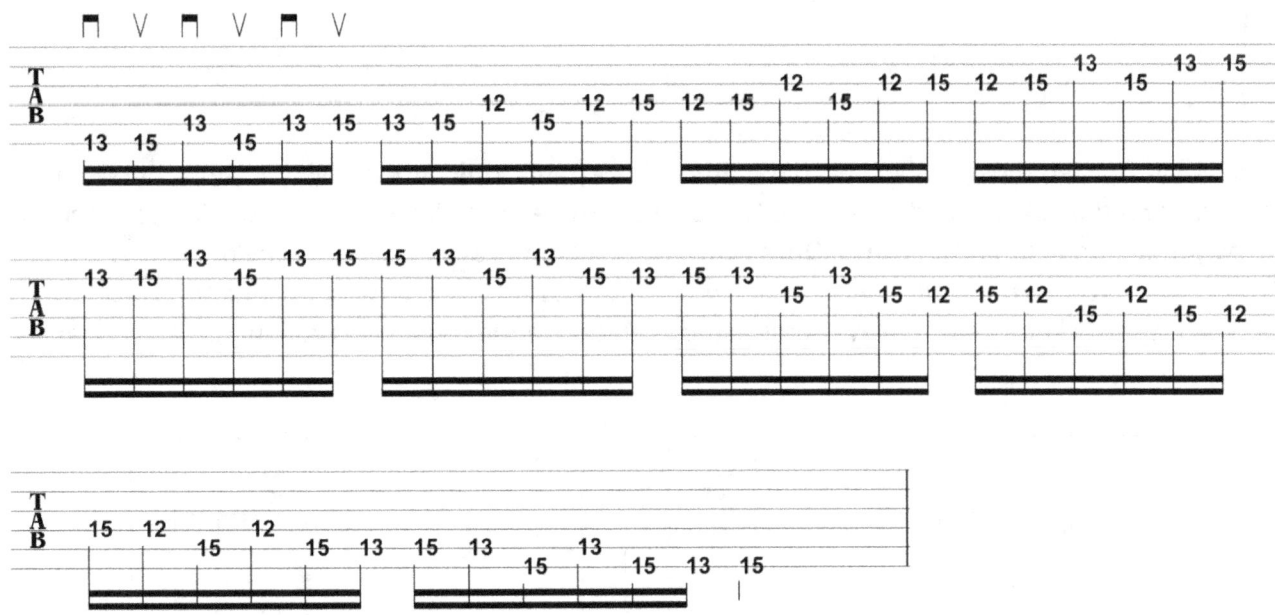

When performing these sequences, be especially careful to prevent any notes from **ringing together**. A particularly troublesome spot for this is during *string crossings*. Aim for **complete separation of sound**, but without any breaks in continuity either. You want **seamless** sound!

Next here's a *4-note* sequence, using **Form #1**; remember to use *alternate picking* throughout!

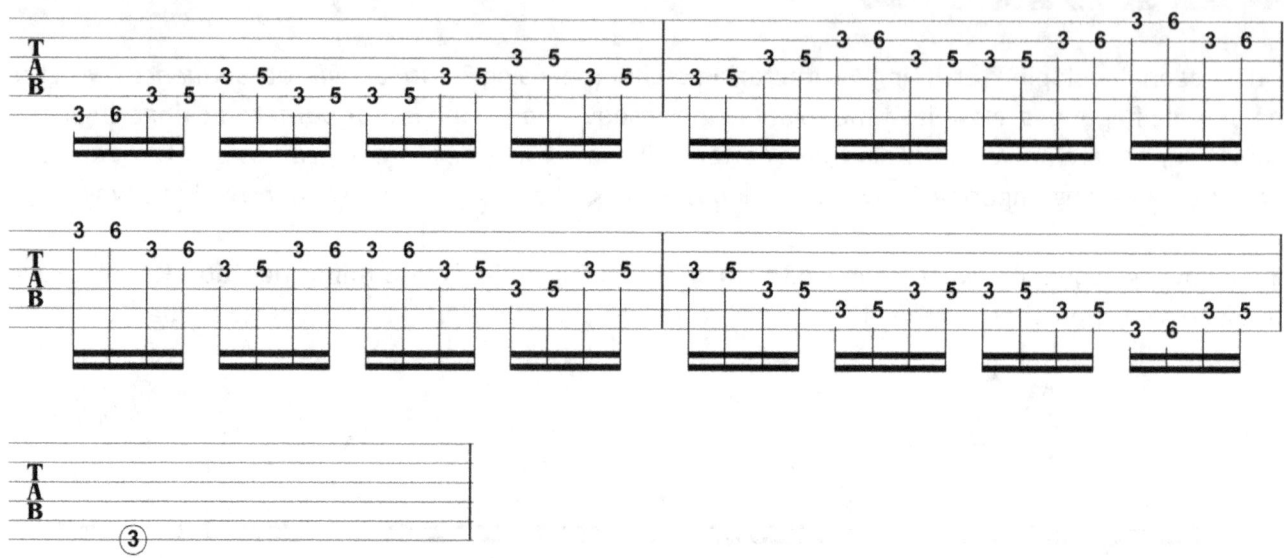

Here's that same sequence, this time using **Form #5**:

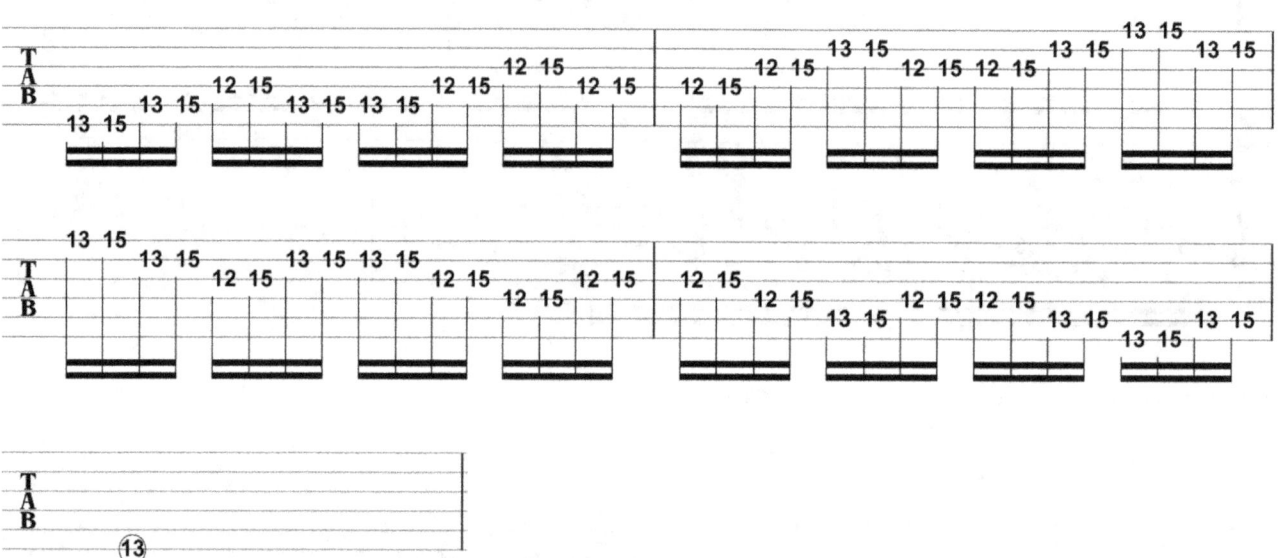

After you've applied those sequences to the **other three pentatonic forms**, give yourself a break - a break*through* that is! - by mastering more **triads**. The next set of major, minor, and diminished triads are played on the **A**, **D**, and **G strings**. Once again, the root note can be found on *any* of those three strings, so you'll have *three different voicings* for each triad. Add these to your existing triad arsenal, and you'll already know how to play chords in **more places on the neck** than probably 95% of guitarists!

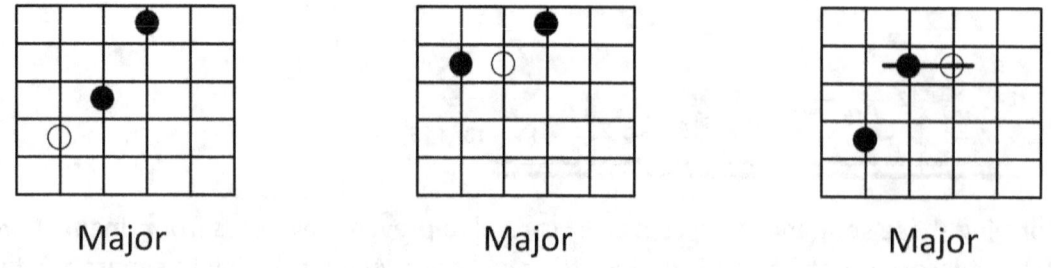

Major · Major · Major

109

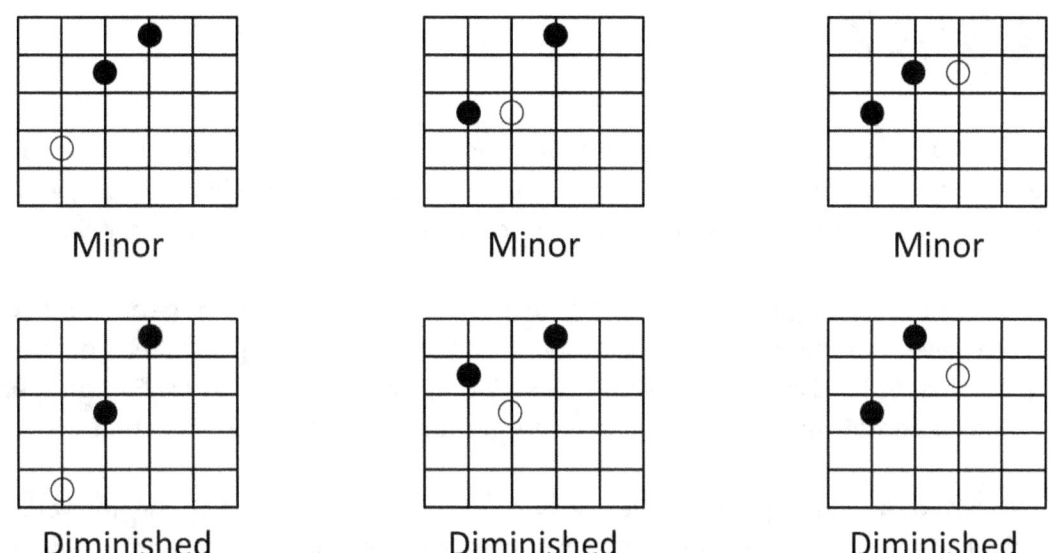

Minor   Minor   Minor

Diminished   Diminished   Diminished

Diatonic time! Best way to practice them, so let's get to it. **Key of A minor**, root notes on **G string**:

A	B	C	D	E	F	G	A
i	ii°	III	iv	v	VI	VII	i

How about **key of D major**, root notes on **A string**?

D	E	F#	G	A	B	C#	D
I	ii	iii	IV	V	vi	vii°	I

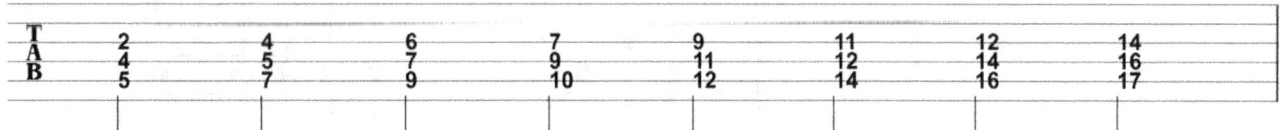

Lastly, let's play all the diatonic triads for the **key of F major** - with root notes on the **D string**:

F	G	A	Bb	C	D	E	F
I	ii	iii	IV	V	vi	vii°	I

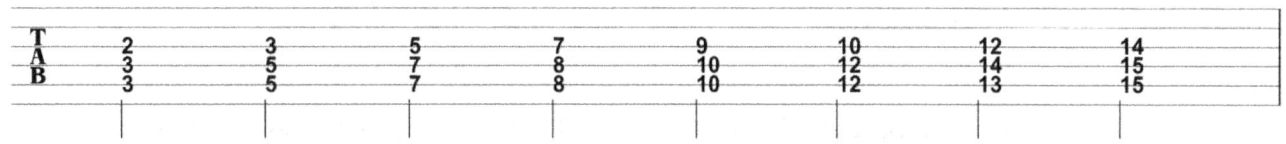

Remember, *keep looking at those root notes* as you climb the neck! If you're using triads with the root note on the G string (like in the *A minor* example), keep looking at that G string as you move from chord to chord. That way, you'll get used to **playing** what you're **thinking**!

MENTAL

Knowing the **location of the root note** within a chord voicing has a clear and obvious advantage: you can use it to play the chord *anywhere!* Using those triad voicings and barre chord shapes, you've been playing A major chords, B minor chords, F# minor chords, F major chords...the sky's the limit!

Luckily, you can just as easily figure out the root note locations within the **minor pentatonic scale**. This will allow you to play *any minor pentatonic scale you want*, all across the neck. Instead of always being locked into the notes of the **G minor pentatonic** (G Bb C D F), you'll be able to play **E minor pentatonic** (E G A B D), **C minor pentatonic** (C Eb F G Bb), **A minor pentatonic** (A C D E G) - any that you want.

Before we get started though, a quick question: *why* would you want to do this? The answer is that we need to *match up* the appropriate minor pentatonic scale **to the riff or song we want to solo over**.

Let's say there's a cool *ZZ Top* song that you want to jam over. The riff clearly has **B** as the main note (you can hear it). You also know that you want the **bluesy rock sound** of the minor pentatonic scale to solo with (it really sounds good over some *ZZ Top*!) The problem is, if you only know how to play the G minor pentatonic, **the root note of the scale will not match up with the main note in the riff** (B). It's like having *two competing centers of gravity*, pulling your ears in two directions. It won't work!

But, what if you could quickly play a *B minor pentatonic* anywhere on the neck? Now, you'll still have that bluesy rock sound you're looking for, but **the root note of the scale will match up with the main note of the riff**. Bullseye! That's why it's so important to be able to move a scale fingering around.

In each of the five minor pentatonic forms, the root note will be found in *more than one place*. However, in order to make it easier to navigate around the neck, **we'll highlight *one* of those root note locations for each form**. The circled notes indicate where the root note is located:

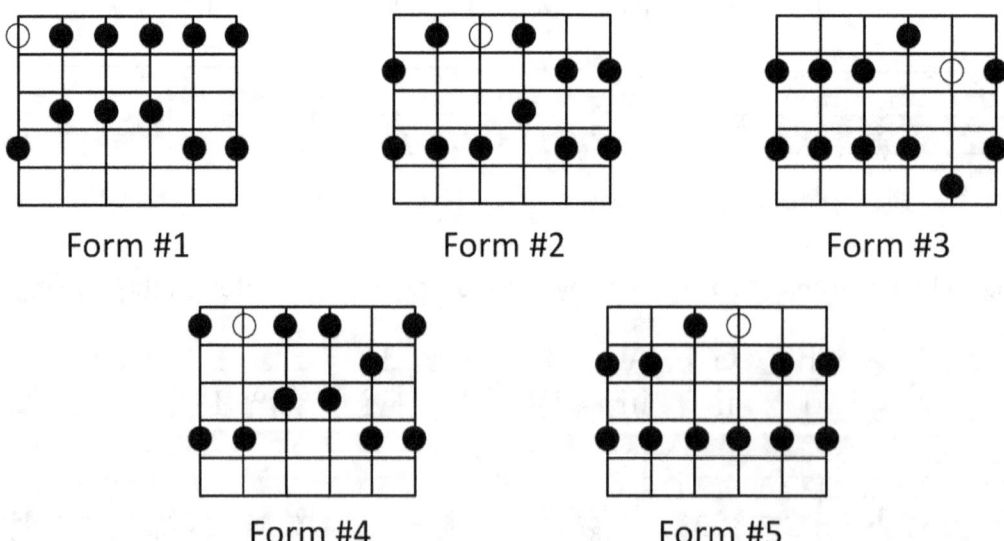

Form #1   Form #2   Form #3

Form #4   Form #5

For example, in the **G minor pentatonic forms** that you've been playing, you'll find that *all* those circled notes are **G**. Try playing through all five forms, pausing at each circled note, and you'll hear it - **they're all G**. What's so cool is, if this works for the G minor pentatonic scale, *the same thing will work for any minor pentatonic*. Let's try it out.

The hypothetical ZZ Top riff had **B** as the main note, so let's try out a **B minor pentatonic**. Also, let's say it's your musical intention to start soloing low on the neck - down by the first few frets. Your task is to **find a B in that area of the neck**, and *match its location* to one of the five pentatonic forms. The B that's physically lowest on the neck (not including the open string) is right here:

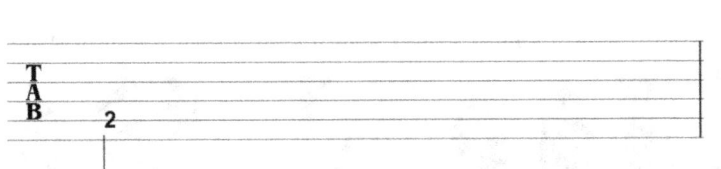
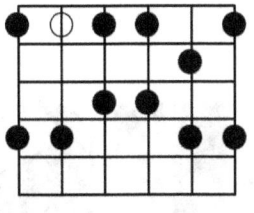

Form #4

You located that B at the **2nd fret**, on the **A string**. In which of the five forms will you always find the root note on the *A string*? **Form #4**. So, if you place your index finger on that B, *your hand is automatically in position to play Form #4.* After jamming for a while, let's say you want to jump to a higher area of the neck, for some dramatic effect. **Locate another B**, this time on the higher frets:

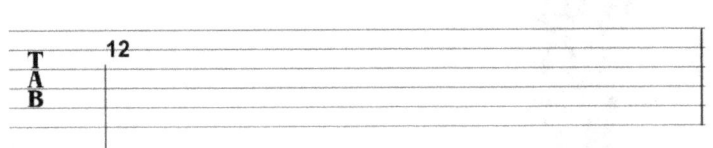
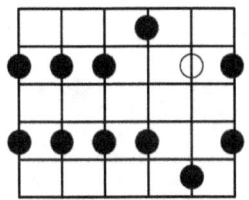

Form #3

You located that B at the **12th fret**, on the **B string**. In which of the five forms will you always find the root note on the *B string*? **Form #3**. So, if you place your finger on that B, *your hand is automatically in position to play Form #3.*

This is an **extremely effective** way to navigate around the neck. If you want to play **E minor pentatonic instead**, all you have to do is find an E, *anywhere* on the neck. Place your index finger there, and you will *automatically* be in position to play one of the five minor pentatonic forms. Simply *match up* the string you're on **with the corresponding form** - #1 for E string, #2 for D string, #3 for B string, #4 for A string, and #5 for G string.

Practice playing the minor pentatonic forms in this way:

1. Choose a root note (like E or B)
2. Find that note on any string
3. Place your index finger there
4. Match the string with the appropriate form
5. Play the form, **starting from the root note** where your finger is, and **ending there** as well
6. Find the root note on another string, and repeat steps 3 - 6!

SESSION 20

PHYSICAL

Starting from the **root note** when practicing scale fingerings is great for both **memorization** and **practical application** (making music with 'em!) This should be standard operating procedure for you from now on; for both the **major scale** *and* the **minor pentatonic scale**.

To get that happy habit happening (alliteration is Metal), here are **all five forms of the A minor pentatonic scale**, starting from the *lowest* possible position on the neck. Each form will start from the **root note** (A):

Form #5

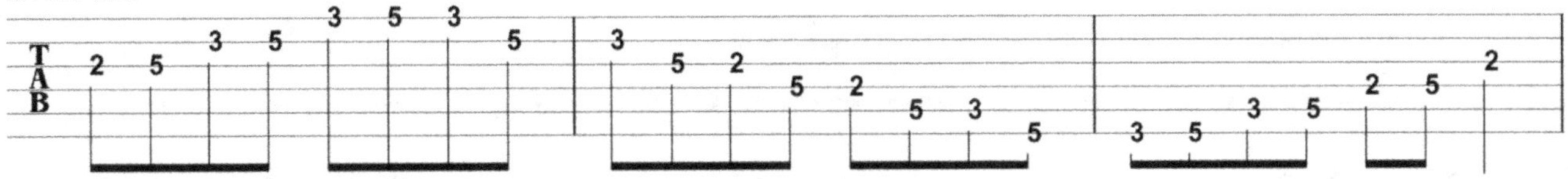

Form #1

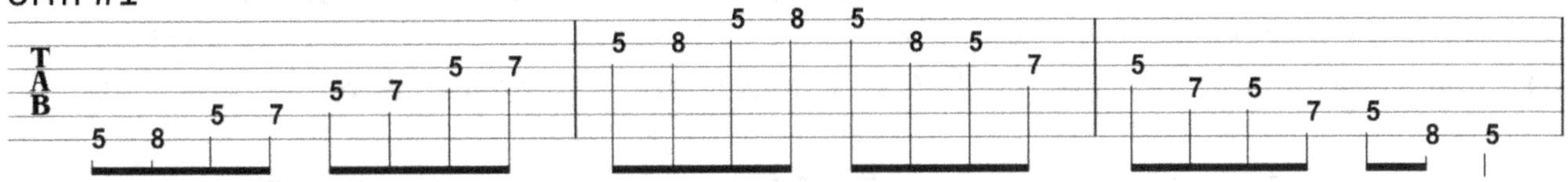

Form #2

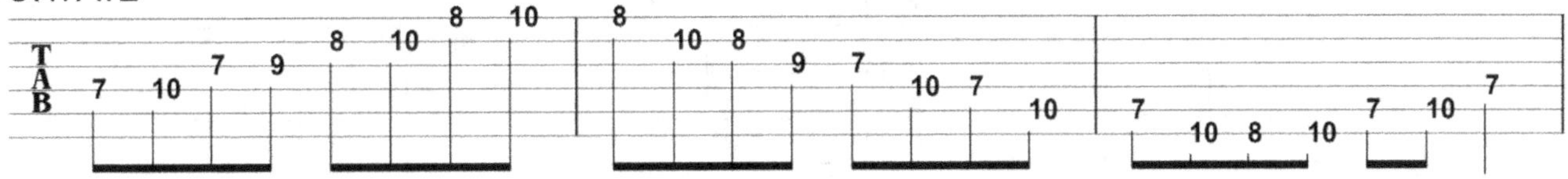

Form #3

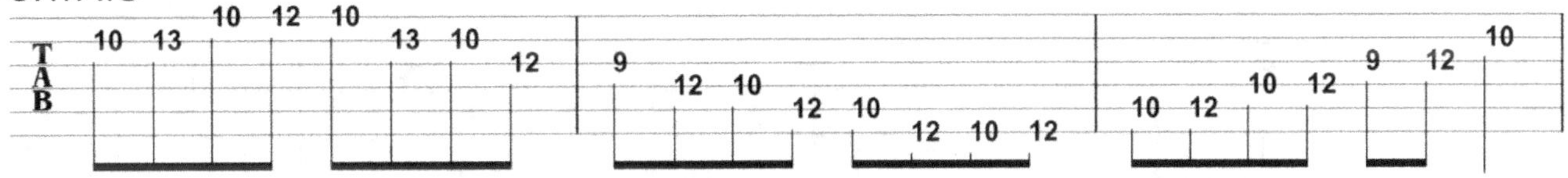

Form #4

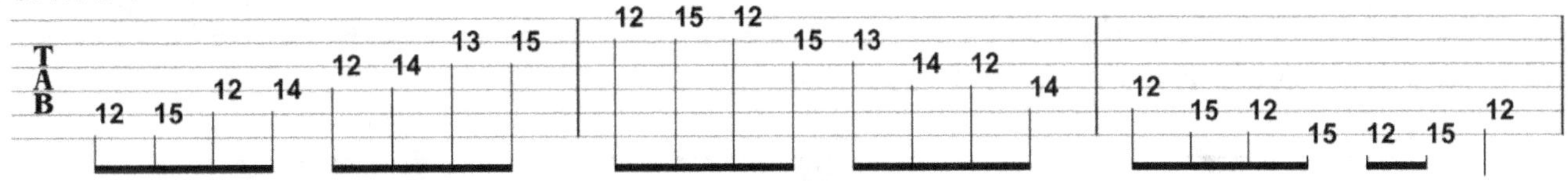

Now for **E minor pentatonic**:

Form #2

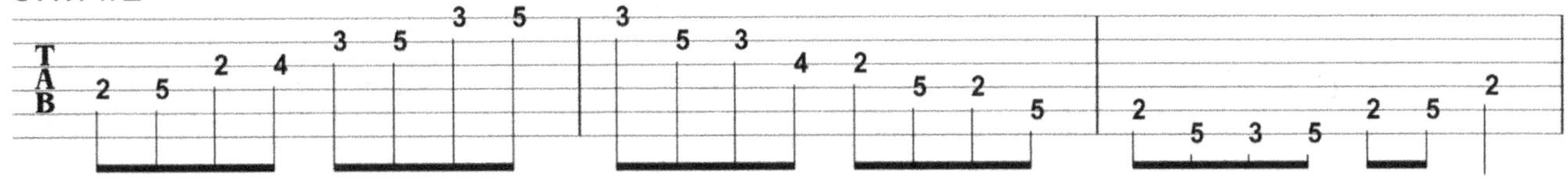

Form #3

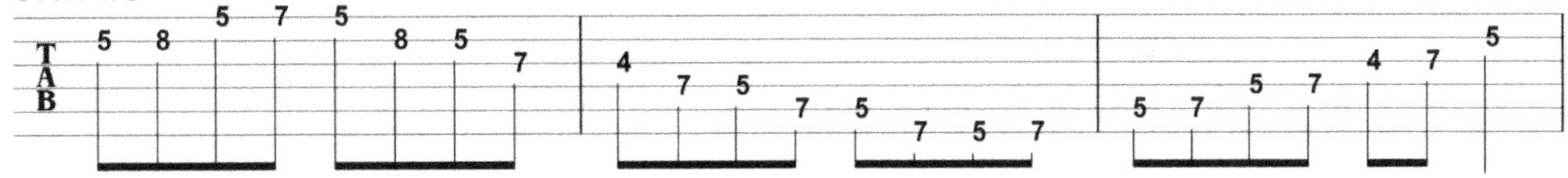

Form #4

Form #5

Form #1

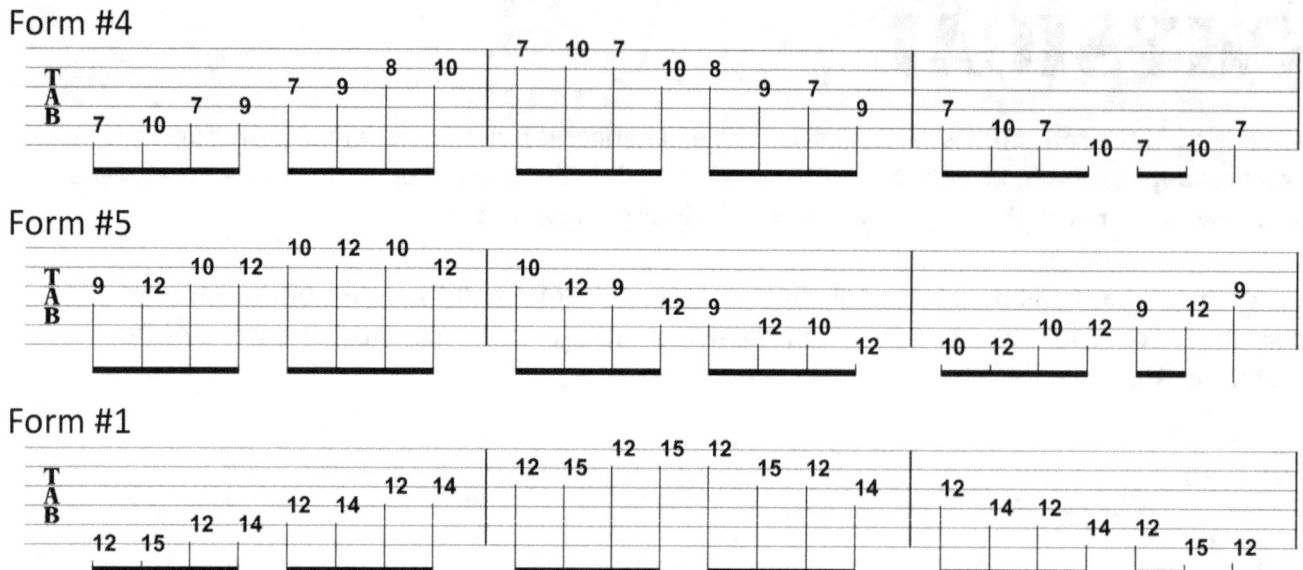

Now that you're starting to feel confident playing scales anywhere on the neck, it's time to put the capstone on your chord knowledge - yes the **final set of triads**, performed on the **E, A,** and **D strings**! Once again, the **root note** can be played on *any* of these three strings, so you have **three voicings each** of the major, minor, and diminished triads. *Bonus* - they're **exactly the same** as the previous ones!

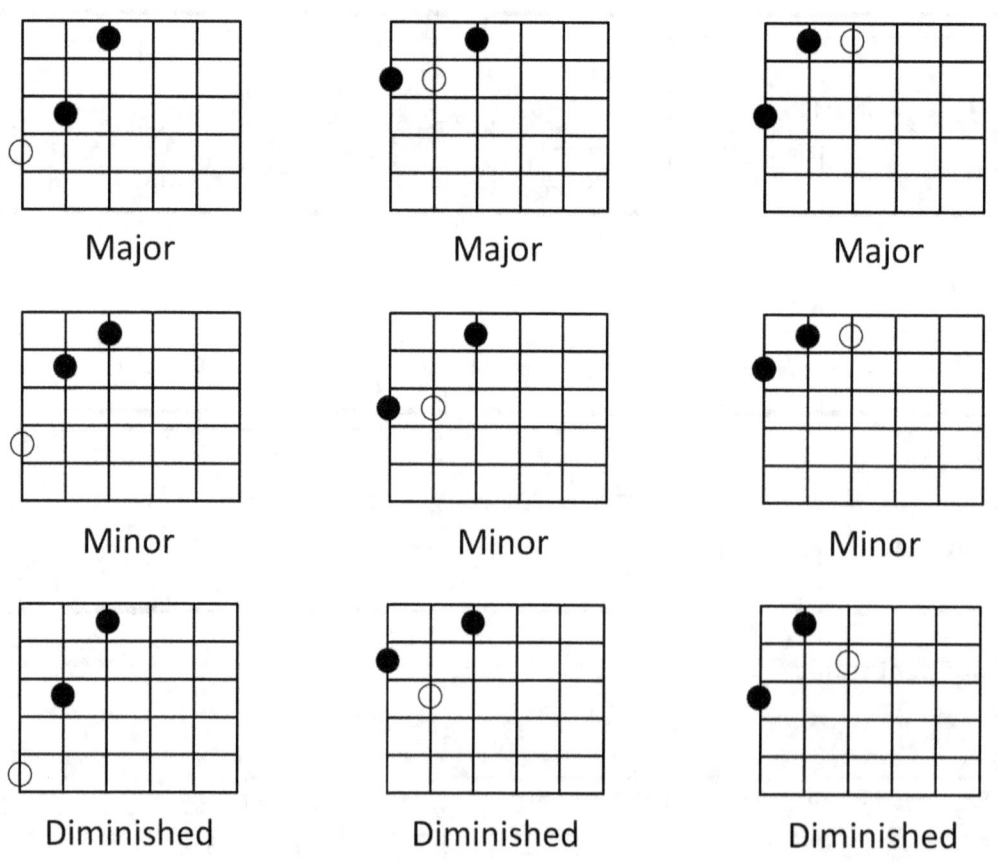

Practice these triads by playing the **diatonic chords** from the **key of E minor**:

E	F#	G	A	B	C	D	E
i	ii°	III	iv	v	VI	VII	i

115

Use the voicings that have the root note on the **D string**:

Next, play the diatonic chords for the **key of A minor**, with the root notes on the **E string**:

A	B	C	D	E	F	G	A
i	ii°	III	iv	v	VI	VII	i

Lastly, play the diatonic chords for the **key of C major**, with the root notes on the **A string**:

C	D	E	F	G	A	B	C
I	ii	iii	IV	V	vi	vii°	I

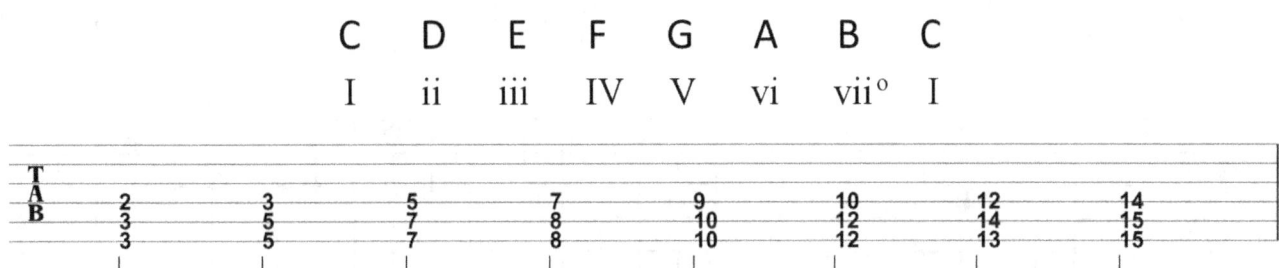

MENTAL

As a beginning guitarist, it can be easy to *"miss the forest for the trees"*. In other words, the necessary focus on patterns, scales, shapes, formulas, techniques, etc., can often overshadow the bigger picture: **making music** with all of it. The term "raw material" has been used several times throughout this book, and it's a great way to think about everything you've been learning.

Triads on the lower strings, along with **power chords**, are often used as raw material for riffs. Here are two examples - riffs constructed from the **key of E minor**, along with a guided tour of each!

E	F#	G	A	B	C	D	E
i	ii°	III	iv	v	VI	VII	i

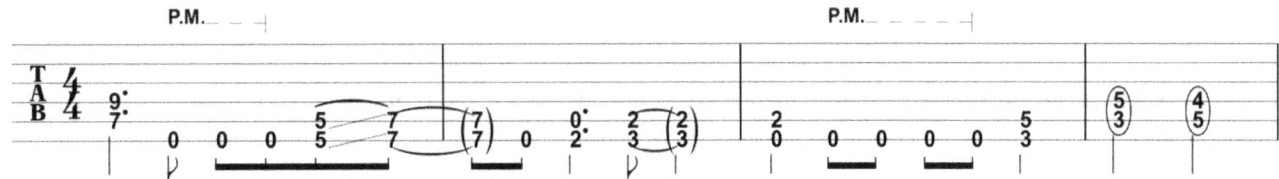

Here's a breakdown of the riff, using Roman Numerals to illustrate the underlying **chord progression** from which the power chords and triads have been based:

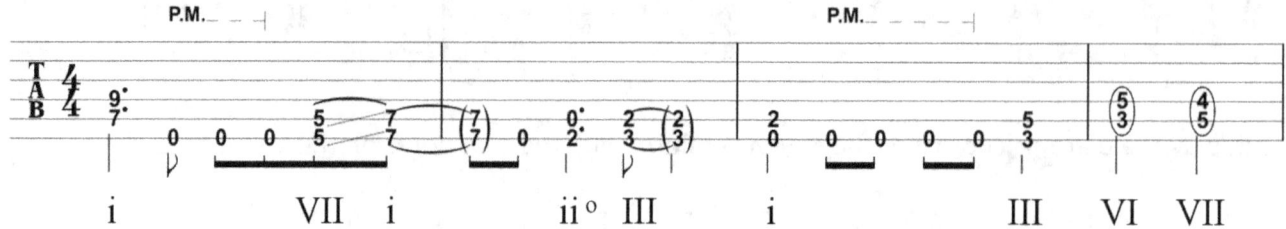

In this first riff, the triad voicings aren't obvious, but they are present - in a stripped-down form! If we **take away** one of the notes from the triad shapes, we're left with a *two-string shape* - similar to a **power chord**. Here are the two-string versions of the triads used in the riff, alongside their "parent" three-string shapes:

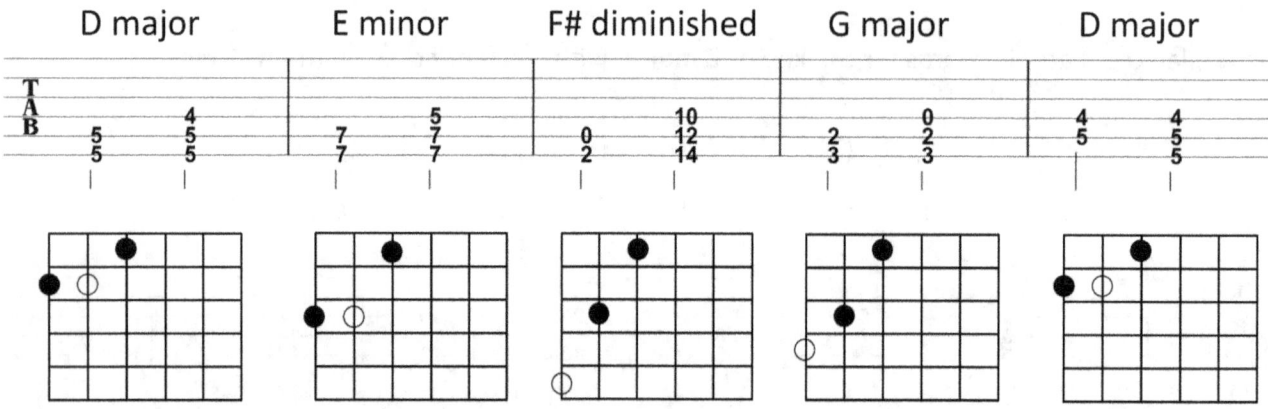

By utilizing two out of the three strings, you can leverage the **more colorful sound** of the triad, while still retaining the heaviness factor of the two string **power chord style** shape. Want the full, three string triad in your riffs? Well, you can do that too! Check it out:

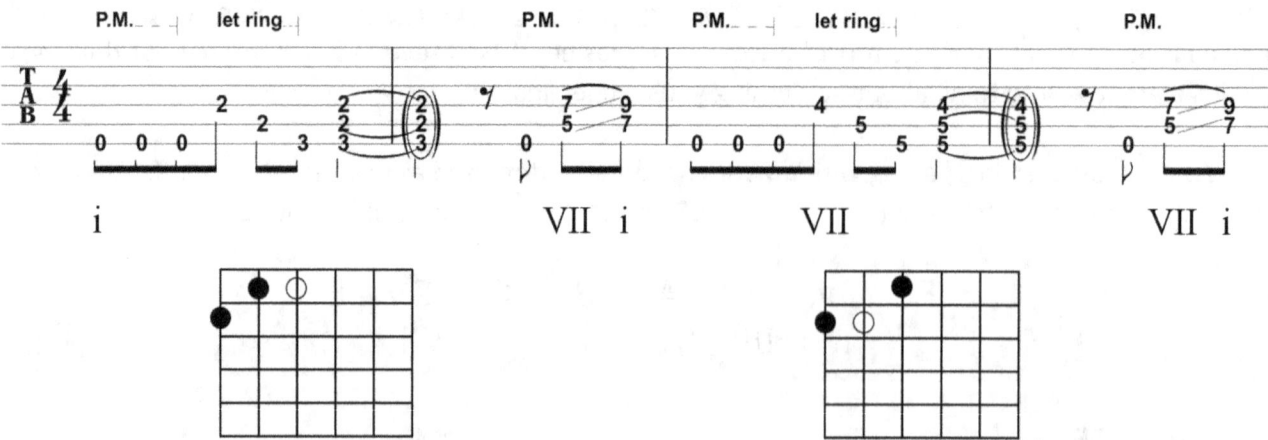

Power chords are great, but using the **E minor triad** with the root note on the D string, and the **D major triad** with the root note on the A string, really makes the riff sound cooler. And the other great thing about all this? Since you know that **the riffs are built from the E minor scale**, what scales do you think you could use to *solo* over the riffs? Why **E minor / G major**, and **E minor pentatonic**, of course!

117

SESSION 21

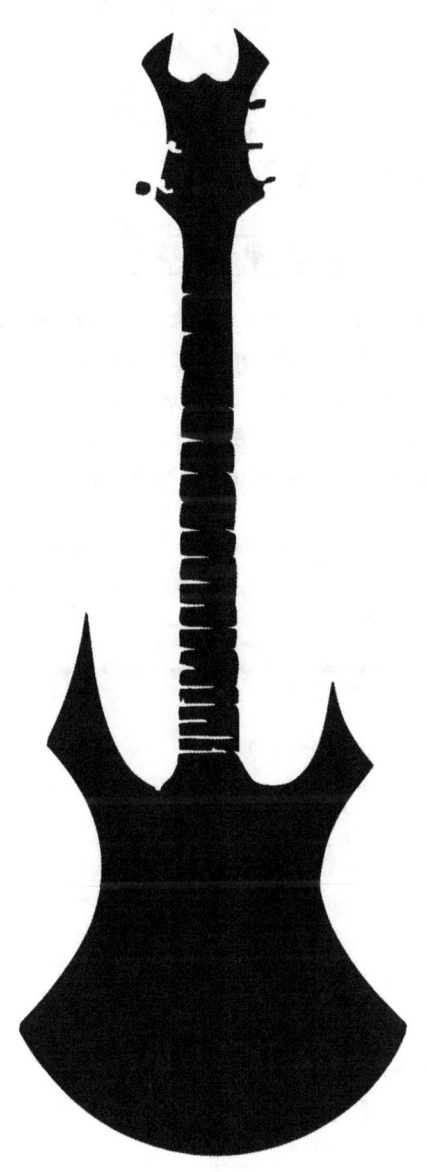

PHYSICAL

Not to be outdone by the *triads*, *barre chords*, and *minor pentatonic scales*, the **major scale** challenges you to a knock down, beat 'em up, barroom brawl! Think you can move those *other* ones around on the neck, and not the major scale? Well, the major scale just called B.S. on that - take it outside, alright?

You know that each of the six major scale fingerings **starts on the root note**, and that the root note is found on either the **low E string** or **A string**. We identify the fingerings based on **which finger** is on that root - *index, middle, or pinky*. This allows you to confidently play a major scale fingering, no matter where you may be on the neck. Here are all six, to refresh your memory:

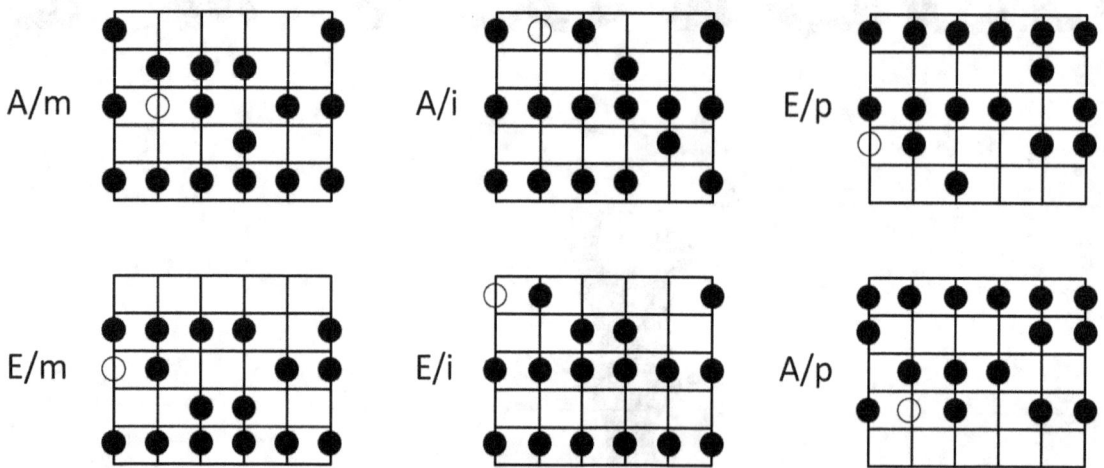

Practicing different major scales is simply a matter of **choosing a root note**, then finding that note *as far down the neck as possible* on the E or A string. On that note, place whichever finger (index, middle, or pinky) allows you to access the **lowest available frets**, without using open strings. Let's play the **G major scale** - here it is, written in TAB. For clarity, each fingering is written ascending only, starting from the root note (G). When practicing, play the entire scale - **ascending and descending, all strings**:

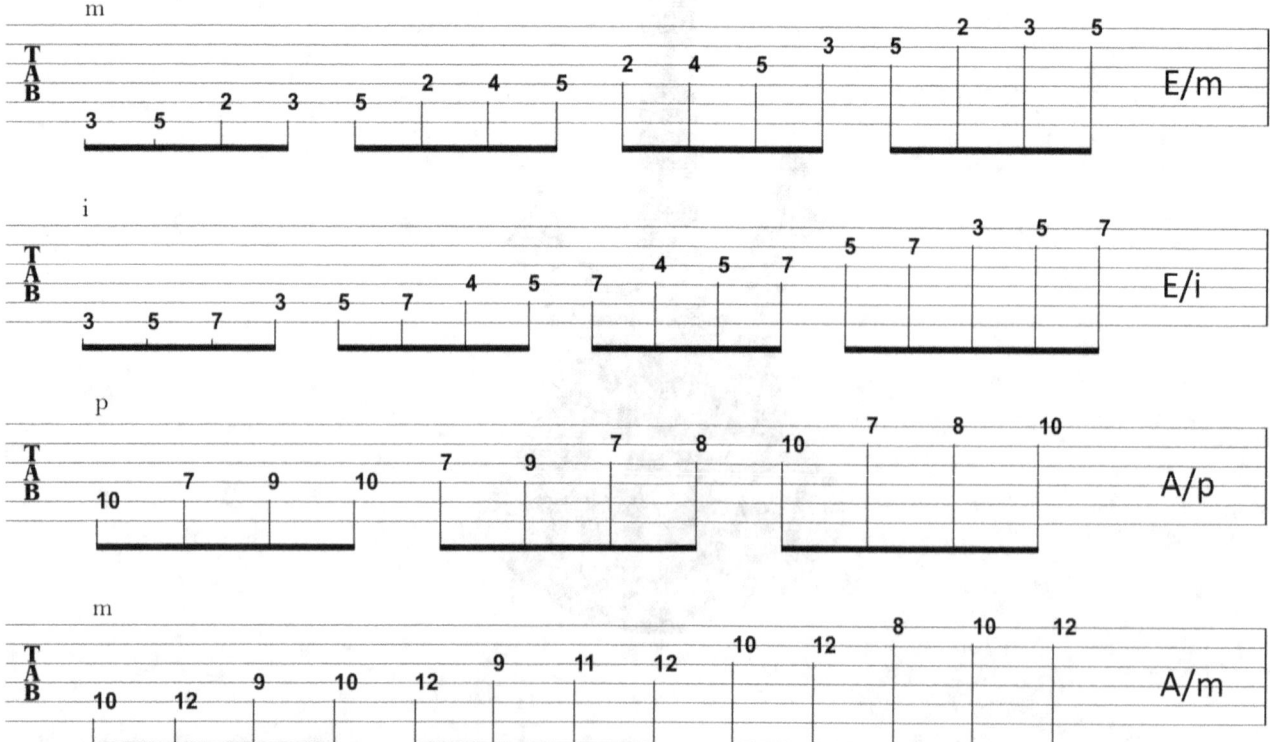

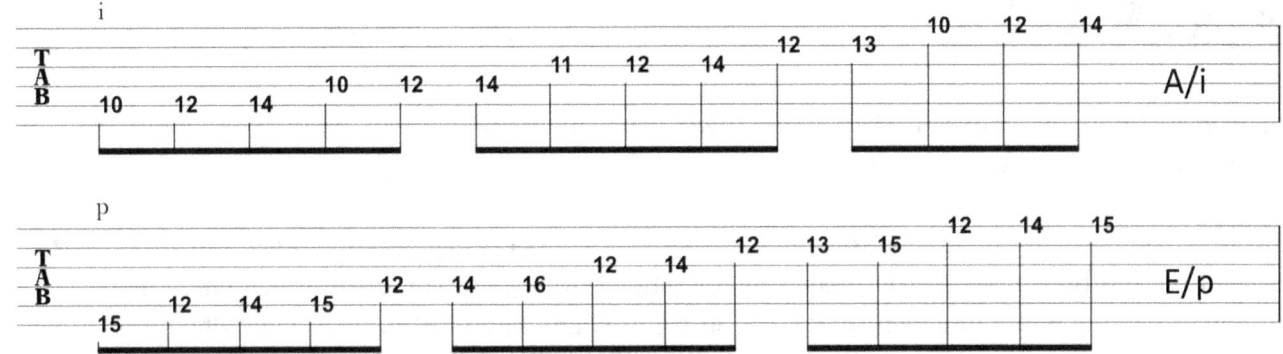

Next, let's play all six fingerings for **F major**:

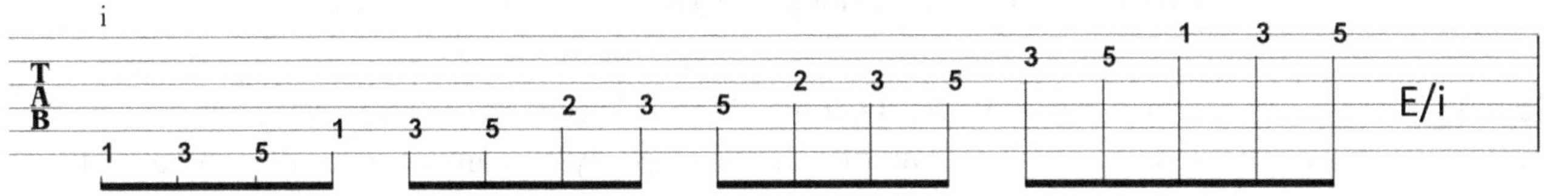

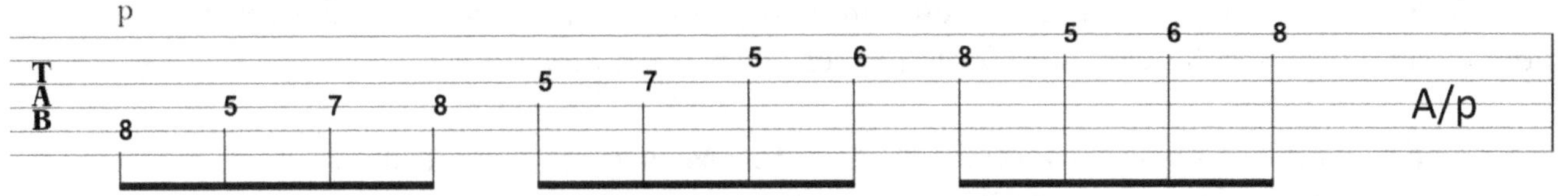

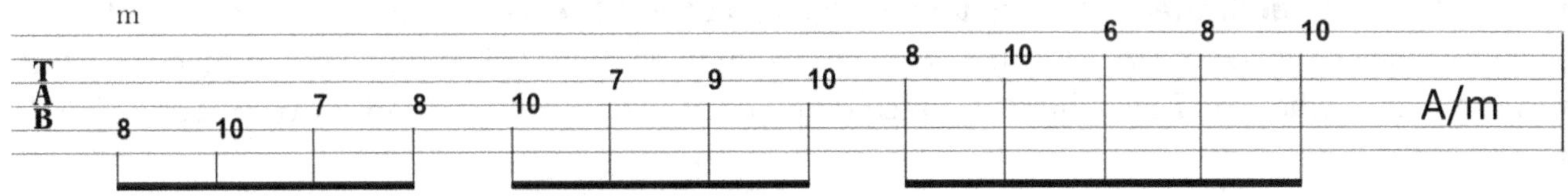

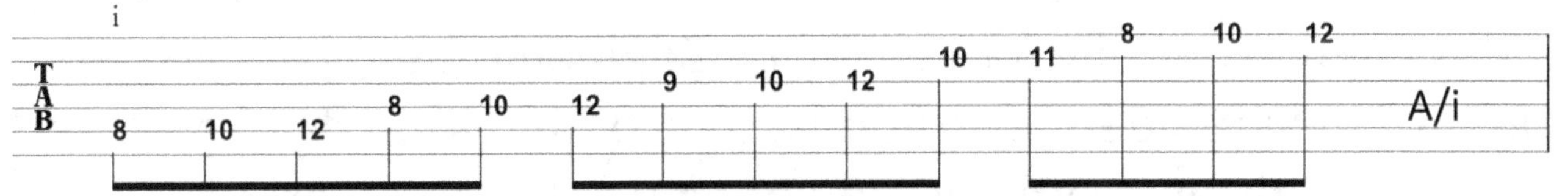

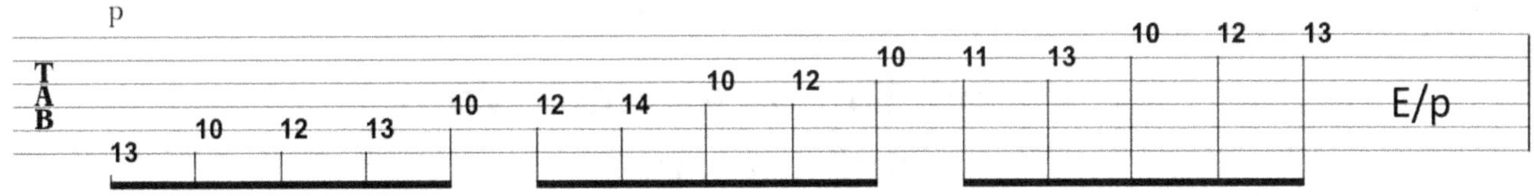

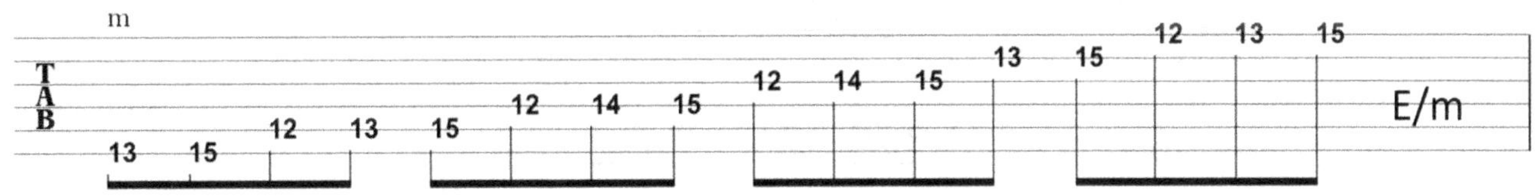

Major scale knowledge - being able to find them *anywhere* on the neck - is **incredibly important**. In fact, it's one of the *unshakeable foundations* for a continuing mastery of the guitar. You should consider major scales (as well as minor pentatonics and triads!) to be an **everyday, routine part** of your practice sessions. These are the "punches and kicks" of guitar - the bedrock skills necessary for developing **deadly guitar-tial artistry**. You must master them, in order to wield your axe with efficiency and force!

MENTAL

You did it. Whether it took you 21 *days* or 21 *weeks*, you've accumulated a ton of experience and knowledge for such a relatively short amount of time.

If you're even anything *close* to resembling an everyday human being (and hopefully, you are!), then throughout this book you've experienced some **guitar triumph**, and some **guitar despair**...some dizzying **six-string highs**, and some cratering, **string-breaking lows**. Music (and especially Metal) is a microcosm of life - so would you expect anything less?

Excellent Job, Guitar Player!

So what's next? Quite a bit, actually. While *Beginner Guitar: No Wimps!* is certainly the most comprehensive and intensive beginning guitar book in the history of mankind, even *this* tome only scratches the surface of what's possible with you and your guitar playing. There's *more* scales out there. There's *more* chords out there. There's *more* rhythms out there. More techniques. More music theory. And most importantly...**more fun**! (and yes, more frustration too).

Like a medieval Inn & Alehouse, **Metal Guitar Academy MGA** will provide respite, rations, and rejuvenation at all future waypoints along your guitar journey. You've been successfully indoctrinated into the **T.N.T. Guitar Strategy : Technique / Neck Knowledge / Theory**™, and have joined an elite phalanx of Beginning Guitarists - those who have chosen to eschew NoClueTube, and instead construct a solid guitar fortification from which to launch their attack against musical mediocrity. Good thinking!

Be sure to check out MGA's other *awesome* **books and courses**, designed especially for advancing Beginning Guitarists just like you. With video demonstrations, tons of details & strategies, and written examples, you *don't* want to miss 'em!

Visit **MetalGuitarAcademy.com**
to find out more...

...and as always...

<u>Keep Shredding!</u>

Brett Miller

Tuning The Guitar

You could be the greatest guitar player on the face of the Earth, but if your guitar was out of tune, you'd sound like the *worst* player in the world instead. So is keeping your instrument in tune important?

You bet your *axe* it is! Here's a simple, step-by-step tutorial for tuning the guitar. It's presented in two parts: using a **tuner**, and tuning by **ear**.

[**Safety Note**: when tuning using either method, take your time and make sure that you're turning the correct peg for the string you're attempting to tune. When tuned to normal tension, a string break is no big deal - it'll go "plink" and just kind of hang there. However, if you've accidentally tuned a string way higher than it's meant to go, the increased tension could cause the string to snap with great force, seriously injuring you or someone around you. Always let the string you're tuning ring out while turning its peg - that way, you'll know if you've accidentally grabbed the wrong tuning peg!]

1. Using a Tuner

Every guitar player should own an electronic tuner, and learn to use it right away. The best kind are the ones that **clip on** to the headstock of your guitar. Here's an example of what they look like; there's a bunch of good ones out there, and you don't need to break the bank when buying one:

Clip the tuner to your guitar, so that you can see the screen. The tuner is designed to measure the vibration of each string when you pluck it; it will then tell you if the string's pitch is **too low**, **too high**, or just right (*i.e.* **in tune**!) Turn on the tuner, and pluck the **low E string**. Be careful to *only* hit the low E string - if you accidentally hit another string as well, it will confuse the tuner.

Look at the tuner screen as the string vibrates. If the string is anywhere in the ballpark of being in tune, you should see a big letter "E" on the screen. There will be some sort of *meter* or *visual readout* on the screen, telling you whether the pitch is too low (**flat**) or too high (**sharp**). Adjust the correct tuning peg for the low E string, either *tighter* (to raise the pitch) or *looser* (to lower the pitch). You should see the meter on your tuner moving in response to this. When the string becomes **exactly in tune**, something will happen on the screen - usually it turns green, or something pretty obvious. That's it! Simply repeat this process for each string, looking for each string name as you go (A, D, G, B, E).

2. Tuning By Ear

Believe it or not, you should just look this one up on YouTube (*gasp!*) Frankly, you **shouldn't even bother with this** until you can use the tuner - it'll just frustrate you (hey, I'm simply being honest!) Tuners are so useful and inexpensive, you should just go get one and learn to use it.

Once you've gotten somewhat used to how each open string should *approximately* sound when in tune, seeing someone *demonstrate* how to tune by ear will be a lot more useful (and less frustrating) than reading about it. Unlike using YouTube to learn to *play* the guitar (a *very* bad idea), using it to learn to *tune* the guitar is fine - chances are, the person in the video will actually do it correctly!

Awesome Guitar Players to Check Out

- Angus Young
- Steve Vai
- Joe Satriani
- Dimebag Darrell
- Alex Skolnick
- Gary Holt
- Christopher Parkening
- Pierre Bensusan
- Al DiMeola
- Paco De Lucia
- John Petrucci
- Jeff Waters
- Eddie Van Halen
- George Puleo
- George Lynch
- Joe Stump
- Yngwie Malmsteen
- Jeff Loomis
- Eric Gales
- Stevie Ray Vaughan
- Chris Poland
- Marty Friedman
- Vinnie Moore
- Brett Miller
- Slash
- Shawn Lane
- Chet Atkins
- Jimmy Bryant
- Jason Becker
- Greg Howe
- Tony MacAlpine
- Randy Rhoads
- Glen Alvelais
- Steve Price
- Andy LaRocque
- Allan Holdsworth
- Frank Gambale
- Sonny Landreth
- Warren DeMartini
- Billy Gibbons
- Stefan Elmgren
- Michael Romeo
- Mattias Eklundh
- Michael Lee Firkins
- Marc Bonilla
- Blues Saraceno
- Neal Schon
- Eric Johnson
- Paul Gilbert
- Nuno Bettencourt
- Chuck Schuldiner
- Steve Lukather
- Django Reinhardt
- Chris Broderick
- Frank Zappa
- Ty Tabor
- Richie Kotzen
- Paul Masvidal
- Michael Amott
- Andres Segovia
- Johnny Colla
- Hank Shermann

The creation of this Mighty Tome was facilitated by Guitarists all over the World, who banded together on Kickstarter to witness its Rise. You know who you are, and out to you I bellow a Fierce & Boisterous *"Hail, Friend!"*

While *all* who supported this endeavor are appreciated, there are some of you to whom a truly Special Thanks is owed. You went above and beyond, and have been a major part of this project!

———— Paul Havig ————
———— Hongwoo Lee ————
———— Dale Ginter ————
———— Christopher Eyles ————
———— Mike Callahan ————
———— Martin Maynard ————
———— Bazza 'Battleaxe' Ledgard ————
———— Luke Martin ————
———— Peter Pakovics ————
———— Jeff 'Hemi' Parker ————
———— Ann ————
———— Nick Luongo ————
———— Adrian Coroi ————
———— Gorodiskiy Eugeny ————
———— Perry Vannier ————
———— DX_Blaster ————
———— Christopher B. Dennett ————
———— Steven Derek Jackson ————